Rory MacLean

was born in Vancouver. He has lived in Toronto, London, the Hebrides, Berlin and Italy. His travel books *Stalin's Nose*, awarded the *Yorkshire Post* Best First Book prize, and *The Oatmeal Ark* were published to great acclaim. *Under the Dragon*, winner of an Arts Council Writers' Award, is his third book. He also writes and presents the BBC Radio 4 travel programme *Itchy Feet*.

Further reviews for *Under the Dragon*:

'Exceptional insight and sensitivity . . . MacLean's talent is multi-faceted; the result is a book with variety of mood and pace . . . I found the "fictionalised" chapters most beautifully crafted and poignant given the need to disguise people's identities to protect them from the government's bully boys . . . Until the Burmese are free to determine their own lives, until a woman such as Aung San Suu Kyi can go about her business then the pages of this wonderful book are as close as I will be getting to Burma.'

ANTHONY SATTIN, *Sunday Times*

'The heart of his book are the personal stories he hears and records in sustained flights of narrative skill and imaginative sympathy . . . they shine with an almost unbearable poignancy . . . [his] attention to the minutiae of Burmese domestic life, and above all his sensitivity to its people's values and thought patterns, lends these narratives their own conviction . . . a book which marvellously extends the conventional confines of travelwriting . . . it is a beautiful insight into this unhappy land.'

COLIN THUBRON, *The Times*

'This is an important book, and an essential book.'
New Internationalist

'Easily the travel book of the year so far.'

Wanderlust magazine.

'MacLean's prose shifts between past and present, truth and, frequently, fiction as he weaves in his stories of four ordinary Burmese women and their extraordinary bravery. His talent lies in his ability to picture, in exquisite detail, an individual life, then pan-out in an almost filmic manner to acknowledge their place in the wider newsworthy events of their country's history. After reading *Under the Dragon*, one can never again see Burma's masses as faceless hordes. MacLean shows Burma to be a country of repression and fear, but also one of great individual kindness and passion.'

Independent on Sunday

'More than a travel book, this is an impassioned plea on behalf of a tragic nation ... Beautifully written, with a powerful sense of involvement.'   *Sunday Express*

'A real page-turner, utterly fascinating.'

HUMPHREY CARPENTER, BBC Radio 4 *Open Book*

'A moving, eloquent account.' PAUL CULLEN, *Irish Times*

'MacLean gives an extraordinary sense of individual hopelessness and radical disorientation under a system of organised absurdity mixed with terror that is contemporary Burma.'   JOHN CASEY, *Evening Standard*

'He takes the reader to the root of the problems of the country; from the corrupt regime itself to the racial relations, prostitution, tourism, drug-trafficking and back. Like a master mat-weaver he keeps the threads tidy to get an artistic work of art which is neat in form but complicated in content. MacLean shows rather than tells his reader what it is like to live in Burma. He does it with humour and honesty. The theme is always black, but he touches his subjects with great care. He expresses his feeling of a cowed and crushed people who can't find words to express their sufferings.' PASCHAL KHOO-THWE, *Spectator*

'Poignant ... a slim, beautifully written travel book, launched on a wave of goodwill, may ultimately be the catalyst which will force Robin Cook, trumpeting a supposedly "ethical" foreign policy, to react.' NEWMAN NOGGS, *Saturday Telegraph*

'A sensitive portrayal of a people who must soon be allowed to emerge from the brutal and senseless repression of decades. It should be widely read.' MICHAEL TILLOTSON, *Country Life*

'Such an extraordinary book ... a stunner ... so deeply felt ... an engrossing narrative.' CHARLES FORAN, *Far Eastern Economic Review*

RORY MACLEAN

Under the Dragon

Travels in a Betrayed Land

Flamingo
An Imprint of HarperCollins*Publishers*

to K

Flamingo
An Imprint of HarperCollins*Publishers*
77–85 Fulham Palace Road,
Hammersmith, London w6 8jb
www.**fire**and**water**.com

Published by Flamingo 1999

9 8 7 6 5 4 3 2

First published in Great Britain by
HarperCollins*Publishers* 1998

Copyright © Rory MacLean 1998

The Author asserts the moral right to be
identified as the author of this work

ISBN 0 00 653082 6

Set in PostScript Linotype Minion with Photina Display

Printed and bound in Great Britain by
Clays Ltd, St Ives plc

CONTENTS

A NOTE ON NAMING

In this book the names of all Burmese who I met have been changed – with one courageous exception. Circumstances and places have also been altered. This is a tragic necessity if real lives are to be protected. The girl with the sensitive hands, Ma Swe with her radio, even the brothers who leaned forward to whisper to me, 'And have you met the Lady?' would be punished if the authorities identified them. These few, altered facts have not changed the essential truth: that the people of Burma wish their horrific circumstances to be known, while their unelected leaders want the reality to be hidden.

In contrast, I have not changed the name of the country. In 1989, in an attempt to obscure their actions, the governing State Law and Order Restoration Council switched the country's official English name to Myanmar. Then, in late 1997, the SLORC transformed itself – on the recommendation of its American public relations advisers – into the State Peace and Development Council. Because the Burmese people, who have scant say in the conduct of their lives, were not consulted about either alteration, I have retained the original names.

It is also necessary to point out that there are no family names in Burma, nor first and second names in the Western sense. Every name is a complete semantic unit. A man called Tin Oo, for example, would never be addressed as Tin or Mr Oo. Forms of address vary depending on the relative social position of the speaker and the listener. Tin Oo would be called *Maung* Tin Oo by his mother, *Ko* Tin Oo by his friends, and *U* Tin Oo when spoken to formally or by subordinates. The prefix used before a woman's name is either *Ma*, which means sister and can be used at any age, or the respectful *Daw*, which translates as aunt. Women do not change their names on marriage.

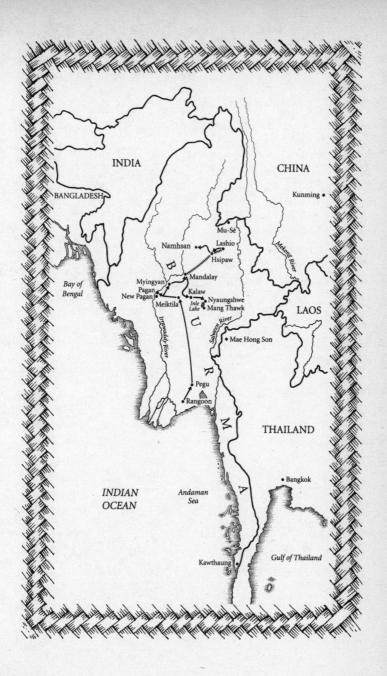

In Every Sense

I CLOSED MY EYES and took a deep breath.

Jasmine. She had wound a white string of fresh blossoms into her hair and let it brush against the copper-brown nape of her neck. I lowered my head and smelt anise. Its sweet scent stirred a memory of two lovers draped around one another in hazy exhaustion. A decade before, beside Kandawgyi Lake I had seen them reading the future in each other's palms, then watched a sandal slip off the girl's tanned foot to reveal the pale brush of whiteness left by a thong.

I took another breath, and the whiff of coffee came back to me. The unhurried widow had drunk it through a straw, perching on a tiny stool, balancing with tidy grace a brick's height above the broken pavement. Her modest *longyi* was tucked and folded around her limbs.

I inhaled again, and the trapped aromas recalled the taste of *mohinga* and caraway, a shock of fiery spices, the recollection of light morning laughter. In my mind I heard the gurgle of wood-pigeons and listened to the rustle of palm leaves in the breeze. I remembered water vendors' plastic cups tap-tapping against their aluminium buckets like the clip-clop of horses' hooves. I summoned back the image of a mother rocking her naked infant to sleep.

Then I took a last, long breath. Now the musty bamboo weave exuded the feral reek of fear. My nose filled with the stink of cordite. I pictured soldiers falling into rank to shoot nurses outside Rangoon General Hospital. I heard bones breaking and women choking as their heads were forced under Inya's waters. I saw the rush of spray from fire-engine hoses clean away the pools of blood.

The memories scorched my senses. I jerked my head away from the old basket. Outside the cold winter rain beat on grimy windows and the sounds of London rose up to return me to the neon-lit storeroom.

My first encounter with Burma had happened by mistake. It was ten years since a long flight from Heathrow had dumped me, exhausted and disorientated, in the soulless chaos of Bangkok airport. I had rushed headlong and bleary-eyed to make a tight connection to Hong Kong and managed to find the departure gate with only minutes to spare. I was the last passenger to board the aircraft. The doors closed. The engines started. I slumped into my seat and promptly fell asleep. Fifty minutes later I awoke not at modern Kai Tak, with electrum skyscrapers gleaming across Hong Kong Harbour, but to the sight of a young woman squatting at the edge of the runway breaking stones by hand. A shirtless, limping man pulled a single baggage cart past a scruffy terminal building. The dilapidated sign behind them read 'We come R goon'. The missing wooden letters lay where they had fallen in the dust. I had caught the wrong aircraft, and couldn't get a flight out of Rangoon for a week.

I have no family link with Burma. No distant relative ever toured the country. I was not weaned on reminiscences of tea plantations or colonial stories about cheeky, teak-skinned elephant boys. But for ten years the memory of that chance visit haunted me. In those seven days the Burmese cast a spell over me, winding themselves into my heart, and leaving behind an ache, a gnawing hunger. A few remarkable women and men dropped into my life. All of them – once away from the ubiquitous police informers – cast aside their gentle, reserved natures to share their stories with me. Time did not loosen or unravel the ties of emotion. Instead they had continued to grip me, as did the untiring, heroic example of Aung San Suu Kyi, leader of the democratic opposition and a prisoner of conscience for much of the last decade. The obsession led me to question why a distant country with which I had no connection had so affected me. It made me wonder what kindnesses hold us, cruelties enslave us, love devotes us to a person, people or place. To me Burma was a paradox, a land of selfless generosity and sinister greed stitched together by love and fear. Its people persevered while accepting life's impermanence, its rulers deified their former leader yet imprisoned his daughter. To try to understand it, I resolved to go back to the country.

I began my return journey by sniffing at a basket in east London. That morning Katrin and I had chased the number 22 bus from the Museum of Mankind, through a gusty January downpour, along Piccadilly. At Swallow Street our umbrella had torn, shredding itself into a tangle of wild tendrils, and a black cab had lifted a gush of water over our legs. The bus had paused at the lights and we scrambled on board, collapsing into a heap of dripping clothing and damp notes.

Our destination lay at the end of its route. Lurking on a forgotten corner of an oily East End street, the brick warehouse appeared as unremarkable as its neighbours. Its innocuous nameplate, BM Enterprises, suggested that it housed a firm of fabric importers or motor-part merchants. No hint was given of the building's true contents. Stacked within, on metal shelves and in boxes, many of them unopened for decades, were not bolts of Chinese cotton or job lots of brake pads, but the treasures of the British Museum's ethnographic collection. For over four centuries British travellers had returned home from Zululand, Bora Bora and the headwaters of the Saskatchewan with sea chests and steamer trunks filled with indigenous artefacts. At first the prizes had adorned the rectories of Gloucestershire and the mantelpieces of Belgravia. But in time their novelty had worn off. Their owners had died or grown tired of dusting the fiddly objects, and the spoils of Empire had found their way to the Museum. There, in the hidden corner of Dalston off the Kingsland Road, African death masks were stored alongside Micronesian penis shields, quivers of Eskimo sealing spears poked at Aboriginal didgeridoos and birch-bark canoes moored beside Burmese baskets.

In the neon-lit storeroom we almost overlooked Item 1950.As3.2.5.

Among many conspicuous treasures, it seemed to offer little of interest. The listing in the catalogue stated simply, 'Basket with lid; as women use for market.' It had been donated to the museum by the widow of a British civil servant. She had probably found it while cleaning out the attic. But instead of turning the page to the rattan cricket cages and hunter's powder horn pouch inset with beetle wings, I hesitated over the entry. The name of the civil servant had caught my eye. It suggested that this basket might be something out of the ordinary.

James George Scott was a bearish man with eyes full of laughter. I have a photograph of him, unshaven, unkempt, smiling outside a canvas tent on the road to Kengtung. In a camera's shutter-snap his whole life seems to be encapsulated, an enthusiastic adventurer ready to toss aside his pith helmet, roll up his sleeves and get down to the business of empire-building. He lived in Burma for more than thirty years in the late nineteenth century, serving as Frontier Officer, helping to map the Siamese border and receiving a knighthood for his contribution to the establishment of British rule in the Shan States. Yet his enduring legacy is not as a distinguished superintendent, aloof and busy with colonial administration, but rather in his books. Scott is probably the only Western writer to have captured the spirit of Burmese society. In his best-known book, *The Burman: His Life and Notions*, he wrote with insight, without condescension or romanticism, at a time when the country's old ways were changing for ever. His work recorded the life and beliefs of a vanishing age: will a Sunday-born man marry well a woman born on a Wednesday? To bring luck, should a house be built on male, female or neuter foundation posts? He asked if a nation which has a voluminous history, almost all of which is pure romance, can be happy. It seemed unlikely that after spending three decades away from Britain this erudite observer would bother to bring home anything mundane.

Katrin waited with me while Scott's basket was brought down from the shelves. We had been married for four years and, much to the despair of her parents, remained of no fixed abode. Her mother tried her best to tempt us into home ownership, clipping out property ads from the local paper and promising us enticing pieces of good furniture. Her father counselled me on rising property values. But instead of being sensible and investing in bricks-and-mortar we chose to look after the houses of absent friends, straining our overladen Escort estate over the Alps, around the Brecon Beacons or into the Highlands every six months or so. We had no jobs to tie us to offices, no children needing to be dropped off at school. Our possessions were scattered from Tooting to Toronto. Our responsibility was only to ourselves, and our families and friends. The travelling life suited us, even if most of our wedding presents remained wrapped up and my papers were in a state of permanent disarray, for it gave us the luxury of time together. We both worked from home, or at least from the place where our suitcases fell open. My pad of paper balanced on my lap, while on hers Katrin wove dyed cane. I snapped pencil leads as she snipped the tips of her withies. She wielded seccateurs where I tried to cut adverbs. At the end of a good day I might have a single black-and-white typed sheet. Katrin would have produced two or three shapely objects of splendid texture and tone. She was happiest in a world of form and colour. She was a basket-maker.

When Scott's treasure was set on the table Katrin was not disappointed. I was delighted. It was shaped like a woman's torso, a full firm chest tapering down to an elegant waist, and my first instinct was to take it into my arms. The basket's busty body was crafted in split bamboo, its dignified posture moulded with gentle curves. Its plaited skin was patterned with precision and the narrow, shaped elements woven into a collar by sensitive hands.

I removed its fitted lid and smelt jasmine and anise, remembered coffee served with lime and the shock of fiery spices. I imagined Scott seeing the basket a century before, swinging by its once-green carrying strap from a young woman's shoulder, resting against her hip, being filled with tender-stew-leaves and fragrant sticky rice. It was feminine and graceful, small-boned and beautiful.

Basketry was probably man's earliest invention. Pottery came later, when woven vessels were lined with clay as protection from cooking coals and hot food. The craft links us to our beginnings and confirms our longing for organisation. In gathering and carrying, trapping or storing, our practical nature has always sought to contain, to try to order life's chaotic tumble of events. A basket weaves together disordered strands to create a new form, becoming a vessel that guards against disarray and uncertainty. A lover's embrace fulfils the same longing for completeness. Limbs entwine like a basket-maker's fronds. Man is stitched to woman, neighbour to neighbourhood, citizen to country, our lives becoming the interlocking strands that together contain and are contained. The individual elements are plaited over and under, twisted and lashed to form a border, making receptacles to enclose a measure of rice, a young family or a whole nation. But the ties that bind also separate. A lover's caress and the bonding of peoples both enfold and exclude. A basket is separated from all but itself. And any weave, if uneven, will exert a pressure that in time frays the edges, unravels the lacing and loosens the bands until the basket comes undone and chaos is restored.

'It's beautiful,' said Katrin, admiring the craftsmanship with a professional eye. 'And so elaborate. But how would it ever carry a day's shopping?'

The basket did seem too small for a trip to the market, but my need for it wasn't domestic. 'I want one,' I told her.

'It's probably a hundred years old,' she said, her realism trying to keep in check my more excessive fancies. 'And the design will have changed. No one will have the time to do detailed work like this any more. We don't even know where Scott found it.'

I looked at the museum's label. It revealed no details of the place of origin. There was no clue either as to the identity of its makers. Although Scott had spent most of his days in the north of Burma, he had travelled so widely that it could have been discovered in any corner of the country.

'The design may not have changed,' I said, my optimism getting the better of me. I hoped that Burma's isolation might have protected its traditions from the worst effects of consumerism's advance.

Burma had been a kingdom – or at least a succession of alternately glorious and anarchic monarchies – for a thousand years, until the

British annexed the country in 1885 and placed it under the Raj. After the Second World War it had enjoyed a brief period of independence and democracy before falling under a repressive military government in 1962. For more than twenty-five years its borders were sealed and its people isolated in a kind of world apart, as the new regime tried to eliminate its opponents and waged a barbaric civil war against ethnic minorities. Then in 1988, the year after my accidental visit, the dictators had put down a popular uprising by killing more than five thousand people. The leaders of the democratic movement who had survived were arrested. But with the temporary release of Aung San Suu Kyi in 1995, the generals had seemed to turn over a new leaf. At least, they were anxious to promote the impression of wanting their country to be united by a force other than fear.

'It's certainly a working basket,' said Katrin, considering its elaborate corners. 'Decoration would have depended on the availability of materials and the plentifulness of food. This would have been made in a good year.'

'So these could still be in use today,' I persisted. 'Look, this has to be a functional feature,' I added, pointing out the inner shell of broad plaited bamboo that protected the outer body's delicate weave.

We considered the statuesque form, the labour of a gifted, anonymous maker. Katrin had a refined sense of adventure, the courage of curiosity tempered by the desire for a long, fruitful life. She knew that a family couldn't be raised in the back of a Ford Escort but, until that time came, she was eager to travel. She also sensed that the basket provided the strand that I needed to follow.

'It's a big country,' Katrin said. Burma is larger than France. 'Where would we start?'

I took another long sniff of the basket. Again its pungent aromas carried me half a world away. I smelt durian and jack-fruit, tasted sweet milky tea, saw boy soldiers in sneaker boots toy with their rifles. Pagoda bells tinkled in my memory and I remembered the warmth of a friend's hand. In all my travels no country had touched me so unexpectedly. It seemed to me that the search for a basket like Scott's would really be an attempt to understand the forces that weave people together. I wanted to try to fathom the needs and fancies, mysteries and curiosities that move the heart. I also needed to see if the Burmese had remained good-natured and quiescent through the last decade of brutal political suppression.

For me only a subjective view enables us to begin to understand – and empathise with – an unfamiliar people and place. So to record the true events I had to go to Burma, in spite of pressure discouraging visitors to the country. The evil unleashed by the country's unelected rulers had to be assessed and articulated. I knew that the journey could be dangerous, and not just for us. The political reality would oblige me to conceal the identities of people about whom I would write. To protect their lives, and to tell the truth, I would have to weave a necessary fiction.

'We'll start at the beginning,' I answered Katrin. 'In Rangoon.'

TWO

Love in a Hot Climate

IN FRONT, BEHIND. In front, behind. She recalled his hands, so large that they had held her as a nest holds a bird. In front, behind. She felt his touch, his lips on her neck and thigh against hip, and let her head roll back in surrender. The gesture had excited him, making her laugh like the bulbuls that hid in the green groves of peepul trees. She felt foolish, always laughing at the wrong time. In front, behind. He had cupped her, clutched her, then found her again. Twist into upright. His urgency had scared her yet still she traced an ear and knotted a finger into a thick curl of fair hair. She felt the white heat blaze out of him. His broad limbs wrapped her to him, pulled her body hard onto his own. In front, behind. Leave the end. Lay in a new strand. He rose inside her, so deep that she thought she might burst, weaving himself into her flesh, coming with a sudden violence that made her want to cry out loud. In front, and behind the next stake. He fell silent, was unable to move, yet held her with no less intensity, his pale skin folding around her own burnished brown. Through the fevered February afternoons it had been that single moment of stillness which had touched her, knitting their fingers together as she now wove her baskets, her small copper hand contained within his palm. In front, behind. She had believed herself to be safe in his arms, as secure as she had felt with her father. The two men of her life – her lover and her father – had protected her. Now both were gone. Ni Ni finished the weave, working the bamboo in pairs, picking up the right-hand stake as she moved around the border, and tried to remember; was that what it meant to love the right way?

It had begun with theft, and ended in ruin.

Ni Ni had grown up alone with her father in two small rooms that opened onto leafy Prome Road. She was an only child because her mother, who had never loved her husband properly, had run off with the refrigeration manager of the Diamond Ice Factory. The manager's cold demeanour had made Ni Ni and the other children shiver. It was his icy feet, they had whispered, which cooled the bottles of Lemon Sparkling and Vimto which no one could afford. But he had been a bolder man than Ni Ni's father, with better prospects. He had also come home at night to sleep, an important consideration for any young wife. The desertion had condemned her father to an existence on the periphery of life, for it had left him not tied to any woman's heart. Yet he continued to try to provide for his daughter. She may have worn *longyis* of plain cotton, not Mandalay silk, and sometimes found no *ngapi* fish paste on the table, but they seldom went hungry. Ni Ni wanted for nothing, except perhaps for less sensitive hands.

Ni Ni ran a small beauty stall from their second room selling lotions, balms and *tayaw* shampoo. Her hands had earned her a reputation for preparing the township's finest *thanakha*, the mildly astringent paste used by Burmese women as combination cosmetic, conditioner and sunscreen. She would have preferred to go to school – pupils at Dagon State High School No. 1 wore a smart uniform with a badge on the pocket – but her father didn't make enough money to pay for the books, let alone the desk and teaching levy. So instead she helped to earn their living by laying her fingertips on her customers' cheeks. She leaned forward, willing from them confessions and complaints, then prescribed the ideal consistency of *thanakha*. Her sensitive touch could also advise them on a change of diet, even tell if they had eaten meat or made love last night. In a tea shop she could pick up a coffee cup and know if it had last been held by a man or a woman. Sometimes though the sensations became too painful and she could not bare even the lightest touch. The breath of air from a falling feather might send shivers to the ends of her fingers. A cooking fire's warmth would scald her. She dropped things. Then she would withdraw, her young laughter disguising adult tears, and wish away her paper-thin skin. She longed to have hard hands like her father.

Every evening Ni Ni's father rode his battered Triumph bicycle into the fiery Rangoon dusk. He worked nights in a central hotel for foreigners near the Sule Pagoda, massaging tired tourist bodies. The hotel collected his fee, paying him only a small retainer, but he was allowed to keep his tips. So sometimes at dawn Ni Ni awoke to the vision of a ten-franc coin, an American quarter or a pound note, tokens that her father had been given during the night. Over breakfast *mohinga* he told her about the faraway places from where the money had come, not with resentment for those who could afford to travel or with a craving to see other countries himself, but out of simple curiosity.

'They are all yours,' he told her with pride, 'so when you marry you can be free to love your husband in the right way.'

'I will always stay here with you,' she assured him in childish devotion, then cheered away poverty's imprisonment. 'The right way is just to care for each other.'

The notes and coins were tucked into the matted walls and Ni Ni's father curled up beneath them, their sleeping room not being long enough for him to lie out straight. She and her father owned the two rooms and two *thin-byu* sleeping mats, a rice pot and betel box, her beauty stall and the bicycle. In a world so large they were content with their peaceful corner of it. Desire did not blind them, like the pickpocket who sees only the monk's pockets.

Ni Ni was thirteen years old when the bicycle vanished. Her father had left it leaning against the gate for no more than a minute. He had woken her with a crisp hundred-yen bill and returned to find his cycle gone. None of the neighbours had caught sight of the thief, not their friend Law San who owned the Chinese noodle stall or even the hawk-eyed gossip May May Gyi. Only Ko Aye, who ran a makeshift barber shop under the banyan tree, claimed to have seen an unfamiliar khaki lorry pass by, although nobody paid much attention to his observations. He had lost an eye back in 1962, and for more than twenty-five years had confused running children with pariah dogs, earlobes with tufts of knotted hair.

All that morning and half the hot afternoon Ni Ni watched her father standing beside the Prome Road looking left and right then left again. He glared at every cyclist who clattered past him. His suspicions were aroused by any newly painted machine. He chased after a man who had turned to ride off in the opposite direction. Ni Ni had been taught that the human abode meant trial and trouble. She understood that the theft, though unfortunate, was not a tragedy. Yet the disappearance of the bicycle made her fingertips tingle, as if she could feel her father's Triumph being ridden far away.

The bicycle is man's purest invention, an ingenious arrangement of metal and rubber that liberates the body from the dusty plod to ride on a cushion of air, at speed or with leisure, stopping on a whim, travelling for free. Its design is simple and its maintenance inexpensive. Yet for all its ease and economy, the bicycle possesses a greater quality. It offers the possibility of escape.

Without his Triumph, Ni Ni's father had to walk to work. He could not afford the bus fare, and needed to leave home two hours earlier to reach the hotel. At the end of his shift he returned long after Ni Ni had risen, ground the day's supply of *thanakha* and opened the shop. Foreign coins no longer jingled in his purse. Tourists grew dissatisfied with his tired hands. Instead of sharing the world with his daughter he slumped, weary and grey, onto his sleeping mat. Ni Ni stroked his brow but the noises of the day – the droning of doves, the throaty hawk of Law San, the call of boiled-bean vendors – began to disturb his sleep. He tossed and turned through the long afternoons. She traded her favourite silver dollar for a small chicken from May May Gyi, but not even aromatic *hkauk-hswe* served in coconut milk could lift his spirits.

Some ten days after the theft Law San scuttled across the street from his stall. His abrupt, sideways walk reminded Ni Ni of a yellow-toned crab. When she was smaller she had believed that Law San cut up his vermicelli with his pincer-like hands.

'*Akogyi*,' he jittered, addressing the older man with respect, 'are you awake?' No voice replied from the dark room, so he added, 'I have found your bicycle.'

'Where?' cried Ni Ni's father, sitting up in the shadows. Ni Ni hurried in from the shop and, in her excitement, dropped a jar of shampoo.

'You remember my cousin who owns the bicycle repair shop in Mingaladon, off Highway No. 1?' said Law San, jerking down onto his haunches. 'I asked him to keep an eye open for your bike. It is a particularly uncommon model, after all.'

'Mingaladon is miles away,' said Ni Ni, scooping the coconut liquid back into the jar. 'No one would ride it that far.'

'That's right,' moaned her father, slumping back against the wall and cracking his knuckles. 'It would never turn up there.' He then added, 'Ni Ni, please make a cup of coffee for our guest.'

She calculated the amount of coffee powder remaining in the jar. 'Please excuse me, but we have no limes,' she told them. May May Gyi could have lent her one but she did not want to be sent away.

'Not for me, no thank you,' Ko Law San replied, shaking a knobbly claw. He was too agitated to idle over refreshments. 'It *is* a long way away, but that's the remarkable thing. Only yesterday a stranger brought into my cousin's shop a machine exactly matching yours. He proceeded with caution at first, asking only a few questions, so as not to arouse suspicion, you understand.'

'And what of it?'

'Well, it turned out to be your bike,' grinned Law San, jumping up onto his feet. 'And I'm pleased to inform you that my cousin has completed all the arrangements. It is yours again.'

'He's really found it?' Ni Ni asked.

'I don't understand,' said her father, his optimism tempered by doubt. 'Did the thief just hand it over?'

'I do not know the specific details, my friend.'

'And what do you mean by "arrangements"? Did your cousin buy it back?'

'I cannot tell you that either,' answered Law San, disappointed that his good news should be greeted by wary questions. 'I know only that you are free to recover your bicycle tomorrow.'

The following morning Ni Ni did not open the shop. Instead she met her father on the main road after he had finished work. Together they caught a line-bus to the northern suburbs. The small pick-up's roof was stacked with caged ducklings and its open flat back crammed full of traders heading to the Highway Bus Centre. Ni Ni managed to squeeze onto the bench between a monk and a conscript. The muzzle of the soldier's rifle rubbed against the acne scars on his face. Her father rode on the tailgate.

The streets of Mingaladon are more pleasant than those of Rangoon's other townships. The tree-lined avenues seem to suffer from fewer potholes. Its houses are in good condition and their gardens better maintained. Even the bicycle repair shop, which sat off a lane behind the Defence Services General Hospital, flaunted an unusual affluence.

Ni Ni spotted Law San's cousin squatting on the front step, a dismantled bicycle between his legs. Her father introduced themselves, but the man did not invite them into his house, despite their long journey, nor did he meet their eyes. 'I am sorry, but your machine is no longer here,' he said, unwilling to look up from a broken gear-changer. He gestured towards a long dark row of spiny acacias. 'It is there, over the road in the military compound.' Beyond the shrubs, behind the barbed wire, against the wall of a barracks, stood the green Triumph.

Ni Ni had been wary of the army since the year two soldiers had tricked a neighbour's daughter. The corporal had addressed his friend as 'Major', and the simple, trusting girl had believed the men to be officers. She had responded to his advances and, after the marriage, discovered that her major was an ordinary soldier. When his unit was transferred away from Rangoon he had left her with a child. The incident never failed to make Ni Ni laugh. In fact it was when confronting misfortune that her laughter came most easily. She had sniggered when first meeting the ice factory manager, even though he had torn apart her family, and thereafter giggled to drive away her father's loneliness. Her humour helped her to rise above disappointment and to act with care, for every act had consequences for the soul's future. But standing in the shade of a palm tree near the compound's gatehouse she suppressed the urge even to smile. She knew that her father would never have brought her with him had he known about the involvement of the *Tatmadaw*. The Burmese army, once a respected and responsible force, had become the country's corrupt ruling class. 'I am staying with you,' she insisted when he tried to send her home. Her concern for his safety was as great as his for hers.

The warrant officer was not in his office, and a sentry directed them along Khayebin Road to the Tatmadaw Golf Club. They were kept waiting outside in the midday sun until he had finished his round. Two Mercedes limousines came and went. When the officer appeared Ni Ni's father bowed, addressed him as *Saya*, teacher, and beseeched him to return to the compound. The young man was irritable. He had been looking forward to lunch and at first feigned indifference to such a minor matter as a stolen bicycle. But he relented, then, on the drive back to the compound, began to rant about the need to uplift the morality of the nation. Ni Ni couldn't understand the relevance of a lecture on personal sacrifice.

'Forgive me, *Saya*,' her father pleaded when they reached his office. 'I am an ill-educated man, but at what are you aiming? Please tell me openly.'

'I am telling you that the thief sold your bicycle to the repair shop, then ran away,' snapped the officer. 'And that if you wish it to be returned, then you must repay the hundred kyat.' At the time a hundred kyat was the equivalent of two months' rent. 'Furthermore I am willing, in the cause of good civic relations, to accept the money on his behalf.'

'*Saya*, are you saying that I must buy back my own bicycle?' Ni Ni was surprised to hear disapproval in her father's voice. He tended to acquiesce in the face of difficulties. 'That does not seem to be the right way.'

'Younger brother, I am trying to help you to find the best way,' said the officer. Ni Ni wanted to hide her tingling fingers in her lap, but they had not been invited to sit down. 'If you refuse, then the bicycle must be sent to the police and a case will be opened. As you know, it will be kept in their care as evidence.'

Ni Ni knew that once it was in their hands, the police would use the bicycle as their own. They would replace its good tyres with old punctured ones, strip the gears and maybe even steal its Flying Pigeon bell. To expedite the case her father would need to make frequent visits to the police station, bringing presents for the detectives on each occasion. His time and money would be wasted. In the end it would cost as much as three hundred kyat to reclaim his bicycle by legal means. The officer knew this too.

'I am afraid that I do not have a hundred kyat today, *Saya*.'

'Of course; it would be foolish to travel with such an amount.' The warrant officer scribbled a few words on a leaf torn from an old diary. 'Please sign this paper here.'

Ni Ni helped her father to read the handwritten promissory note. He asked her to repeat its words to him twice. 'But *Saya*, there is no mention of the bicycle here.'

'That is not necessary. This paper says simply that the repairman has loaned you one hundred kyat and that you will pay him back – by way of myself – at the end of the week. When you return with the money, you may have the bicycle.'

'The law comes out from their mouth, not from the book,' Law San said later that day. He had loaned the money to Ni Ni's father, aware that there was little prospect of repayment in this life. He hoped that the act might perhaps gain him merit in the next one.

'We do not own our home, our children, even our possessions,' hissed Ni Ni's father, making light of a Buddhist precept. 'They are only given to us for a short time, or until they fall into the grasp of the *Tatmadaw*.' He and Law San had learned that the thief from whom the cousin had bought the machine had been a soldier. The warrant officer had become involved not to right a wrong, but because he had not wanted the soldier alone to profit from the robbery. He had seized the bicycle so as to get his own cut.

'*Malok, mashok, mapyok*,' Law San sighed. 'Don't do anything, don't get involved, don't make yourself trouble. That's what I advise, *Akogyi*.' In the end both he and his cousin had lost a hundred kyat. 'Let's get back to work.'

Later Ni Ni tried to comfort her father, asking him about massage oils and encouraging him to teach her his techniques. Although it stung her hands she massaged his shoulders, chatting to him about her dowry of coins, but his thoughts drifted away from the Prome Road. The soldiers' crime had kindled his discontent.

It was towards the end of that summer that Ni Ni's father lost his job. He was accused of discussing politics with foreigners, an allegation invented by a younger masseur who coveted his post. The hotel manager dismissed him without a hearing. It was better to sack a man than to risk trouble with the authorities. The irony was that Ni Ni's father, while kneading bronzed Swedish backs and easing tired Thai muscles, had indeed been criticising the regime.

In the spring of 1988 Burma's military government had suppressed a small demonstration with bestial brutality. Peaceful protesters were beaten and driven into Rangoon's Inya Lake to drown. The *Lon Htein* riot police stormed the university and arrested truckloads of students. In prison men were tortured and women gang-raped. Forty-one students suffocated to death in a police van. The official inquiry found that only two protesters had died, further incensing public opinion. A curfew intended to control the students misfired. Stall-keepers were prevented from reaching the markets. Food became scarce. A *pyi* of rice tripled in price over the summer. The daily wage of a manual worker remained fixed at 6.50 kyat. People could no longer afford to eat.

The resignation that July of General Ne Win, the despot who had wielded absolute power for twenty-six terrible years, came as a complete surprise to the nation. The Burmese had as a rule accepted both misfortune and bad government with stoicism. Suddenly it seemed that they *could* unravel themselves from the economic decline and arbitrary cruelty. There could be an end to the reign of terror. A general strike was called in the hope of dislodging the rest of the military government. On 8 August – the auspicious 8.8.88 – a million hungry, hopeful people took to the streets without fear, with only elation in their hearts. Ni Ni's father walked among them, pushing his bicycle.

On the day of the strike Ni Ni was told to stay at the shop, not that there was anyone to buy her lotions, as even loquacious May May Gyi had joined the marchers. Ko Aye sat with her for an hour, few people needing one-eyed haircuts either, and told her of the importance of the strike. His enthusiasm made her feel foolish. She had asked to go with her father, but he would not listen. They had argued for the first time, just as he and her mother used to argue, and her fingers had quivered. Ni Ni wondered if her mother and the cool ice factory manager had joined the demonstration.

She ate a little rice at midday and tried to nap through the hot afternoon. But sleep would not come, and so, unnoticed by Ko Aye, she stole away into town. She hoped to catch sight of her father, though not of course to be seen by him, but in the central Maha Bandoola Park there were too many people. They poured in from all directions, cheering, clapping, marching in their thousands towards the city hall. Dockworkers walked alongside tailors, air force pilots joined hands with housewives. Students formed human chains around groups of soldiers, protecting them from the marchers, shouting, 'The People's Army is our army!' Three columns of monks carried their alms bowls upside down, to show that the whole nation was on strike. Ni Ni walked behind them, alongside pupils from Dagon State High School No. 1, her right fist raised too, calling '*Do aye*!' – our cause – and watching out for her father.

'You have never seen anything like it,' rattled Law San in the early evening. He had returned home soon after her, so excited by the unprecedented events that he cooked up a steaming cauldron of

Shan hkauk-hswe and passed around free bowls of the noodles. Her father had not been with him.

'We walked at the head of the Prome Road demonstrators. Your father carried the portrait of Aung San on his handlebars.' Aung San was the national hero who led the struggle for independence from British colonial rule and from the Japanese occupation in the 1940s. 'There were township banners from Yankin, Bahan, North and South Okkalapa, everywhere.'

Student leaders had made spontaneous speeches beneath the Sule Pagoda, their banners calling for democracy, for an end to one-party rule and for freedom for political prisoners. In the late afternoon the Rangoon district commander had appeared on the portico of the city hall. He had ordered the people to disperse, threatening that otherwise his troops would open fire.

'But there were too many of us. The crowd just grew and grew,' thrilled Law San. He could not contain his amazement. 'We chanted, "This is a peaceful demonstration. No provocations," and General Myo Nyunt went away. He just went away.' People found the courage to take hold of their destiny. 'Then a young man unbuttoned his shirt and addressed the troops. "Shoot me if you dare!" he said. I tell you, Burmese soldiers will not shoot Burmese civilians. The government will cave in. It will collapse tonight.'

'And my father?' Ni Ni asked. 'Is he all right?'

'All right? Of course he's all right.'

Ni Ni laughed, both out of nervousness and relief. 'Then why didn't he come back with you?'

'Because he couldn't tear himself away, Ni Ni. And I understand him. I understand him well. This is a lucky day in our history. He will be home later. Have another bowl of noodles.'

But Ni Ni's father didn't return, not that night or the next day. Instead terrified neighbours stumbled up the Prome Road, their *longyis* stained with blood. In hushed, hurried tones they recounted the horror of the massacre. Not long before midnight, army trucks loaded with troops had roared out from behind the city hall. Armoured cars had driven into the heart of the crowd. Soldiers had stepped down from their vehicles, taken up position and opened fire. Machine guns had cut savage swathes through the mass of unarmed civilians. Hundreds had fallen as they ran to escape. Monks who stood their ground had been bayoneted. School children had been beaten. A scattering of lost sandals had littered the gory pavement around Bandoola Park.

Ni Ni stopped every passer-by outside the house, asking if they had seen a man pushing a bicycle – 'A green bicycle, with a Flying Pigeon bell.' But they simply shook their heads or hurried past her without a word, or fell into trembling as they tried to speak. No one had seen her father. She retreated into her room, her hands tucked up into her armpits. She curled up on her mat, unable to move, to touch or be touched. She tried to remind herself of the Buddha's saying, that anger can be held with a heart of kindness, but when May May Gyi visited in the late afternoon Ni Ni cried out in pain as she tried to take her hand.

'He can ride very fast,' Ni Ni thought, to comfort herself on the drive back into town. 'Faster than any soldier can run.' In the pick-up no one spoke. The passengers were too frightened. Two women wept. Their lips trembled but they did not make a sound. Only the lick of tyres on wet asphalt broke the silence. Barricades had been set up all over the city. The Toyota navigated around the new checkpoints, and between the cairns of broken concrete piled at the places where people had been killed. The twists and turns made Ni Ni feel nauseous.

'He will have cycled away and be hiding somewhere.'

She searched for him first outside the city hall. She touched the black asphalt and shivered. The dead and dying had already been thrown into lorries and driven away under the cover of darkness. Rain and water hoses had washed away the stains of butchery. The square was deserted, except for the passing khaki trucks filled with soldiers. Their rifles pointed outwards, and behind them Ni Ni glimpsed women with bound hands. She darted around the park, praying that she would find her father's bicycle leaning against the railings. Instead she caught sight of a band of defiant demonstrators emerging from beside the Foreign Trade Bank. A gunshot rang out and their fighting peacock banner fluttered to the ground. Ni Ni had never before seen a man die. He lay curled on the glistening stones as if asleep, and she wanted to shake him awake. A second report echoed off the buildings and the remaining protesters took to their heels. She too ran, but in the opposite direction, hoping that the sniper would not notice her in the sudden downpour.

Along the backstreets, down the alleys and in the deserted open-air market she searched for places where her father might be hiding. She tucked herself under a flight of steps, in a place too small for her father to fit, while a *Lon Htein* patrol passed the Theingyi bazaar. In the flats above she heard the muffled whispers of people confined to their rooms, imprisoned by fear, nursing wounded bodies and disbelief.

Outside Rangoon General Hospital the bereaved thrashed through the crowd, hunting for missing relatives. A dozen students crouched on the pavement, bleeding from bayonet gashes. A mother cradled her son. His smart high school uniform was shredded and his body stiff with rigor mortis. The naked male corpses with shaven heads were monks whom soldiers had stripped of their robes. Medical staff hammered a banner above the emergency unit: 'Doctors, nurses and hospital workers who are treating the wounded urge the soldiers to stop shooting.' The words were written in blood. Ni Ni watched a group of nurses gather to demonstrate against the killings. They stepped forward carrying the national flag. A *Tatmadaw* truck approached them. There was a single shot, then automatic-rifle fire. The soldiers sprayed the hospital building with bullets. Ni Ni stole into its dank corridors, running past dying marchers and bloodied white tunics, looking for the cyclist with hard hands, touching nothing, lost and afraid.

'He is waiting,' she later told May May Gyi while grinding *thanakha*. It had been madness to try to look for her father, so Ni Ni had returned home. 'Lying low until it is safe to come out of hiding.'

'Maybe he has escaped with the students to Thailand,' the gossip suggested, not wanting to smother her own optimism. Her son had not come back either, and she hoped that he was among the thousands of demonstrators who were fleeing to the border. 'But it may be some time until your father can return.' May May Gyi knew that the beauty stall alone brought in little money. 'You're almost fourteen now, Ni Ni. You should try to find a job.'

The girl shook her head and did not smile. 'I will wait too,' she replied. The laughter had been stolen out of her.

Ni Ni was wrong in thinking that she had time. Late one Thursday evening the lights went out in the houses on either side of the Prome Road. At first no one paid any attention to the blackout. The country's electricity supply was erratic. Then seventy-five heavily laden army trucks rumbled along the road, carrying from the port crates marked 'Allied Ordnance, Singapore'. The weapons and ammunition were a gift from the state arms company of a fraternal nation. They would enable the regime to reinforce its power at a time when it hadn't the money to buy guns. The military government had not been dislodged. Ne Win, in spite of his sham resignation, still retained control.

'I must wait,' Ni Ni repeated to herself. But the following week she was evicted from her home, along with most of her neighbours. The shady old trees that lined the sleepy road were cut down. Prome Road was to be widened into a four-lane highway to give the battalions of Mingaladon faster access to the city's centre. Ni Ni gathered up the rice pot, betel box and *thin-byu* sleeping mats. The soldiers who turned her out stole her eucalyptus oil. She only just managed to hide her dowry of foreign coins in a purse under her *longyi*.

The regime, which had torn apart the ties of family, declared its main objective to be the non-disintegration of national solidarity. The *Tatmadaw*, which had used fear to divide neighbourhoods, pledged itself to community peace and tranquillity. The local Law and Order Restoration Council offered to support and protect the new orphans, if they condemned their dead parents in public. Ni Ni refused to cooperate, and so was denied the woven wall mats needed to build a shelter in Wayba-gi, the new 'satellite zone' on a barren plain under the airport flight path. Her home had already been seized, so it could not be taken away again, and she had no job to lose. Others were not so independent, and the *Working People's Daily* carried their notices. Husbands denounced wives for singing freedom songs. Mothers disowned their children for being 'absconding and misled students'. To uphold the 'Noble Traditions' of the new *Tatma-daw* government it became necessary to abandon those one loved.

Ni Ni borrowed two wall mats and built a lean-to at the side of Law San's half-finished stall. She threw herself into the physical work, even though it stung her hands, assisting May May Gyi to make her tiny shack. Then she lashed Ko Aye's mirror to a post. It had tended to fall down every time the delta-winged aircraft passed overhead, making his occasional clients even more wary of the wandering scissors.

She was good with her hands, Law San observed, watching her earn a few kyat by helping a couple to build a cooking-oil shop, and that evening over noodles he told her, 'I have a cousin.'

Ni Ni looked unamused.

'A *second* cousin who is employed by a construction company. He is always on the lookout for able-bodied workers, especially with the new projects about to start.' At the height of the uprising, in a gesture at once callous and surreal, the government had announced a number of cooperative ventures with Western firms to build tourist hotels. 'I could have a word with him.'

'My father will come back soon,' said Ni Ni.

'Ma Ni Ni, even if he does return . . .'

'*When* he returns,' she insisted, raising her voice. 'I know that he will. I can feel him.' Ni Ni lifted her hands from her lap and showed Law San her palms. They were the colour of mohur blooms, flushed blood-red by a rash of worry and hope. 'I can feel him riding his bicycle.'

'I mean when he does return,' Law San corrected himself with gentleness, 'he won't have a job. There will be no money.'

Ni Ni did not answer him, never having mentioned her dowry. She knew those savings needed to be preserved. But if she could make a little cash she might be able to reopen a beauty stall. Then she could help to support her father.

'You need a benefactor,' Law San told her.

The girls swarmed up the scaffolding, stacks of bricks and palettes of mortar balanced on their heads, bodies swaying under the weight, building the five-star hotel. They dropped their burdens on the upper floor, where tourists would one day dine in the skyline restaurant, stretched their stooped spines, then climbed back down to collect the next load. If they could afford them the older girls, who were aged up to eighteen, wore working gloves. The younger ones covered themselves in *thanakha*, and copper-skinned tracks of perspiration lined their slender arms. Ni Ni didn't bother with either precaution. She let the cement dust dry her hands, her fingers become callused and her skin grow dark from the sun.

Law San's second cousin had been kind to her, giving her work, favouring her above the other applicants. He appeared to be patient too. The first time she had held a brick she had dropped it, sensing the scorching heat that had baked it. Law San had warned him of her physical tenderness, so he waited, without shouts or complaint, as she steeled herself and picked up the coarse clay blocks one by one. She eased eight of them onto her improvised turban, balanced the load with her throbbing hands, then mounted the bamboo steps. Ni Ni taught herself to bear the splinters and sprains, to endure the chafe of masonry, and soon the rough labour began to scour the sensitivity off her fingertips. She did not allow pain to weaken her body. Her attitude won the respect of the other girls and even encouraged the younger labourers conscripted onto the site. Law San's cousin tried to show his appreciation by giving her less arduous tasks – mixing cement or sorting timbers – yet she never took advantage of his kindness. She always carried and stacked more than her fair share. But at night in her room she blew cool air onto her hands and sobbed. She was frightened, and alone.

One hot morning when Ni Ni was emptying baskets of concrete into wooden frames, casting the pillars which would contain the hotel's executive business suite, she felt his eyes upon her. The attention unnerved her but she was anxious to please him, so hurried her work. She tripped over a loose metal rod and dropped her basket. Its wet load slopped across the scaffolding, fell two storeys and almost hit the site supervisor, a starch-white English architect who managed the project for its overseas financers. In an instant all movement stopped. The ant column of children froze on the ladders. Carpenters held their hammers in mid-stroke. Shovels hovered above sand piles. It was as if the workers were machines that had been disconnected from the electricity supply. The surprised architect stared at the damp grey lump setting on his shoe and dabbed a spot of concrete off his thick spectacles. He raised a wary hand to shield himself from the glare and squinted at Ni Ni. He seemed about to speak, then instead retreated like a water-rat into the cool shadow of his air-conditioned office. Law San's cousin, on the other hand, did not withdraw, but waited until Ni Ni found the courage to lift her eyes. 'Come and see me at the end of the day,' he said. It surprised her to detect a hint of satisfaction in his voice.

The afternoon dragged, weighing down on her like a double burden of gravel, and everyone avoided Ni Ni. She kept herself busy, pouring twice her daily quota into the frames, trying to regain Law San's cousin's approval. He did not speak to her, or even glance her way, and it was only long after the other girls had left to go home that he called her into the office. She waited, standing, while he completed the daily report.

'This is an awkward situation,' he pronounced, laying his leaky biro onto the blotter. 'I gave my word to my cousin that I would help you . . .' He sucked on a cup of stewed China tea. '. . . but this morning's unfortunate incident has created difficulties for me.'

'I am grateful to you for your kindness,' said Ni Ni, her breath shallow and sharp. 'I am truly sorry for my error today.'

'The supervisor was furious,' continued the cousin, ignoring her distress. 'More angry even than he was the day the swimming pool cracked and would no longer contain water.' He plucked a single green tea leaf from between his teeth. 'I tried my best to pacify him.'

'I thank you for your care, *Saya*.'

'These foreign advisers are difficult devils,' continued Law San's cousin, warming to his theme. 'They talk about high standards, but all they are really trying to do is to measure the East with a Western yardstick. It can't be done, of course, and their frustration makes them ill-tempered.' He shook his head. 'He wanted to dismiss you on the spot.'

'I apologise for the trouble that I have caused you. If you wish it then I shall leave.'

Law San's cousin rose to his feet and slipped around the desk. He considered Ni Ni's poor, dusty clothes. 'Your figure would be flattered by a finer *longyi*, Ma Ni Ni.' She found his manner immodest and lowered her eyes. 'One made of silk, perhaps?' He stepped closer, running his eyes over her. She turned her head away and for a moment he did not speak. 'Your hands,' he then asked in a tone at once both casual and calculated, 'are they really so sensitive?'

'Not now,' lied Ni Ni, hardly breathing. 'The work has hardened them.'

Law San's cousin twisted around to reach for the tin tray on the desk. A second teacup, chipped but unused, rested on it. 'Let's see then,' he said, holding the tray between them. 'Who last drank from this cup? A man or a woman?' When she did not respond he ordered, 'Take it.'

Ni Ni took the cup and rested it in her palm. She ran an index finger around its rim and stroked its side with her thumb. 'A man,' she answered.

'Correct,' laughed the cousin. 'A man who drinks from two cups. This man.' He stretched to take her hand but she pulled away from him. 'You have a very sensitive touch.'

The door swung open and the architect fell into the room. 'My God,' he swore, stumbling over the rough threshold, 'who the hell made that?' Because his name was Louis the Burmese had nicknamed the Englishman U Lu Aye, which translates unsuitably as Mr Calm.

'I thought you had left for the evening, Mr Louis,' said Law San's cousin in English, startled by the supervisor's agitated entrance.

'On my way out,' he replied. Then, recognising Ni Ni, added, 'Almost literally.'

'I have told this girl of your anger, Mr Louis. Your great anger.'

'Missed me by this much,' said Louis to her in hesitant Burmese, holding his thumb and forefinger half an inch apart. 'You'd better aim more carefully next time.' He swayed a little and Ni Ni smelt alcohol on his breath. 'Because I'd prefer a swift death.' When he blundered out of the room, instinct made her follow him.

Dusk had tucked itself around the quarter, and single lightbulbs glowed like honey-pale stars in the surrounding tenements. Across the half-built ballroom the nightwatchman's brazier cast golden shadows which danced to the rhythm of unheard music. Louis missed his step and plopped down in the dust, losing his glasses on the descent. 'One day this will be the finest hotel in Rangoon,' he announced to the world in general, then added to Ni Ni, 'and you can come here to dance.'

'I doubt Ma Ni Ni will be able to return,' said Law San's cousin, 'once her work is completed.'

'Can't see why not. I'm sure she's a very fine dancer,' said Louis, regaining his feet. 'So fine, in fact, that she shall be the first woman to dance in the hotel.' He bowed deeply, almost toppled forward and slurred in drunken formality, 'Daw Ni Ni, as a price for failing to murder me, I request the pleasure of this first dance.'

Before Ni Ni could react Louis took her into his arms. He swept her off the steps and across the rubble-strewn floor, humming a tuneless waltz. They took a turn round the ballroom and skirted the roofless dining hall. Ni Ni, who had once seen Western dancing in a travelling cinema show, did her best to hang on. She had matured early so had a lithe, graceful figure, though in his present state Louis would be hard pressed to say if she was thirteen or thirty. They swung through the hotel's reception area, then collided with a cement mixer and fell into a pile of sand. Louis dropped her like a soiled handkerchief, then hiccoughed.

27

'I wonder,' he asked, lying with his feet in the air, 'could you two help me find my specs? I can't see a damn thing.'

They looked under the steps and around the tool store. As they searched behind the office Louis rolled onto his stomach and, with a sozzled groan, buried his head in the sand. The nightwatchman brought over a dim gas lamp, which spluttered and blew out. 'I can't find them without a torch,' said Law San's cousin. Then Ni Ni felt them in the dark.

'Thank you,' said Louis, blinking like a mole. His clothes were filthy. He seemed about to say something more, but turned instead and tripped away into the night.

'U Lu Aye does not seem so very angry,' said Ni Ni, her head spinning.

'No. Not any more,' said Law San's cousin. 'Because of my efforts. You are lucky, I hope you appreciate that.'

'I am grateful,' Ni Ni repeated.

He watched her for a moment then said, 'I will drive you home.'

'If you will forgive me, I prefer to take the bus,' she said.

'It's late. It will take you over an hour to reach Wayba-gi now. I will have you there in ten minutes.' When Ni Ni shook her head Law San's cousin clamped his hand around hers. 'Ma Ni Ni,' he hissed, 'I can do much to help you, but much more to hinder you. I wish you no harm. I ask only for you to attend to your duty.'

'My duty?'

'It is your duty to care for your benefactor.'

'No,' she answered, shaking her hand free. 'No.' And ran away into the night.

There was no sign of Louis the next morning, but Law San's cousin was much in evidence. The care which he had appeared to feel for Ni Ni had drained away with his wounded pride. Rejection can twist the kindest heart, but when it also challenges tinpot authority the response can be spiteful. The cousin turned on Ni Ni with a wry vengeance, ordering her to dredge the sludge from the gully behind the site. He told her there were no spare tools, and she had to clear the filth with her bare hands. The other workers noticed the change in him and questioned Ni Ni until, over midday rice, she confessed to his approach. The older girls scoffed and turned back to their bowls, while her contemporaries laughed. 'Your turn had to come around sooner or later, Ma Ni Ni,' said Way Way, who had worked on the building for almost six months. 'He had a go at me in my first week.'

'But he doesn't treat you so badly,' said Ni Ni.

'Not now,' she shrugged, reaching for the fried garlic.

'Do you remember Ma Thet?' said another labourer. 'She went with him just to get a ride in his saloon.'

'Don't look so surprised, Ni Ni,' said Way Way. 'It was a Toyota.'

'I've never ridden in a saloon,' said the new girl from Dagon Myothit.

'But now Way Way spends her spare time with Tin Oo,' observed one of the older girls. Tin Oo operated the site's cement mixer. 'I've noticed that his machine always needs to be serviced at the end of the week.'

'It doesn't hurt and it keeps him happy,' said Way Way, shaking her head. She was not yet fifteen years old but already her hair had lost its youthful lustre. In six months it had become dull and brittle. 'Then he gives me ten kyat. Can you imagine? A whole day's pay earned in a few minutes. Sometimes a very few minutes.'

'Ten kyat?' said the new girl.

'Life is so hard, how can we be anything but kind?' said Way Way.

All afternoon Ni Ni considered running away. If she had a bicycle she could escape north, along the route which her father might have travelled, into the hills east of Inle Lake, to try to reach Mae Hong Son. Or she could try to find a fishing boat heading to Kawthaung and walk through the jungle to Thailand. Way Way knew a man who had promised to find any girl work in Bangkok, as a waitress or a chambermaid he had said, and earn enough to buy new clothes, maybe even a watch. She tried to organise her thoughts while carrying lime to the mixing barrels. The heavy work made it difficult to think. Her shoulders ached from the constant stirring, her hands were burnt by the caustic earth, and Law San's cousin kept shouting at her, ordering her to perform her proper duties, until the tears began to roll down her dusted cheeks and drop into the wet plaster.

Towards the end of the day she was carrying bundles of hemp cord across the upper level when a sudden cough from the cement mixer distracted her. Ni Ni missed her footing, lost her balance and the bundles fell off her head. She managed to catch hold of the scaffolding but the cords unravelled down the face of the building, roping together some workers, lashing others apart. The accident enraged Law San's cousin, who sprinted up the ladder and, standing above the girl, began to flog her with an end of rope. Ni Ni did not resist him. Instead she cried with the realisation that there was nothing she could do. There was no chance for her to run away alone, to flee to the border, even to hide in Wayba-gi. She had no resources to eat without wages, no chance of finding another job, no possibility of escape. She knew that she was trapped.

'Stop,' said the architect.

'I beg your pardon, Mr Louis?'

'Stop beating this girl.' The commotion had flushed Louis out from his office. He too had mounted the ladder, climbing up faster than anyone had seen him move in any direction. He placed a hand on the cousin's shoulder.

'She is a lazy and disobedient worker. I know her type, and only harsh discipline will improve her behaviour.'

'I don't want to interfere,' Louis stammered. 'But she's only a child.'

'These women are my responsibility. They need not concern you. Please do not trouble yourself.'

'No. You are being unkind,' said Louis. He was not comfortable involving himself in the disagreements of others, yet he found himself stepping between the cousin and Ni Ni. He held out his broad hand to her. She hesitated, then pulled herself to her feet. 'Please gather the rope,' he said.

The men returned to the office. Their raised voices could be heard echoing across the site. At dusk as the workers laid down their tools Law San's cousin appeared at his office door. 'Ma Ni Ni,' he called, loud enough for all to hear, 'do not come back tomorrow. Your work here is finished.'

On the street Ni Ni counted out her meagre pay. Fifteen pyas per day had been deducted for rice. At least she had her dowry of foreign coins. They would pay to get her out of Rangoon. She tried to catch sight of Way Way. She had decided to find the man who could arrange work in Bangkok. She would go away for a few months, work hard, then return home with enough money saved for her and her father to make a new start. But instead of Way Way's lacklustre hair, it was a blond head which she saw bobbing towards her above the departing crowd.

'I'm sorry,' Louis said. Ni Ni stared down at the ground. She didn't know what to say. She worried that conversations with foreigners had to be reported to the police. 'I'm full of good intentions,' he continued. His poor Burmese made her want to smile but she resisted the temptation. 'I never meant to get you fired.'

Ni Ni shuffled her feet then rubbed her nose, even though it didn't itch. Law San's cousin had gone back into the office. The new girl from Dagon Myothit had been called in to see him. The other labourers were gathered at the end of the street, pausing at the cigarette stall or waiting for buses. She saw no sign of Way Way. No one seemed to be watching them.

'You were trying to help me,' said Ni Ni. Louis had to lean closer to hear her voice above the dying gasp of Tin Oo's cement mixer. 'I must be grateful.'

'Can you get work somewhere else?'

Ni Ni looked up into his eyes, as blue as the hot season sky. He seemed to be concerned for her. He seemed to want to help her. He understood nothing of her country. 'I have a plan,' she answered, looking away.

'Good. Plans are good. Mine never came to much, so I admire someone who has confidence in their own. Look, I am sorry,' he repeated, then added, 'Here,' and slipped an envelope into her hand. 'I enjoyed our dance last night.' Inside the smooth, clean white envelope Ni Ni found two hundred kyat.

The next day she planned to return to the site to find Way Way. She put on her favourite *longyi* and a borrowed muslin blouse, and took the time to gather her fine black hair into a knot around a comb at the back of her head. She pressed a thin coat of *thanakha* on her cheeks, then paused to consider her clear almond eyes in Ko Aye's mirror. She turned this way and that, moving her slender figure with refinement and economy. She took a small piece of red crêpe paper, wet it with her tongue and rubbed it on her lips.

On the walk from the bus stop a car stopped beside her. She hurried on, fearing that it was Law San's cousin. Then she heard its electric window slip open, and recognised the voice that said, 'Ma Ni Ni?' She hesitated. 'What are you doing back here?'

'I've come to look for my friend,' she answered. 'She promised to help me to find work.'

'It's too hot to even think about work,' said Louis. 'I'm taking the day off. I've been here for six months, and all I've seen is this damn building site.' He stared at Ni Ni and she turned away, suddenly self-conscious. 'Is your friend expecting you?' he asked.

'No.'

'Then come with me to the Shwedagon. You can see her tomorrow.'

Ni Ni shook her head. 'I can't do that.'

'No one need know,' insisted Louis. 'Please come. I'd enjoy your company.'

The world looked picturesque from inside the air-conditioned car: Rangoon's decaying colonial buildings appeared charming, the passengers riding on the roofs of overcrowded buses seemed quaint. Her seat was so soft, and the ride so smooth, that Ni Ni felt as if the wheels had left the road and the car was gliding up toward Shwedagon's great gilded pagoda. She could not bring herself to speak. A guitar concerto played on the stereo. A traffic policeman saluted as they drove past the Deaf and Dumb School.

They didn't climb up the slowly rising steps with the Burmese pilgrims. Instead Louis guided Ni Ni into the lift which was reserved for military officers and foreigners. She paused at the gate, expecting to be turned back by an indignant armed cadet, but no one asked her to explain herself. Being with Louis made her feel safe. At the top he tipped the operator ten kyat, less than twenty-five American cents.

Temple bells tinkled on the golden *hti*. The diamond orb at its tip flashed in the sunlight. The faithful strolled and murmured around the worn stone walkway, stopping to meditate, to offer flowers at the smaller shrines and to recite the Buddha's teachings. Monks walked arm in arm and youngsters squatted on the cool marble slabs. Like St Peter's in Rome and the Kaaba at Mecca, Shwedagon was a centre of pilgrimage. Yet for all its sanctity it ordained no severity. The atmosphere that prevailed was both intimate and communal, exhilarating and serene. Buddhism remained a constant solace, in spite of the recent turmoil.

They circled the platform twice in silence before Ni Ni stepped forward to pour water over a chalky Buddha image – one glassful for each of her years, plus an extra one to ensure long life – then lowered herself onto the stones to pray. As she tucked her legs beneath her Louis saw for an instant the pale soles of her tiny feet. Their nakedness stirred him, as might the touch of a stranger in a darkened room.

Six months earlier he had left England in search of the unfamiliar. He was young – twenty-six – and not long out of university. He had not taken a year out, so as to complete his degree sooner. His discipline had earned him a First. Nothing disrupted his rigid ambition. Every morning he laid his pens out on the desk in a neat row. When his practice offered him a promotion overseas he had leapt at the opportunity. He could advance his career, and unwind.

'Burma is an economic tiger cub,' the firm's senior partner had told him. The Asian economic crisis was still far in the future. 'Business there is going to take off like a skyrocket.' Then he had added with a wink, 'You'll have fun, too.'

Louis had bought a mosquito net and a year's supply of Paludrine. He had enrolled himself in an immersion language course and read Collis, Orwell and Maugham. He wanted to be a part of that boom, to help to modernise the country brick by brick, but he hadn't counted on the heat. From the moment of his arrival in Rangoon it had exhausted him. The dazzling white light had blinded him and the poor hygiene had made him ill. He had contracted bacillary dysentery and spent his second month in bed. His girlfriend had cancelled her visit. His methodical organisation had uncoiled.

Having reached this most extraordinary country, Louis began to pine for the familiar, to look for signposts which would help him to orient himself. He rarely strayed from the building site and his company villa. He ate Welsh rarebit in the British Club rather than ginger soup on Anawrahta Street. His weekends were spent in shady rooms reading other travellers' tales. He lived apart from the city, until his urgent hunger, stoked by the scalding climate, drove him in search of company. The few women at the British Club were all attached or unavailable to a transient, so his eyes turned to the Burmese. It was all so easy, he told himself. His relative wealth, and their lack of liberty, gave him power. In them he found the reassurance of the familiar, yet grasped their gentle difference: taut breasts, slim hips, supple hands and a lightness of movement that reminded him of birds fluttering in a cage. No one, not his accommodating hosts or their irresponsible government, cared to stop him.

On her knees, her back towards him, Ni Ni bent forward in supplication, and touched her copper-brown forehead to the cool white marble. Louis was gripped by the desire to possess her.

The child returned to his side. 'The Buddhist comes to the pagoda to rejoice in the good deeds of others,' she ventured, trying in her way to thank him. 'And in one's own fortune to be able to do good deeds.'

'Do you know Somerset Maugham?' he asked. It did not occur to him that she might never have been able to afford a book. 'He once wrote that Shwedagon was "a sudden hope in the dark night of the soul". I just remembered that now.'

He took her out to dinner. Ni Ni had never before been to a restaurant, apart from Law San's noodle stall, and she ate with caution. Louis explained each dish and ingredient to her, guessing at the translation of words that he didn't know: prawn, mayonnaise, lemon meringue pie. She listened but was hesitant with her own words, speaking only once, and then about Buddhism. She didn't mention her father. Louis filled the quiet with talk of university, London, central heating and his job. When she reminded him of her need to find work he interrupted her. 'Please don't go to Bangkok,' he said. She leaned forward, willing him to talk, hiding her desperation. 'Stay here. I will look after you.' Her manner made her seem eager not to disappoint him.

After the meal, sitting in the dark in his car, he asked her where she lived. Ni Ni was unsure whether to tell him, so he took her home. It was that simple. They were both alone.

His eyesight was so poor that without his glasses he could not see the hand in front of his face. In bed he removed them and caressed her by memory, recalling the bodies of past lovers from Basingstoke and Bassein, hardly knowing the tender presence in his arms. Ni Ni too loved by touch alone, but her fingers trembled with new sensations: a rough graze of stubble, the tension in his thigh, his weight so heavy upon her. All her other senses were numbed. She was the unformed strand of desire, pliable and easy to mould, and Louis shaped her in his great white paws. He wove her slim legs around him, lifted her petite hips towards him and lashed her feather-light sex to his own. At first he took her with gentleness, handling her as another caged bird, whispering soft vows, until the heat and frustration swelled up inside him and he tore deeply into her flesh, making her bite her tongue so as not to cry out. She hid her face in the pillow, muffling her tears, afraid.

Louis knew that Ni Ni was young, very young, and wondered at himself for a moment. He was hard-working, loved by his parents, from Berkshire. At home he bought flowers for his grandmother and made donations to Children in Need. His designs favoured open-plan architecture, not the hierarchical structures which set in stone the tentacles of power. He was not at home, but he reasoned that he could still do good. I can help this one, he told himself. I can give her a home, a bed and a start in life. It's almost an act of charity, he lied, gripping at her pliant flesh. He slipped the pillow aside to kiss the damp eyes.

In all her life Ni Ni had never been praised, never been told that she had done well, yet now his lips were on her nipples, on her stomach, caressing her with charmed words. Louis's loving overwhelmed her. Its ferment had brought pain, but now he was promising to look after her, to protect her. And though her voice remained stifled by the months of fear, she sensed that her hands should express her gratitude.

'I think we will move to a cold country,' he whispered later, his voice pulling her back from the edge of sleep. 'In the far north, where it never does anything but snow.'

'Snow?' she breathed, soft, aching, uncertain.

'We'd live in an ice house.'

'I don't want to live in an ice house.' She didn't want to disagree with him but her father would never find her in the north.

'Every morning before going hunting, you'd chew my boots to soften them. I'd chase polar bears and whales for our supper. We'd have a herd of caribou, a fleet of kayaks, a pack of huskies.'

Ni Ni raised herself onto her elbow and touched a cool hand to his forehead. 'It was too hot for you at Shwedagon?'

'In the summer the sun would never set. Our children would grow up to be strong hunters and trappers and we'd spend all our evenings in our sleeping skins, rubbing noses by the open fire.' He sighed, 'We'd be cold. Cold.'

Louis shivered and held Ni Ni. She abandoned herself to his embrace. As sleep rose up to claim them it did not seem right to her that he dreamed himself away to a cold country. If he expected them to share their bodies, she wanted his thoughts too to be there in the strange warm bed.

In the morning when he left for the site he asked her to wait for him. At dusk when he returned she taught him how to walk. He had wanted to make love first, but she resisted. He only agreed to the lesson on the condition that they took off their clothes.

'When you walk, be where you are,' she told him.

'I am here.' He stood at the head of the villa's shuttered lounge. Evening sunlight criss-crossed the room's inky blue shade. 'But you are too far away, Ni Ni, way over there.'

She moved forward out of the half-light and removed his glasses. He stretched out to touch her and she sprung back. 'Don't feel me; feel your feet on the floor.'

Louis felt the smooth teak floorboards and balanced himself upon them. He pictured the room about him: the palmy etchings of colonial Rangoon, the deep wicker armchair, Ni Ni's tight form tucked into the silver shadow by the old campaign chest. Then he saw himself, prickly skin on a bony frame, short on hair and energy, a gaunt, sun-bleached English architect dislocated in the tropics, wearied by battle with the elements. Ni Ni must have noticed the furrows wrinkle his brow, for she said, 'If you do not care for yourself, how can you care for others?' So Louis tried to let her quiet enter him. He pushed aside his worries. 'Walk,' he heard her say.

He lifted a foot, felt the pull of calf and bend of knee, sensed his ankle pivot and his weight shift as he began his tread. He took the second step with even more care, swinging his other foot forward, feeling the warm air brush against his body. His toes met the floor, steadied him, made him aware of his poise. He walked the length of the room, a path of twenty paces, then returned. As he paced a thought surfaced to distract him, a flashback to the night before of Ni Ni cowering in a corner to unbutton her tapered blouse. She had released her hair so that it fell over her shoulders. 'Come back to your footsteps,' she whispered, recalling him to the present.

He walked on, measuring each step, relaxed yet alert to every movement, each footfall. He discovered the shape of his soles by the way they met the floor, felt the hard bone of his heels and detected the pull of his tendons. The rhythm of his breathing held his attention and then, with each swing of his arms, the minute outward twist of his wrists.

Louis was a stranger to Ni Ni. His white, hairy figure was foreign and unfamiliar. His gestures were abrupt and his movements unrefined. His snarled tangle of pubic curls repelled her. Yet as she watched his progress – the tensing then relaxing muscles, the rise and fall of his chest – she believed that for all his differences Louis shared something with her father. He was weak. He too was a man lost because he was not tied to any woman's heart. The revelation made him seem less unknown, less the beast who had torn her out of childhood. 'Open your heart,' the monks had once taught her, 'and you will realise that you belong.' As Louis trod the hardwood pathway she willed herself to believe that there could be a kind of safety in his frantic passion. The thought helped her to accept that she could belong in the shuttered company villa, in the springy bed, with him. He was her escape, if she was willing to pay the price. She watched his half-blind walk and told herself, 'This is the man I must love properly.'

Ni Ni reached out her arms and, from across the room, traced the outline of Louis's moving figure. She sketched the curve of his spine with her thumb, and the man shivered then missed a step. 'Don't stop,' she hissed from behind the chest. She was frightened, but moved forward to walk behind him, her hands hovering above his waist, feeling him and being felt. He sensed Ni Ni's hands on his chest, gliding over his ribs, even though her fingers did not touch him.

He turned at the end of the lounge and tried to carry on but his pace faltered, his breathing quickened. 'Walk,' she said, and he stepped forward again. She slid backwards before him, stroking his hips without brushing his skin, her distant touch feeling the cool of his buttocks and heat of his loins.

'Walk,' she repeated as his legs grew taut and heavy. Her fingers tingled as she wove them around his shaft without touching him. Ni Ni's alarm and wonder mounted as he began to swell in her detached caress. Louis groaned and rose with his longing. He reached blindly into the void to find her. Instinct made her pull back. She laughed, once again at the wrong time.

'Ni Ni,' he begged, 'where are you?' She retreated from him, fleeing just beyond his reach. 'I can't see you.' Around and around he turned, grasping at her indistinct shadow, aching to grip her flesh. 'Come to me,' he ordered. The anger in his voice stifled her laughter and she obeyed him. He seized her, turned her and took her from behind, lifting her up against the armchair with his fierce thrusts until she bled again and he collapsed, sated, empty, upon her. Then she hurt, *amè*, she hurt, but she felt safe.

The next day Ni Ni moved in with Louis. She had no family who might have warned her. Law San understood that everyone simply did their best to survive. Ko Aye received her sleeping mats. May May Gyi was loaned the rice pot. Louis's kitchen boasted more saucepans and woks than were on sale in the whole of Bogyoke market. In Wayba-gi she left behind the villa's address and the betel box, to be kept until her father's return. All Ni Ni brought with her was the cotton sack of coins and her few worn clothes, which Louis stripped off her that evening. They tumbled on the shreds, ripping the seams of the threadbare cloth, then, while the flush of their copulation was still on her, he dressed her in a new silk blouse and a Chinese silk *longyi*. Its rich salmon-pink complemented her high colour. 'It costs nothing,' he said as she gazed at the unfamiliar reflection in the full-length mirror. Then he told her that she was beautiful.

For the next few months Ni Ni's life hung between innocence and barbarism, caring and abuse, East and West. In Burma physical contact is an intimate matter. Men and women do not touch in public. Her actions further distanced her from her society. She ceased to belong. To compensate for the loss she convinced herself that she was tied to Louis, that his convenient liaison was love. He did nothing to dissuade her. When he arrived home they coupled urgently, on the sofa, in the bed, even once on the hallway floor with the front door still ajar. Afterwards they washed, sometimes dressed again, and ate in the glimmering dusk. Across the low table he took her small hands, kissed each finger in turn and told her that she made him happy. She believed that they would be together for ever, or at least until her father came home. Louis knew that it would end.

There is evil in every man and woman. It courses through our veins, beneath the silk dressing gown or battle fatigues, ready to sweep aside compassion. Our civility determines whether or not we act upon the baseness, whether we restrain it or unleash it. Louis tried to contain his by locking it away in the villa. He and Ni Ni never went out together. He isolated her as Burma had been isolated by its military rulers. Their months together melted away as multi-party elections were held across the country. The generals, outraged by their humiliating defeat at the polls, annulled the results. But their refusal to relinquish power went all but unnoticed in the strange bed. Ni Ni surrendered her innocent heart to Louis. She felt herself protected. She once again made the mistake of thinking that she had time.

One Saturday morning in May Ni Ni awoke to the mutterings of rainless thunder. It was the end of the dry season and all Burma was waiting for the western winds that would bring the monsoon. The earth was parched and every breeze stirred the dust, hanging gritty veils across the dirty streets. The thunder seemed to encircle all of Rangoon. Ni Ni, her head lying on Louis's chest, heard his voice rise out of its rumble.

'I've been asked to go home,' he said, his inflexion flat. 'My work is done here.' She said nothing, but he felt the tension brace her body. 'I didn't tell you sooner because I, well . . .' His weakness appalled him, but he gave himself up to it. 'You'll be all right.'

'The building isn't finished.' Her woman's whisper quivered, then broke. She sounded like a child again. 'Not yet.'

'My part of it is.'

The hotel's superstructure had been completed. A Singapore contractor had been appointed to coordinate the fitting out. An English supervisor was not needed to oversee the installation of the wall and ceiling panels. The French interior designer was already on site.

'Ni Ni, you're young,' Louis prattled, turning his unease into platitudes. 'You've learned a lot, and your whole life is in front of you.' He did not ask her, a fourteen-year-old orphan, to come home to England with him.

Ni Ni slipped out from under the sheet, her lightness leaving no impression on the mattress to show that she had ever laid beside him, and crossed the room to the wardrobe. She opened a lower drawer, burrowed under her fine new clothes and found the bag of coins. She knelt beside the bed, unsure if Louis wished her to return, and emptied out the money onto the pillow. There were silver quarters and Dutch guilders, Deutschmarks and a Canadian two-dollar bill. She arranged her funds with care, sorting them according to colour and size, not by value or nationality, and said, 'My father saved these for me. Every day for over five years.'

Louis roared with laughter. He sat up in bed, pulled the orderly display toward him and did a quick calculation. 'About twenty dollars, I'd say. Although I don't know what the yen is at today.' He chuckled again. 'Five years, you say? My poor Ni Ni.' He shook his head. 'And where is your father now?'

Ni Ni cried out in a sudden burst of emotion. She threw herself onto the coins and then at Louis, her nails raised like talons. She pinned him down to the bed and tried to scratch his chest, his arms, his face. He could have tossed her aside, but instead he gripped her hands. He locked her feet to his own. She yelled at him, casting off her reserve. Her tears rained down onto his cheeks as she sobbed out the story of the theft of the bicycle.

'It's only a bike,' Louis laughed in his bungled Burmese. 'What can a bloody bike cost here?'

It was then, as she unravelled her pain, that Ni Ni finally understood how she had been used. She knew that it was the end, that she had never been safe. She tried to pull herself away, to get off him and run out of the villa. But he held her to him. Her outburst had excited him. And despite her cries and pleas, he took her one last, terrible time.

'One day my father will return,' she told him later, gathering up the small change that had been scattered across the bed. 'You need not worry about me.'

Louis was not worried, though he did wonder what had come over him those last months. The girl was so poor, so gauche. He hated himself, but it didn't really matter; he was leaving. He wanted her out of the house, but hadn't the nerve to tell her. Instead he took his wallet off the bedside table and pulled out two hundred-dollar bills. 'Here,' he said, impatient now. 'These will help you get by until he comes back.' He put them into her bag and added, 'I want you to forget me.'

'I will never forget,' she said, straight-backed and serious, no longer a child.

Prostitution does not exist in Burma; at least it cannot be mentioned in the press. The Burmese kings had a history of taking numerous wives, and religious sites always offered the service of 'pagoda servants' to pilgrims. Neither custom still exists today, officially. The girls on the steps of pagodas sell flowers and candles, religious requisites, not physical comforts. The royal *zenana* has been replaced by the executive escort agency. But both traditions remain part of the culture and, as a result of the smallest misfortune, a woman can become trapped.

Louis's dollars, though worth a fortune to Ni Ni, didn't last until the end of the monsoon. Soon after her return to Wayba-gi she fell ill, and May May Gyi spent the money on medicines which did nothing to improve her condition. No drug seemed capable of restoring her energy, no tonic would lift her spirit. Buddhists are taught that they are responsible today for what they will be tomorrow. Every man and woman is answerable for their own actions. But Ni Ni's sense of duty had left with Louis's departing aeroplane. The roar of its engines had shaken the satellite town. Like her father before her she brooded through the airless, vaporous afternoons, not hearing the rain drumming on her roof, ignoring May May Gyi's encouragement, even turning down Law San's offer of *Shan hkauk-hswe* noodles. The past was memory, the future might only be fantasy, but she had no love in the here and now. Ni Ni did not feel anger, wished no vengeance, and when the money ran out, when there seemed to be no other choice, she went in search of Way Way.

Way Way's friend promised to find her work in Thailand as a dishwasher. The wage he promised was double that which she could earn in Rangoon. He paid for her bus ticket to the border, where she was met by a Thai driver. There were five other women in his car: two Burmese, two Shan girls with milky-white complexions and a single, silent Chinese. On the road to Bangkok the driver paid a uniformed man at a checkpoint. In the brothel Ni Ni was given a number and told to sit in a windowed showroom. She toyed with the hem of her blouse when bypassers stopped to stare at her. The first man who took her in the *hong bud boree sut*, 'the room to unveil virgins', paid the owner 120 baht – less than five dollars – and tipped her the same amount. During that month she was sold as a virgin to four more clients. She was allowed to keep her tips. They were the largest she was to receive over the next four years.

The friend had been an agent. The debt which enslaved Ni Ni was his fee, plus her transport, clothes and protection money, compounded by 100 per cent interest. She was required to wear high heels and a mini-skirt instead of her silk *longyi*. In lieu of money she received red plastic chips; one for every client. Each morning she counted them twice to calculate the amount that had been subtracted from her debt. She kept them under the cement bunk on which she was forced to prostitute herself. Under it also was the secret door to a locker where she hid during police raids. The abrupt arrival of a dozen armed officers never failed to alarm the brothel owner. More often though the policemen came in ones and twos after work. However they arrived, the girls were always theirs for free.

The cubicle measuring six feet square was her home. Here Ni Ni slept and worked, twelve hours a day, seven days a week. Only two days a month were allowed off, during her period. The clients were mostly Asian, although Westerners paid for her too, flying in from Frankfurt and Brussels on 'sex bomber' package holidays. She served five or six men each weekday. On weekends she often had as many as thirty customers.

The demand for new faces dictated that every few months she be moved to a different brothel. Each was the same as the last. The neon-lit rooms were dingy, the walls always stained grimy grey along the edge of the bunk. There were never any proper toilets. Once, in one cubicle she thought she heard the sea, though it could have been a passing *tuk-tuk*, and from another, if she stood on the bed and peered through a grille, she could make out the graceful spires of the Royal Palace. The frequent displacement left her no time to get to know the other girls or to consider escape, especially as she never knew where she was incarcerated. Those who did run away were often caught by their police clients and returned to be punished, or locked up for months without trial, subjected to abuse, in a Thai immigration detention centre. The few who managed to reach Burma risked the possibility of arrest for 'illegal departure', and even, it was rumoured, execution if they were found to be HIV positive. Their only choice was to work until they were told their debt was paid, then to rely on an agent to escort them back through the checkpoints and over the border.

The years crept up on her, ageing Ni Ni's firm young body. Men chose her less often, and those who did were less particular. One client put a gun to her head when she asked him to wear a condom. It wasn't because she was afraid of pregnancy – she had often paid the owner's wife to give her Depo-Prevera injections – or even because he was filthy. It was simply that he frightened her. In life there is a path of fear and a path of love, and Ni Ni had been unable to follow the latter one alone. The owner threatened her with a beating if she ever came out of the room before her client again.

Ni Ni's hands touched and stroked and satisfied the men, but she felt nothing, sensed nothing through the empty years. Only sometimes in an Englishman's clumsy white embrace did she remember Louis. But he never came to rescue her. At eighteen she was over-handled and utterly misused. Her life had been stolen. She had lost control of her body. She possessed nothing more than a sense of hopelessness.

It is estimated that two million people are employed in Thailand's sex trade. The business is probably the most valuable sector of the tourist industry, which itself exceeds all exports as a source of foreign exchange. In 1988 4.3 million people visited the country, three-quarters of whom were unaccompanied males. But it is local patronage that makes the greater demand. Half of all Thai men have their first sexual experience with a prostitute; three out of four have visited a brothel. The majority of commercial sex workers are natives, but there are also Filipinos, Indonesians, even Europeans – five thousand Russian prostitutes are working in Bangkok. And every year ten thousand Burmese women, young and infection-free, are trafficked across the border, enticed by false promises, imprisoned by debt bondage. Their great hope is to go home, but their greater fear is deportation.

Often, in the quiet of morning when Ni Ni was left alone, she fell into the same dream. In her cubicle a miniature black spider, no bigger than a pinhead, crawled up her hand. She watched it spin between her thumb and forefinger a silky thread which glistened and grew until it twisted together her five fingers. She felt its tickle as both her hands were enmeshed. The bonds became tighter and she tried to free herself. But the industrious spider, so friendly and engaging at first, continued its labours, stitched its weave, wrapped the corners, until all her body, the bunk on which she lay, even the red plastic chips were wrapped in its cobweb, dusty and dirty, and her life was snuffed out.

It was from this dream that Ni Ni was awoken by the sound of English voices. The Crime Suppression Division – in cooperation with the Commission for the Protection of Children's Rights – raided her hotel in an operation stage-managed for the world's press. The girls were arrested and interrogated for the cameras, though they were not asked questions about the brothel owner. He had been allowed to go, along with the pimps and the clients. Ni Ni and the other Burmese nationals were sent to the penal reform institution in Pakkret, from where they were deported. In that brief period when Rangoon sanctioned repatriation, no brothel agents or Thai border-patrol officers could lure the women back to Bangkok's red-light districts. They were not harassed in local jails or raped in reform houses. There was no need for them to buy their release papers. The Shan and hill-tribe prostitutes, not being ethnic Burmans, were less fortunate. The Burmese authorities forbade their return because they were members of a racial minority. They, like the fresh-faced girls who arrived every morning at Bangkok's Northern Bus Terminal, were left to their fates in Thailand.

On the flight home Ni Ni caught sight of golden Shwedagon. She watched the red earth of Rangoon rush up to meet the aircraft. She saw the delta-winged shadow flash over the dusty plain. She was taken to the North Okkalapa Female Police Training Academy. A doctor tested her blood. There were injections and tablets to be taken every day. The girls were told that they could go home as soon as their parents came to collect them. Some families were too poor to travel to the capital. There was no one to claim Ni Ni, and almost a year passed before she was released from the barracks.

In front, behind. In front, behind. She worked the bamboo in pairs, picked up the right-hand weaver, moved it around the border. In 1994 Ni Ni had returned to Wayba-gi to find neither news of her father nor word from Louis. Her old neighbours had either died or been moved on. She needed to find work, and might have fallen back into prostitution, for in the intervening years the local sex trade had expanded to serve tourists and businessmen at the new hotels, but for the assistance of a foreign charity. In the absence of any government aid, it had established a sheltered workshop to reintegrate those who had been repatriated into society. There in its peaceful studio Ni Ni trained to be a basket-maker, picking up the right-hand stakes, weaving the frayed strands of her life back into order. Her small, sensitive fingers produced the workshop's finest, most detailed work. The other women, who had chosen to learn to become secretaries or tailors, teased her, for the Burmese word *hpa* translates as both basket and whore. But Ni Ni worked on unbothered, even volunteering to draw other vulnerable girls into the training programme, so that they too might have a choice, so that they need never be trapped. In front, behind. Shape the form, trim off the ends. In the last summer of her short life Ni Ni had discovered that there were three things which matter most.

First, how well did she love?

'With both my hands,' she might have answered, not lifting her eyes from the weaving, but laughing at herself for an instant.

Second, how fully did she live?

'As best I could,' she could only reply.

Third, how much did she learn to let go?

'Not enough. Not enough.'

There is an old story of a poor woman who came to Buddha weeping. 'O Enlightened One,' she cried, 'my only daughter has died. Is there no way to bring her back to me?'

Lord Buddha looked at her with compassion and replied, 'If you bring me a basket from a house where neither parent or child, relative or servant has ever died, I shall bring your daughter back to life.' The woman searched for many months, travelled to many villages and towns, and when she returned Buddha asked her, 'My daughter, have you found the container?'

The woman shook her head and said, 'No, I have not. The people tell me that the living are few, but the dead are many.'

THREE

Ties of the Heart

'YOU ARE RATHER LATE, MY DEARS,' said Colonel Than in clipped Sandhurst English, tucking his burnished pocket watch back into his robes. 'We shall miss tea.' He let go of my hand then bowed to Katrin, a monk being forbidden to touch a woman, and his small round spectacles caught the reflection of sweating French oilmen and cool Taiwanese traders. 'Charmed girl, may I introduce myself as someone who still maintains a soft spot for the British Royal Family and the people of UK.'

'And of Canada,' I reminded him, shouting above the screech of the next arriving aircraft.

'Another nation to prosper from Imperial rule,' he assured us, and whispered when Katrin turned away to pick up her rucksack, 'If I may be permitted the compliment, your woman is a cracker. You are the luckiest man in the worlds.'

'Thank you,' I said. Than's fine eye for ladies was at odds with his faulty ear for language.

'It is never good for a man to be alone. I am glad that you are now wed,' he continued with parade-ground projection. 'If you would care to follow me our taxi cab conveyance awaits.'

Colonel Than, properly Khin Mg Than, Colonel (Ret'd) Artillery Regiment, strode forth into the throng, his step purposeful, his back bent like a storm-lashed palm. His black umbrella, its tie broken, flapped wildly at his side. Ten years before, in the same arrivals lounge, I had stumbled off my mistaken flight and into his care. 'It is my duty to offer a helping hand to visitors,' he had announced, then added in a conspiratorial tone, 'My dear, I have just had the good fortune to be graciously smiled upon by the Duke of Hussey's daughter.'

'The Duke of Hussey?' I had asked. I would learn later that Than considered it his responsibility, as a former King's commissioned officer, to scoop up lost anglophones.

'Of course,' he had replied, pleased to illuminate a colonial's scant knowledge of the British aristocracy. 'The Chairman of the BBC; Marmaduke Hussey.'

We followed his short, rust-robed form past the hotel touts and German package tourists, out of the low terminal building and into the dazzling afternoon light. At the time of our first meeting the Colonel had been a devout Christian, exchanging Christmas cards with the Bishop of Rangoon and singing God's praises as the senior chorister at St Mary's Cathedral. But after the 1988 uprising he had converted to Buddhism, 'because I needed to know my people better'. Over the following decade we had become faithful correspondents, even though he could rarely afford the bribes demanded by the postman to deliver my letters. His outspoken missives on the other hand had always reached me, though in envelopes slit open by prying censors. The often incomprehensible turns of phrase must have baffled them, while preserving him, but they helped me to see how strong loyalties – like poignant memories – sometimes do not age. Instead they hold their value and leave their mark on the present.

'I try to instruct the younger monks,' he had once written in his stilted, archaic English, 'by embracing and receiving with open arms any and every one who wishes on his or her own account to listen.' It was a miracle both that he had survived the years of terror and that he had received word of our impending arrival.

The humid Rangoon heat engulfed us in viscous air, turning our walking into wading, our city shoes into leaded diving boots. I smelt jasmine and diesel, heard cicadas and sirens. A boy with black mica eyes took hold of my sleeve and asked, 'Change money? Sell clothes?' A dozen children with shaven heads held out grimy hands and wailed,

'Bic! Bic!' Than swept them all out of our path with brash confidence.

'Handicrafts aren't my kettle of tea,' he declared, uncertain of the sanity of our travelling halfway around the world in the hope of tracing a basket. 'So my intelligence gathering will be cronky at best.' He woke our driver, who was dozing beneath a vast hand-cut billboard. It read, 'Enjoy the Distinctive Myanmar Quality: Smiles, Warmth, Peace and Abundance'. 'All I know is that almost every occupation in our country requires baskets. We have a mess of different sorts. Drive on,' Than told the driver, 'it's high time for tea.'

The dusty taxi whisked us away from the airport and onto broad Prome Road. There did seem to be baskets everywhere: atop women's heads and on bicycle handlebars, used as cradles and colanders, fashioned into furniture and braided around saplings as protection from goats. We saw vast bamboo shoppers and dainty palm-leaf whisks, plaited hats and a wheelbarrow with woven sides. A multi-storey basket loomed out of the polluted haze. The undulating lines of bamboo scaffolding created the illusion of movement. A glittering, sequinned sign acclaimed the glory of the Sedona Hotel, the biggest of the new tourist developments overlooking Inya Lake. At the foot of the woven hoarding a girl knocked chunks of grey mortar off old bricks before stacking them in a platter basket.

Katrin leaned forward, her shirt sticking to the baking back seat, and handed Than a photograph we had taken at the museum store-room. 'Hello,' he chirped. 'I know this type.'

'It was found towards the end of the last century, somewhere in Burma.'

'The design is damn familiar.'

It was a response, though not an idiom, that we would hear often over the next four weeks.

'Then you can place it?'

'Not me, gentle good woman. But calm your worries. I know a chap who can.'

Ten minutes later the taxi swept into the Kyimyindine township and, avoiding the potholes, stopped in front of the School for the Blind. 'Here,' Than stated with authority, 'baskets are made.' But once we were inside the cool building he began to apologise. The school was closed. The pupils had been sent away until the monsoon. The basketry tutor had gone to the monastery for a week's retreat.

'That is unfortunate but not a problem,' said Than as we drove away along Kaba Aye Pagoda Road. 'I had the forethinking to make a contingent plan.'

'Maybe we should go to the hotel first, Colonel?' I suggested. 'Our flight was quite tiring.'

'My dear, there's a rush on,' he insisted. 'Time is precious and your visa only lasts for one month. You'll understand the need to chop-chop when you reach my golden age.'

Our second stop was the Mayangon Orphanage School. Children waved at us through the barred windows as we turned into the drive. 'Baskets are made here as well,' Than declared with undiminished confidence. 'And I am certain that their caff can rustle up a sterling pot of tea.' But the school director was out too. The inconveniences seemed not to bother Than, for much the same reason that Burmese travellers never ask for arrival times. 'Anticipation tempts fate,' he counselled.

When Katrin went off to inspect the deserted workshop Than nodded after her and said, 'A fair filly my dear, but, alas, you have no children?'

'Not yet,' I told him.

'Forgive me for asking, but is your elegant and petite wife unbearable?'

'Not in the least, Colonel.'

'I am fond of children, not only human beings but also animals, all over the world, which has become not very wide nowadays, and I would make a kindly uncle.' He touched my arm. 'You should drink malted milk, my dear. It is good for all ailments from my own experience.'

In the workshop the smiling caretaker told Katrin of a Baptist mission near the airport. 'Good show,' enthused Than, though he was disappointed to miss tea. 'Now we are making a fine progression.' We turned the car around and headed back north.

Thirty minutes later Saw Taung stared beyond the Colonel's left

shoulder and said, 'Baskets? Of course we do baskets.' We had found
the Self-Supporting Karen Mission at the end of a leafy lane of
woven-walled houses and open drains. 'Our work is the finest in
Rangoon.'

We stumbled through the pitch-black rooms, our blind guide
having no need of electric light, and I wondered how we would show
him the photograph.

'It is the handles and bases which go first,' explained Saw Taung,
leading us into a murky workshop. A row of weavers, each wearing
dark glasses, laboured in the shadows, repairing broken multi-
coloured plastic shopping baskets with cane strips. 'We can fix them
for half the cost of a new one.' He walked across the room, knowing
its measure without a stick, and took hold of a restored shopper in
his pudgy pale hands. 'Feel that quality.' The weaving felt neat and
exact, but it was too dark for us to see any detail. 'Maybe you've
watched our ads on television?'

The government promoted the mission's work around the time
of International White Cane Day. In return the blind craftsmen and
women offered to renew the generals' wives' baskets. The offer was
not taken up, because Louis Vuitton and Hermès did not sell plastic
shoppers. Nevertheless the generals showed their appreciation by
arranging for the craftsworkers to be fed for a week or two.

'Our repairs are only meant to be ordered through government
shops,' Saw Taung explained to us, his right hand twitching in the
dark, 'but if you have brought a shopper all the way from England
then I could make an exception.'

We thanked him and told him about the real object of our quest.
'Not plastic, then,' he said, disappointment in his voice. 'We like
working with plastic because of the wonderful colours.'

'This one is yellow and orange,' volunteered one of the blind
workmen. A poster pinned above him read, 'Make money from the
happy eyes and compensate that money to the blinds'.

Katrin described Scott's basket to Than, who translated the details.
Saw Taung listened carefully and nodded. 'It sounds traditional,' he
said flatly.

'It was found over a hundred years ago.'

'Then I am sorry. Such work takes too much time. No one can afford to make such a complicated piece any more.'

On the drive into town we felt disappointed, as well as drained by the heat. The Colonel on the other hand seemed delighted, humming to himself a few bars of 'Rule Britannia'. 'You should be thankful,' he said cheerfully. 'Everyone recognises the basket.'

'But no one can place it,' sighed Katrin.

'You must not want this too much,' said Than, slipping seamlessly from imperialism to Buddhism. 'It is not good to pray and ask for anything. One has to do good deeds and transmit pure, clean radiation to all corners of the earth, below and above.'

'Radiation?' I asked.

'*Mettá*, we call it. A sort of loving kindness. A universal kindness.'

We turned onto Prome Road and drove into a traffic jam. The SLORC traffic policeman had turned his back on the waiting cars. An ice lorry fumed at the head of the queue, its load melting away in the afternoon sun. Grey clouds of exhaust puffed from an idle Win cigarette bus. Two girls yawned under parasols in the back of an ancient pick-up truck. It was 27 March – Armed Forces Day – and distorted martial music warbled from a distant loudspeaker.

'I am sorry, my dears,' apologised the Colonel, 'but the delay is because of the parade in Resistance Park. "The *Tatmadaw* Shall Never Betray the National Cause",' he quoted, without a hint of sarcasm. But when our driver stepped out of the car to light a cheroot Than hissed, 'This lot had bugger all to do with our liberation.' Once called Resistance Day to celebrate the start of the campaign to expel the Japanese, the date had been hijacked by the regime to substantiate its erroneous claims of legitimacy. 'They stole it, like every damn thing else in the country.'

A fruit vendor working the queue offered us grimy bagfuls of sliced papaya. Then a gleaming khaki Jeep with a flashing red light and four yellow-kerchiefed, rifle-toting soldiers escorted a black Mazda VIP 929 saloon around the snarl. Our driver slipped back behind the wheel.

'Listen please, Burma is a faithful country,' Than told us now that he could again be overheard. 'We try to refrain from all evil, to do what is good, to purify the mind. This is the Buddha's teaching.'

The SLORC policeman flourished a salute at the official limousine's tinted windows and then, almost as an afterthought, deigned to let the other traffic proceed.

'Here, please,' Than said to the driver. 'This will suit me fine.' He climbed out onto the Pyay Road and, while straightening his robes, offered to help us search for the basket again the following afternoon. 'I wonder,' he added, 'if you received my last letter?' He cast a cautionary glance toward the driver.

'I'm sorry,' I replied. I had been too hot, and too rushed by Than's anarchic runaround, to remember the gifts. 'They're in here somewhere,' I said, rummaging in the bottom of our bag.

'I favour simple cooking,' Than told Katrin. 'Poached eggs and sausages with mashed potatoes; a throw-up to my days as a gentleman-cadet at the RMAS.'

'A throwback,' I suggested, though many Burmans might disagree, and passed him three glass bottles and a jar.

'But you have kindly imported from England that most essential ingredient! Yes, thank you. Crosse & Blackwell Fruit Sauce.' He examined the jar. 'And this is most excellent too. Coleman's. You appreciate that I am still quite young so very much care for the adult mustard. Now please will you forgive me for not providing you with tea-like refreshment but the driver will converse you to your hotel. I must call on old pals who have gone over to the other side of the world.'

'America?' I asked.

'No, my dear. Comrades-in-arms who long ago went for a Burton beer.' He flapped his umbrella toward the mauve bougainvillaea that marked the Pyay Road war cemetery. 'And who are now pushing up daffodils. I always drop by when I'm in this part of town,' he explained before leaving us.

A helicopter shuddered overhead and, passing within sight of the Shwedagon Pagoda, we heard the marching song of the loyal *Tatma-*

daw. As we paused at a traffic light for another military convoy the driver asked us what our nationality was. All afternoon he had given no indication of having understood our conversation. I told him, then pointed out the window and said, 'That's quite a contrast. The military here, and Buddhism there.'

'I'm sorry,' he replied, feigning incomprehension, 'but sometimes my English isn't too good.' The light changed and we moved forward, not to exchange another word.

Night fell and shutters were thrown open to catch any breath of wind. Apartment blocks, which had been sealed against heat and sun by day, spilt their lives and washing lines out onto the street. Families sat cross-legged on broad armchairs of woven rattan, watching vast colour televisions, eating crispies and peanuts. As Katrin and I picked our way around the pavement living rooms, around old men reading newspapers and children asleep on bamboo mats, I tried to reach back to the Rangoon of ten years ago. I wanted to recall my first visit, to hold its mirror up to the present day. Vignettes did come back to me: the squawk of parrots and quarrel of sparrows in the trees; the laughter of an outspoken friend who had vanished one Sunday evening; the cries of beggars in the darkness, 'Please, saah. Give us food. We have nothing to eat.' I wanted to remember and to write them down, every thought and encounter, so that they would not be forgotten, so that I might hold onto the memory for ever.

Rangoon became Burma's young capital in 1885, when gunboats completed Britain's conquest of the country. A century before, King Alaungpaya had named the city Dagon, or 'end-of-strife', to celebrate his dynasty's military invincibility. He would have been displeased by his descendants losing it in the Anglo–Burmese wars. During their brief stewardship the British transformed the city into an imperial capital and major port. Its strategic position, facing the ocean and served by a river navigable for nine hundred fertile miles, enabled the country to become the world's largest exporter of rice. It was a way-station for KLM, Air France and British flying-boats.

Its high literacy rate was a source of national pride. Then in 1942 the Japanese invaded, and half a million people fled for their lives. Three years later, at the end of the Second World War, the 'scorched earth' policy practised by both the invader and the Allies had rendered a third of all cultivated land unusable.

For the next forty years Burma was a place out of time, unable to progress, racked by rebel insurgents and impoverished by Ne Win's disastrous 'Burmese Way to Socialism'. Paddy fields lay fallow. Majestic buildings were left to rot. Everyday goods became unavailable. Once the rice bowl of Asia, the country began to import food to feed its children. By 1987 it ranked among the world's ten poorest nations. When I arrived milk was too scarce to be left in jugs on tea-house tables. A single bottle of Johnny Walker Red Label whisky sold on the black market would finance a week's travel, including flights, accommodation and food. Writers scribbled their stories on strips of paper torn from the blank margins of old newspapers, and shopkeepers made paper bags by pasting together sheets from wormy issues of the *British Medical Journal*. The desperate, destitute conditions had incited the 1988 uprising, which was crushed by the heinous massacre.

An ice vendor hauling oversized blocks flecked with rice-chaff insulation lay down his load to shake our hands. From street kitchens women smiled at us, pausing from mulching curry into fistfuls of noodles, pressing through the flavours with their fingers. Diners squatted beside them, eating over open drains on kerbsides stained by sanguinary pools of betel-nut spit. Chilli-spiced mango slices glistened beneath candles flickering in cellophane bags. A *palata* vendor waved, then slapped a thumb of dough onto his platter and shaped it like a pizza. He slipped it onto the griddle, cracked an egg on top, then flipped and cut the fried flatbread into bite-size mouthfuls with a pair of old scissors. We pushed through the busy night market, stepping over a display of second-hand Thai denim, and into a noisy biryani bar illuminated by car-battery lamps. We squeezed onto a table beside a young Indian family. A shy, walnut-skinned woman looked down at her plate. Her husband in a sweat-stained singlet offered to buy our dinner. 'Friends. First time. Myanma Drinking Water,' said the restaurant owner, placing a plastic bottle before us. His white teeth flashed and a mouse-sized cockroach ran up the wall.

'I don't understand how after all that has happened these people can still laugh,' I said to Katrin. 'Don't they remember?'

'What has changed since 1988?' she asked me.

'Everything and nothing. Back then there was no Pepsi or high-rises. No one had a television. Now there's much more food. But somehow all the changes feel physical, superficial.'

'The Burmese want to survive, like everyone else,' said Katrin. 'Maybe it's better to be quiet and alive than outspoken and dead.'

'You heard Than this morning. I don't believe that the people's acquiescence has been bought by reruns of *Dallas* and a few extra measures of rice.'

We watched the family eat with their hands, using fingertips bunched like utensils, organising and mixing the *puris* and *dosa* on the stainless steel *thali* plate. The owner came over again to ensure that we were enjoying our meal.

'The *biryani* is delicious,' said Katrin.

'You are welcome here,' he nodded, pleased that we had chosen to visit his restaurant, his country. 'You would like some more water? It is on the house.'

'Thank you, yes,' I replied. The night air cloaked us like a wet blanket in a sauna. 'But only if we can pay.'

'It is good that you see our life,' he said, choosing his words with care. His three sons paused from cleaning dishes to come up too and stare at us. 'To us you tourists are like the stars in the night sky. We hope a little of that light will shine on us.'

On the drive back to our hotel the bus did not use its headlamps. The street lighting too had been turned off, to conserve electricity. A stranger riding with us tried to pay our fare. We walked the last few hundred yards past soldiers standing guard under *hkayayban* trees. Children darted out between the passing cars to gather the falling star-flowers. One youngster, bolder than the rest, held my hand. 'You very beautiful,' he told me, too bashful to look at Katrin.

'And you are very handsome,' she replied.

'I love you bye bye bye,' cried the other children, running away with their embarrassment, then threading the collected blossoms into garlands for their mothers to sell in the morning.

'So where to tomorrow?' asked Katrin. The evening air smelt of caraway and rattan, like the inside of an Eastern basket.

'I want to find out more about Ni Ni.'

'Do you really mean Ni Ni?' she asked, raising her eyebrows. 'Or her story?'

'I mean the Rehabilitation Centre,' I replied, correcting myself. 'Colonel Than promised to arrange it.'

The next morning I was woken by memory. An eerie song echoed between the musty buildings, rang off crumbling walls, reached up into our hotel room. The deep, clear voice eased me out from a dream of industrious spiders and rare birds. I stood on the bed and looked out at the dawn.

'*Pe-byouk*,' called the voice. The sky was tinged by the flush of morning, and from a distance the singer looked no more than eleven or twelve years old. '*Pe-byouk*,' she called again, her words pealing along the urban chasm. On her small shoulders she carried a yoke. Two lined bamboo baskets swung at her waist. '*Hawdiga hawdiga.*' A yawning customer stepped out from a doorway, a banknote crumpled in her palm. The singer set down her load in the dust and spooned out a measure of beans. *Pe-byouk* are boiled beans, the staple food – along with rice – of a hungry people. Cyclists wheeled around the pair, carrying yard-high stacks of government newspapers. A raven dropped from a palm tree to pick at the rubbish adrift in a fetid alley. A few kyat changed hands and, before the young street vendor twisted herself back under the yoke, she paused to catch a loose strand of her hair. Only then, in that very feminine movement, did I realise that her slight frame and the soft morning light belied her true age. The singer was no child, but a mature woman. Her deep voice alone had not been checked by malnutrition. She called out again, her sales pitch more music than words, and carried on down the hot road. I remembered the same song, sung by her daughter or niece, on a similar street at an earlier dawn.

'We're not against prostitution,' explained Simon Zehnder, a pragmatic Austrian with deep-set eyes. He spread his broad hands as if to embrace the five hundred women and children who had been helped by the Centre in its four years of existence. 'It's a part of society.'

Colonel Than, who seemed to know everyone in Rangoon, had told us, 'Zehnder is a white-moustached rhinoceros in spectacles. If you go up his nose he'll attack.' I had promised not to irritate him and asked the Colonel to join us at the meeting. 'I'll take a rain check on that recce, my dear,' he had replied.

A taxi had carried us west past Virgin Land Tours and Travel, beyond the signs for Foster's lager and Pulpy C fruit drink, to the low-slung white building behind a green hedge. Katrin and I had left our sandals at the door and walked barefoot across the polished floor into the sparse office.

'Our approach is pragmatic,' continued Zehnder, leaning his chair back against the blank wall. He was a big man dressed in a pressed white shirt and black trousers. 'We simply want to offer people a choice.'

In a lifetime of charity work he had cared for the orphans of war and famine, escorted humanitarian convoys into Bangladesh, watched friends die in Cambodia and East Timor. His compassion had been aroused when reading newspaper reports of the Burmese government's execution of former prostitutes found to be infected with the HIV virus. At the time aid agencies – like all things foreign – had been banned from the country. But his rhino-like tenacity had ensured that the Centre became the first non-government organisation to be granted access to Burma.

'But how could I, a European male, win the trust of the women?' he asked. 'It was Ma Aye Min who ensured our success.'

Ma Aye Min, the Rehabilitation Centre's manager, perched on the edge of the bamboo sofa. 'We think of ourselves as enablers,' she said, 'enabling people to think for themselves.'

She had been born into a wealthy Rangoon family, grown up with security and a good education. But rather than flaunt her advantages they had made her aware of those less fortunate. She had trained as a social worker, become the rising star of the Ministry of Health, until rapid promotion had taken her away from case work. She had paid off her bond and left the ministry to continue to work with individuals in need, and Zehnder.

'The families we deal with have no money,' said Ma Aye Min, an eagerness speeding her speech. 'When Simon says that he has no money it means, maybe, that there is only ten dollars in his pocket. When I say it I might have a hundred kyat. But they have nothing, not even two kyat, and sometimes no father, never any state benefits, living with four or five relatives in a room so small that the men cannot lie out straight to sleep.' I recalled Ni Ni's father curled up beneath his worthless coins and banknotes in the tiny room on the Prome Road.

'Into this world the girls grow up, full of ambition and natural desires,' she continued. 'And because there is no money they have to work, from the age of ten or eleven, helping to run the family cooking-oil stall, trying to make a few kyat each day just to buy food.' She ducked her head, trying to hide her mouth behind her hands. 'Under these circumstances, if the slightest problem befalls them, if a thief steals their food or the mother falls ill, they are thrown into a desperate situation. The girl must look for – how to call him? – a benefactor to lend her, say, three thousand kyat. This loan must be paid back *every* evening, so the girl will buy two or three sacks of rice to sell by the *viss* on the pavement, and give him 3,500 kyat at the end of the day.'

'From which he will give her a hundred kyat for herself,' added Zehnder, staring at us over his spectacles.

'Or she might get a job on a construction site, carrying bricks and sand. It is very physical work and there are many men there, and often this is a girl's first experience.'

'They hang around tea shops and talk to friends and often they just fall into it. They grow familiar with the benefactor or a builder and keep on fulfilling his wishes and that's it.' Zehnder snapped his fingers. 'The parents don't ask any questions because the money buys the family a new cooking pot or pays for a younger brother to go to school.'

'A younger brother?' asked Katrin.

'Yes,' nodded Ma Aye Min. 'The girls have nothing. They're trapped, and often see their actions as the only means of escape.'

'It's our job to make things seem less inevitable to them.'

At first the Centre had counselled only the commercial sex workers repatriated from Bangkok, then it had extended its care to their families, their friends and in time to other vulnerable women on the point of being drawn into Rangoon's own burgeoning sex industry.

'How do you find them?' Katrin asked Ma Aye Min.

'Sometimes I go out into the neighbourhoods. Sometimes they are introduced to me by girls who we've already helped. But wherever it begins I have to be very careful in my communication. For example I never wear gold earrings or bracelets, but often the girls, who claim to be poor, appear wearing jewellery or an expensive shirt. At first I thought that they were misleading me and I asked them how they could afford it. They started to cry and told me not to be sarcastic with them. Then I began to understand that their appearance was an illusion, a wish to give a good impression. They would have borrowed the shirt from a neighbour, the bracelet from a friend. I show them that it is not necessary, that I am interested in them as individuals, and next time they wear normal clothes.'

'It can be difficult to restore their individuality, especially if for years their only identity was as a number in a brothel window.'

'They offered to help people and were abused, so when real help comes they are suspicious of it.'

'And you can't simply tell them "Don't do it,"' I said.

'If I did they certainly would go straight out and do it doubly,' laughed Ma Aye Min, raising her hands again to cover her mouth.

'In the beginning they're always reluctant to trust us.'

'No, instead I say, "Please consider this alternative," and we offer them training and guidance.'

'Or money,' added Zehnder. 'The first women all wanted to start businesses, so we helped them to set up spice stalls or snack stands but it wasn't a success. They had no schooling and the businesses failed because established traders were jealous and undercut the new competition.'

'They failed too when a child fell ill and the capital was needed for medicine. When you're so poor you're desperate. The basics are just not there.'

'So we learned to concentrate on education, offering vocational training here at the Centre, teaching the women how to weave baskets in a sheltered workshop.'

'Simon then pushes them, demanding better and better work, guiding them, for I, like the girls, find it difficult to plan ahead. It is a flaw in the Burmese character,' admitted Ma Aye Min. 'And you know, they begin to do really good work and we tell them so and it makes them cry.'

A young woman in a salmon-pink *longyi* slipped into the room carrying a tray. She knelt beside the table and poured four tiny cups of tea. Ma Aye Min thanked her as she withdrew, but her eyes remained lowered throughout the episode.

'We share knowledge; we never impose it,' Ma Aye Min continued, her voice softer. 'You see, I too have a great deal to learn.' Her humility, and the acceptance that understanding requires an exchange, touched us. 'I look after five hundred girls now, and they're like our family. They look after me too; they're quiet when I'm quiet, excited when I'm excited. I'm unmarried and I don't have – or need – anyone else.'

'Only last week one of the first women we helped came back,' said Zehnder, 'in her company car. We'd paid for her to go on a secretarial course and she found work with a joint-venture company.'

'But another girl from the same group fell back into prostitution. An old client from Bangkok recognised her and threatened to reveal her history unless she slept with him. We lost her, I'm afraid.'

I wanted to ask Zehnder and Ma Aye Min if they remembered Ni Ni.

'Ni Ni?' he might have replied. 'Of course. She came to us from Bangkok in the first group of ninety returnees. Half of them were diagnosed HIV positive.'

'She was a quiet one,' Ma Aye Min might have added, 'but I think she rather enjoyed being teased by the other girls. Everyone likes a little attention. She died in our first year.'

'We never knew much about her, other than her skill with her hands. She rarely spoke about her past.' Zehnder might then have pointed to a finely woven container on his desk. 'That's one of her baskets there.'

'Maybe you'd like to meet the girl she trained?'

We walked back across the polished floor and through a shaded almond tree courtyard. In a large, bright, open studio dozens of young women sat around long workbenches making bamboo baskets. We were introduced to a young maker with sensitive hands. She could have been Ni Ni's student. I didn't see the need to ask her about the past, for her careful, detailed weaving kept a memory alive. Katrin showed her the photograph of Scott's basket.

'I am pleased to have met you,' said Ma Aye Min, her eye on the clock. 'Thank you for being interested in our work. But please will you forgive me; I cannot be late for an appointment.'

'Forty years ago when I first came to South-East Asia,' said Zehnder as we returned to the main building, 'Thailand was a modest country where men never touched women in public. Then came the American soldiers on r&r leave from the Vietnam War, and now in the clubs in Bangkok girls dance on counters and tables with numbers pinned to their petticoats, letting customers push money up inside them.' He considered us again over his glasses. 'Burma today is like Thailand was: a virgin land. Soon the jumbo jets will fly to Rangoon direct from Frankfurt and Los Angeles. The drop-outs who now live in Goa or Pattaya will come here too – for drugs, cheap living and that virginity – bringing with them their shit. Already I see Western businessmen with pretty Burmese girls on their arms, and I know that the man is only here for a few weeks or months. So when he flies away, what becomes of the woman? Is she a prostitute? Why blame the female because she expresses love or needs money? Who is wrong here?'

At the door we found our shoes and shook Zehnder's hand. 'There are those who disapprove of my working in Burma, of cooperating with this government,' he said, not releasing his grip. 'So I ask them, "Are you a politician or do you want to help people?" I don't believe in forced labour or torture, but these girls must be helped. And their leaders must be given time to learn to think another way.'

That afternoon in the Maha Bandoola Park a man wearing a loincloth walked a treadmill to drive a ferris wheel. Above him its young riders squealed and chattered without a care in the world. Colonel Than sat nearby on a bench in the children's playground, reciting Pali texts. 'Ahoy, my dears,' he hailed as we approached him through the clouds of exhaust fumes rolling off the Sule Pagoda traffic circle. 'How did you get on?'

'We're off to Pagan,' I told him.

'A dusty place of spooky memories,' he replied. 'It used to be bewitched by *nats* and bandits, now it's the tourists who haunt it. Why do you want to hare all the way up there?'

I told him about our visit to the Centre. Ni Ni's student – or, at least, the woman who could have been Ni Ni's student – had recognised the basket in the photograph. Its weaving had reminded her of the old Pagan style. We knew from his books that Scott had travelled to the ruined city at the end of the nineteenth century, so it seemed to be our most sensible destination. 'There's an express bus going as far as Meiktila tonight,' I said.

'Fair enough,' said Than. 'You've got on your shoes so we'd better pull up our socks. You'll need to change money.'

In Burma, where organisation is often languid and careless, bureaucracy has the complexity of the Gordian knot. 'The hotel offered us 118 kyat to the dollar,' I said as we strolled around the *chinthe* lion sculptures of the Independence Monument. 'They told us we'd get 120 kyat on the street, but I thought it might be risky.'

'That is not a right thing,' said the Colonel with a dismissive shake of his umbrella. 'On the street you can get at least 126 kyat. Follow me.'

He led us out of the park and across the street into the Myanmar Foreign Trade Bank. The vast marble hall echoed with the din of a dealing floor. Tangles of anxious men clutched illegible slips of paper. Cocksure money-changers shared unheard jokes with army officers. Behind the counters, few of which had signs, employees drank from flasks of China tea and gossiped with friends. A snarl of customers surged up to a desk, pushed around its side to plead with the uninterested teller then, as if by instinct, twisted away to the opposite counter. Colonel Than uncoiled a path to the unmarked Travel Section and showed our travellers' cheques to the clerk. She ignored him, unlike the helpful black marketeer who examined them with care and directed us to the next window. There, after five minutes' pleading, our passports were examined and the cheques exchanged for 'effees', dollar-denominated Foreign Exchange Certificates that enabled the government to tax and control foreign currency. The attentive marketeer, who had waited beside us with the courtesy of a Swiss hotelier, then escorted us back onto the street and down a quiet alley to negotiate. Burma's official exchange rate was fixed at six kyat to the American dollar, but the rate was twenty times that on the free market. From his Air France shoulderbag the dealer extracted a six-inch stack of two-hundred-kyat notes. He also gave us his business card. The money to finance our month of thrifty travel – a modest $250 – was enough to house and feed a Burmese family for a year.

'The earning of pence is a small thing in comparison with the joy of life,' Than pronounced on our way to the Strand Hotel, 'and material things themselves are an illusion of the temporal flesh. You have observed how many citizens of this poor country have new television sets and top-notch high-fidelity apparatus?' We had noticed, and had felt it seemed to be at odds with a culture which had no tradition of materialism. 'It is because the Burman no longer trusts the banks,' Than explained, gesturing back at the Foreign Trade building.

He said that few Burmese held bank accounts, as the government often levied arbitrary taxes on savings. Nor did they keep their earnings in cash for, in 1964 and then again in 1987, the year of my last visit, certain denominations of banknotes were demonetised. On both occasions private savings were eliminated, impoverishing the general public.

'Overnight 80 per cent of our money became worthless. So now the wise Burman buys commodities, not to keep but to sell when cash is needed. Like money-changing it is not legal,' sighed Than, 'nor is it illegal.'

The Strand, he told us, had once been the wardroom of the Royal Navy. The hotel had been built at the end of the last century by the owners of Singapore's Raffles as a comforting colonial outpost. British administrators, teak traders and writers had eaten roast beef in its dining room. The wives of plantation owners had taken suites while they were in town to buy prams or gramophones. In his last Burmese days Scott would have sipped gin and tonic in the lounge. But after the war the hotel had been nationalised, and become a shadow of its former self. On my last visit my order at the bar for a long, cool drink had produced a measure of warm, neat spirit. There had been neither tonic nor ice in the hotel for over a month.

'The reception staff used to know me well,' Than announced as we were ushered into the restored lobby, 'but times have changed.' The hotel had undergone a five-year modernisation programme financed by the Dutch-Indonesian owner of the luxurious Amanresorts group. Now, instead of the echoes of Empire, its air-conditioned bars and equally cool staff brought to mind any other five-star Asian hotel. The Strand was comfortable once more, but it was characterless.

I offered the Colonel a farewell drink, but it being after noon, and he being in monk's robes, he turned me down. 'In any event I haven't touched the demon refreshment since I was with the RNVR in Ceylon. A very nice novelty it was back then too.' So while the waiter poured tea we sat on the bamboo sofa and watched the traffic grind along the waterfront. As soon as we were alone, Than leaned forward to whisper, 'There is another reason for those televisions, my dears.'

'What's that, Colonel?' I asked, thinking of George Orwell. It could have been in this lounge, while on leave from the Indian Imperial Police, that he had dreamt up Big Brother and doublethink. The thought reminded me of an old joke. *Burmese Days*, based on Orwell's time as a policeman here in the twenties, is a good book, but not as good as his second novel about the country, *Nineteen Eighty-Four*.

'After the uprising our generals embraced the whole hog of capitalism,' said the Colonel. 'Foreign investment poured in, teak and oil drained out. Now we have factories and refineries and millionaire soldiers and a small middle class as rich as Midas. They placate the people with hi-fis to keep clear of politics and try their damnedest to create an effluent society.' I considered correcting him, but thought better of it. 'And you young things are the newest resource to be exploited.' Than considered the Strand's restored glory. 'The military works with foreign entrepreneurs "on a mutual benefit basis" to promote tourism,' he explained. In three years the number of hotel rooms in Rangoon had grown over four times. 'Did you see today's *New Light of Myanmar*?' That morning's leading article had celebrated the most recent hotel opening.

'Secretary-1 of the State Law and Order Restoration Council Lt-Gen. Khin Nyunt,' the article had reported, 'pressed a button to formally open the signboard of the Yuzana Garden Hotel.' Each paragraph had begun with the name of an officer present, arranged in descending order of rank. 'Secretary-2 Lt-Gen. Tin Oo . . . Minister for Hotels and Tourism Lt-Gen. Kyaw Ba . . . The Commander-in-Chief (Navy) and the Commander-in-Chief (Air) . . .' Every man at the ceremony had held a military title.

'Colonel, so far we've been welcomed with open arms,' I said. 'Don't the Burmese blame us – if you like, the children of former colonists – for these last years?'

'The Burmese forgive easily, my dear.'

'But don't they think that we could have done more to help? Your government has taken so much from you, yet there is no sense of revenge.'

'I told you once that the Burmese never understood *Hamlet*. I hoped that you would appreciate that now.'

'It is an honourable virtue, a lack of vindictiveness. But if the Burmese always forgive, how can the system ever be changed?'

The Colonel gazed out through the tinted glass towards the harbour. 'Our situation today is like Rangoon's weather,' he sighed. 'A great rainy downpour that bubbles our hopes down the drains, then sunshine making everything looking picture-perfect. But really all is withering in thirsty drought, terrible dry-season drought.' He glanced over his shoulder. 'At least the Lady is devoted to healing our country.'

'You have met her?' I asked, excited, curious. The Lady was Aung San Suu Kyi.

'We all know her,' whispered Than. 'Her example is always with us.' Then he thumped the arm of the sofa. 'How I wish I could join you young things on your jaunt. But instead I will transmit my *mettá* to you every day in prayers so no catastrophe, no cyclones or typhoons can reach you from any direction whatsoever.'

We thanked him for his time and guidance, even though it had not been of much use.

'I am just a lonely old *bhikkhu*, or wayfarer, a leaver of home and family, striving for knowledge to help liberate other good citizens from suffering. Send me an SOS if I can provide any further assistance,' he offered, standing up to bow to Katrin. 'Tally-ho and safe footsteps, charmed girl,' he said to her, then whispered in my ear, 'Remember my dear, she is one who knows how to rock the cradle. Travel well.'

There is a deep sadness in Burmese travel; not for the traveller himself, who can come and go as he pleases, but for the Burman who is tied by fear and penury to one place, prevented from unravelling the filaments and strands which have formed his remarkable country. Yet the sadness does not come from the native people, in spite of their bondage. They appear to be free of envy and greed, seem to be at peace with themselves, remain cheerful, modest and happy. They smile, while telling a tragic story of eviction and execution. Rather the sadness comes from the outsider, the lucky traveller who is allowed to enjoy the places that a resident cannot visit. It gripped Katrin and me as we boarded the Leo Express bus that evening, and stayed with us long after the completion of our journey.

'We pray and wish for the physical and spiritual comfort and well-being of our passengers throughout the journey,' soothed the soft, on-board welcome. The pre-recorded English had an Oriental overlay. Its vowels sounded as rounded as Burmese lettering appears to the Western eye. 'May our voyage together tonight be blessed with calm and peace.'

A squat traveller, wearing a drab suit and bright betel-stained tie, swayed down the aisle and fell into the seat across from us. A light shower of dandruff settled on his threadbare shoulders. The young man beside him, who had been listening to an English-language programme, switched off his shortwave radio and looked away. Our yellow-robed stewardess turned up the bland music as the passengers, who were mostly prosperous Burmese, settled into their books and magazines. A lone, heat-blanched Englishman sat at the back of the bus reading a two-day-old *Financial Times*. All were travelling overnight on the new private service to Mandalay, except for us. We planned to disembark at dawn to catch a local connection to Pagan.

We cruised through the early-evening traffic, past the ignoble White Bridge where protesting students had been drowned in 1988. Inya Lake was now best known to businessmen as the site of the International Business Centre. We drove north along the Prome Road, where Ni Ni could have lived with her father, past the airport and poor Wayba-gi, onto Highway No. 1. I caught sight of the Tatma-daw Golf Club beyond the Defence Services General Hospital. A convoy of new khaki Chinese Lanjian pick-ups drove into the military compound in Mingaladon. Hilux line-buses, crammed with com-muters and traders, coughed and spat their way towards the grimy suburbs. Ancient lorries without bonnets or doors, their engine blocks bolted onto bare chassises, blazed along the dusty shoulder. The stewardess turned on the video player.

Hidden away in the folds of mountains which reach down like the fingers of a hand from the heights of Asia to the sea, Burma has always been a nation apart. Its high ranges squeeze the country between India and China, cramming the diverse peoples into the deep river valleys of the Irrawaddy, the Chindwin, Sittang and Salween. Its borders contain one of the world's most complex racial mixes: twenty-one major ethnic groups, divided into seven divisions and seven minority states, speaking over a hundred languages. The Burmans, who dominate the Irrawaddy's vast, fertile flood plains, make up two-thirds of the population, but even their majority is not homogeneous.

'I feel like Rip van Winkle,' volunteered the squat businessman, nodding out the window. Along the rutted roadside women and children toiled in labour gangs. 'The country has been asleep for decades.'

'I imagine they wish that many things had changed,' said Katrin. We had read that local authorities maintained the right to call on 'voluntary' labour in lieu of taxation. Children were paid about one dollar a week to work on projects 'for the benefit of the community'. The improvement of the fifty-mile stretch of Highway No. 1 between Rangoon and Pegu, a popular tourist destination which featured the famed Great Golden God Pagoda, had earned it the name of 'the road of no return'. According to Amnesty International, on this road two workers had been executed by their military supervisors after they had tried to escape. Another had been beaten to death with a hoe.

'This is the tradition in Myanmar,' said the businessman, using his country's new official name. 'People give their labour voluntarily and patriotically for the love of the Union.' We watched a young boy, wearing only a short kilted *longyi*, struggle under the weight of a basket filled with stones. 'I lived in Australia for twenty-seven years, so I realise that it can be difficult for Europeans to understand.'

'It is terrible to see.'

'I agree. That's why most work is undertaken when there are no tourist buses passing. There must have been some sort of slip-up.'

Katrin looked around to see if there were any unoccupied seats, but the bus was full. She turned away, slipped on her pair of slumber goggles and pretended to sleep. 'You lived in Australia?' I asked.

'Here's my card,' he smiled, passing me a business card and dislodging another downpour of dandruff, 'Michael Naga of Naga Insurance. Maybe you've heard of the firm?' I shook my head. 'Then you've never been to Perth. I left Myanmar back in 1962, when the country began its march towards socialism. I didn't fancy the walk so stowed away on a boat heading down under and claimed political asylum.'

'You left your family?'

'Of course,' he shrugged, his gestures smoothed by vanity. 'We stayed in touch at first, until we started speaking different languages. How could they understand about health care and Christmas holidays and buying a second family car?'

'It must have been difficult, living your life disassociated from your past.'

'I don't know about that,' he replied, 'but it sure was right grabbing the opportunity to come back.'

To encourage the country's development, and in the hope of repairing the damage wreaked by the failure of Burmese socialism, the government had offered a general amnesty to its former adversaries – especially if they were successful businessmen. Those who returned to the country, and who took the precaution of aligning themselves with a SLORC minister, grew wealthy with alarming speed.

'We're building three shopping malls in Mandalay now,' Michael gloated, with a fearless confidence. 'Construction insurance is my niche.'

The coach lurched over single-track bridges, dipping and rising like a ship at sea. As dusk settled around us dim hearth-fires became visible in the distance. Our headlamps caught bullock carts and trishaws in their glare. They, and all manner of broken-down vehicles, appeared like apparitions in the colourless beam of light before being swallowed up again by the night. Michael fell asleep, a copy of an American self-help paperback, *The Leader in You*, on his belly. On the video a sci-fi kung-fu thriller, made for the Asian market in English with Japanese subtitles, was playing.

Around midnight the bus stopped at a roadside restaurant for dinner. Vast bowls of rice had been laid out on refectory tables and the passengers pounced on the food. Michael served himself two portions of chicken curry and broke off a hand of stubby, plump bananas. 'Everything is included in the price of the ticket,' he explained, 'so eat all you can.' There were endless flasks of tea and platters of palm-sugar cake on offer. The restaurants, which were equipped with toilets and snack stalls like open-air motorway service stations, had sprung up to serve the long-distance coaches. The inno-vation impressed Michael. 'It's ventures like this,' he pronounced while eating, 'that will create our new middle class. These are the entrepreneurs who will build up our prosperity.' I didn't know who had financed the building of the restaurants, though later we learned that Leo Express was owned by the son of a Kokang drug trafficker. 'But it will take time,' Michael warned me. 'You saw the country ten years ago. Come back ten years from now. You won't recognise the place. Rip van Winkle will have become an insomniac.'

'And will there still be child labourers then?' asked Katrin.

'It's churlish to talk about politics. We want to make politics an unfashionable subject.'

'By concentrating only on making money?'

'Initially. Then democracy will slip into place and every citizen's life will be improved. Capitalism first, democracy second; that is the Eastern way.' As he stood to return to the coach Michael stowed half a dozen pieces of cake in his jacket pocket. 'It is necessary to work the system if one is to survive, but to succeed one needs opportunities.'

We managed to change seats with two Mandalay traders returning from a shopping trip in Rangoon, and settled into the back row.

The Englishman reading the *FT* did not meet our eyes. But the night's conversation and the seesaw movement of the bus conspired to deny us sleep. 'I find it hard to comprehend,' Katrin whispered without removing her goggles, 'that every foot of this road has been built by hand.' Rock had been broken into gravel, gravel laid onto the road base, the base pounded and tarmac poured by bare hands. When we stopped later at a level crossing to wait for the northbound 'Up' train to pass, I crouched in the headlights and touched the road surface. Meanwhile the women slipped off into the shadows on the right-hand side of the bus. The men relieved themselves in the darkness to the left.

Michael caught my eye as we climbed back on board. 'Look me up when you reach Mandalay,' he suggested between mouthfuls of palm-sugar cake, 'and we'll do lunch.'

'Not a chance,' replied Katrin.

At Meiktila we stumbled through unlit, silent streets from our sleek, express coach to the pre-war bus gate. Drivers dozed in their cabs, and passengers who had arrived long before dawn to find a place waited on the hard bench seats. Apart from the odd colonial rail line and the expensive air service, which was priced to exclude all but foreign tourists and rich entrepreneurs, the only way to travel in the country was by line-bus. Leo Express and Myanmar Arrow ran between Rangoon and Mandalay, but elsewhere there was nothing other than aged pick-up trucks fitted with wooden benches. The roads along which they clattered were often unpaved, always single-track, and to pass vehicles needed to pull over to the shoulder. Transportation, like most systems in modern Burma, had been structured to hinder communication. Rather than linking, it isolated towns, individuals and thought.

Day broke to find us moving but unable to move, packed in with thirty other travellers. Our limbs were jammed between sacks of vegetables and boxes of reconditioned car parts. A child slept across our laps. There wasn't enough room for me to crane my neck around to catch sight of the arid, scorched plain beyond the pick-up's metal frame. Not that I was missing much. Once I spotted a spindly, pathetic eucalyptus plantation, but otherwise there was only a barren wilderness of stony ground, laced by the dust-dry gullies of last year's monsoon.

For two monotonous, grinding hours the scene remained unchanged, until tall, slender toddy palms came into view, the first verticals in a flat landscape. At the morning tea stop we watched farmers guide long bamboo ladders to the trees, then, with charred pots suspended from their waists, climb the elephant-grey trunk to topknots of broad, splayed leaves. There, a hundred feet above the ground, the long tubular nodes were bound together like bundles of oversized genitalia and, in a strange sexuality, the toddy milked into the perfectly round orb of the suspended collecting pot. The toddy juice, either boiled and sweet or fermented into alcohol, was sold in the shaggy, thatched hamlets, alongside rectangular-lidded baskets woven from the palm's fringed, pointed leaves.

The morning and the miles dragged on, our backs and arms ached, until, after seven bone-jarring hours of travel, a serrated line of hills cut the horizon. The landscape became dotted with gleaming, bleach-white *stupas*. According to Scott, 'Jerusalem, Rome, Kiev, Benares, none of these can boast the multitude of temples, and lavishness of design and ornament' to be found in Pagan. We had arrived in 'the most remarkable religious city in the world'.

At a scorched crossroad we hobbled off the back of the pick-up, numbed by the journey and dazzled by the noonday sun.

'Hello my friend where you go?'

'What country? What your name?'

The rising heat wrung the colour from our vision and we blinked at the shimmering silhouettes of half a dozen horse-drawn carriages.

'This is my horse-cart. You see pagodas?' asked a lean young man at the reins.

'You German?' enquired another, patting the skeleton of his under-fed mare. '*Bitte, wir gehen zusammen. Sehr billig*,' he begged.

There were no trees to offer respite from the sun. The only shade was under the carriages' canopy. 'We need a bed first,' I managed to say, as feeling began to creep back into my legs.

'Good bed clean hotel fried egg breakfast no problem,' gabbled a child, taking Katrin's hand. 'Please madame,' she pleaded, 'come with me.'

'Come with me, my friend.'

'*Freund, wir gehen zusammen.*'

We chose to ride with the quietest boy. His horse did not seem to have been maltreated. As we trotted past ancient temples crumbling away into the bare, tinderbox plain I gave him the name of our hotel, recommended by Colonel Than. 'What is your name?' I asked him.

'Soe Htun,' he replied. It was his first day on the job, but he overcame his shyness to ask, 'Please sir, later we go to temples?'

Anawrahta, the first great Burmese king, was an Asian Crusader, determined to purify Burmese Buddhism by capturing holy scriptures and relics. In 1047 thirty-two white elephants carried into his capital, Pagan, his sacred booty along with 'such men as were skilled in carving, turning and painting; masons, moulders of plaster and flower-patterns; blacksmiths, silversmiths, braziers, founders of gongs and cymbals, filigree flower-workers; doctors and trainers of elephants and horses ... hairdressers and men cunning in perfumes, odours, flowers and the juices of flowers'. Anawrahta's military victories, financed by agriculture and the rich trade with India, China and Malaya, heralded Pagan's golden age. He and his prospering subjects were inspired to build magnificent monasteries and temples, earning merit for their patrons and assuring them a better life after reincarnation. Thirty thousand prisoners were pressed into the frenzied building of pagodas. They too had 'given their labour voluntarily and patriotically for the love of Burma'. Over 250 years the officers and rulers built thirteen thousand temples and *kyaungs* on the arid curve of the Irrawaddy. 'The towers are built of fine stone and then one of them has been covered with gold a good finger in thickness,' wrote Marco Polo; '. . . really they do form one of the finest sights in the world, so exquisitely finished are they, so splendid and costly'. But this extraordinary undertaking impoverished the kingdom. Asia's greatest city became vulnerable to Mongol invasion.

The popular view of Pagan's demise evokes a fanciful vision of Kublai Khan's hordes ransacking and looting the royal city. In truth its end was the result of complacency and exhaustion. Burmese rulers never developed a bureaucracy capable of maintaining control without a strong army. The centuries of supremacy had made the military indolent. The last king, Narathihapate, was so frightened of invasion that he tore down all of the city's wooden houses to construct fortifications. On discovering a prophecy under one of the ruined buildings that predicted his downfall, he fled from Pagan. In 1287 the Mongols took over the deserted city, and for half a millennium its ruins were cursed with bandits and evil spirits.

The dusk was filled with the tinkle of temple bells, countless tiny chimes stirred by the evening breeze. Two thousand pagodas remained standing in the Pagan Archaeological Zone, and foreign visitors paid $10 to wander the dusty roads between them, dwarfed by the dark brick ruins, trying to imagine the glory of the lost city on the barren plain. After an afternoon nap, Soe Htun had taken us to the Thatbyinnyu, a monumental square temple laced with a maze of inner passageways and flanked by guardian figures. Katrin and I had climbed its narrow steps to a resplendent Buddha image. From the upper terrace, two hundred feet above the ground, it was possible to conjure up the bustling ancient city eight hundred years below. In our imagination the smell of cooking rose with the murmur of voices. The wind carried the Pali chants of meditating monks. Villagers bathed in the Irrawaddy, boys splashing girls, women crouching in the grey waters, their bare shoulders touched by the rosy light of the evening. Trading barques from Ceylon and Siam swayed in the swells. We watched the sun set beyond the river's great arc and the lush green trees dissolve into black. A full moon rose above the hills to the west while below, in our fancy, ten thousand lamps were lit and ten thousand meals prepared. But then, as the star of a high-flying aircraft strobed overhead en route to Jakarta or Singapore, my imagination failed me and I became aware of an absence.

Pagan has not remained uninhabited since the days of the Mongols.

Earlier in the twentieth century farmers returned to settle among the *kyaung* ruins. A village had developed, and during my first visit to Burma I had eaten in a family restaurant and stayed up until dawn watching a local *pwe* festival. But from our peaceful, idyllic eyrie Katrin and I spotted no sign of the marketplace or tumbledown food stalls. There were no bamboo houses, villagers or school, only new hotels and sightseeing guides. The site had been transformed into a museum for tourists.

On the ride back to our hotel I asked Soe Htun what had happened to the old village. 'Kublai Khan destroy,' he replied. 'Rape and pillage all of old Pagan. Very bad man.'

'No, more recently than that,' I said. 'Maybe last year? Two years ago?' Soe Htun turned to stare at me and I thought for a moment that he hadn't understood. 'There was a town here when I last visited.'

'No town, no sir,' he replied, fidgeting with the reins. A furtiveness had crept into his behaviour. 'A few farmers, maybe, but no town.'

'Ten years ago I stayed at a place called the Mother Hotel. And I remember a sign at a restaurant which said, "Be kind to animals by not eating them".'

The cart turned off the track and onto a new tarmac carriageway. A gust of wind from a passing tour bus filled with Taiwanese holidaymakers almost blew us off the road. For a moment the only sound was the clip-clop of hooves on the tarmac. 'Today is my first day as horse-cart driver,' Soe Htun said. 'My grandfather buy for me. It is our business, you understand.'

'We wish you success,' said Katrin.

'It *must* be success,' he insisted. 'You see I hoping many tourists come to Pagan so one day I can buy a cart for myself.' It seemed unlikely; the horse and cart would have cost Soe Htun's grandfather the equivalent of two years' salary. He would also have had to bribe local officials to secure one of the 160 tourist horse-cart licences. 'My grandfather take 30 per cent of my daily money so not leave much for saving, but one day I will make prosperous.' He took a breath. 'That is why it is important not to talk about some things.'

There was no further mention of the missing village. As the cart

passed under an avenue of tamarind trees Soe Htun asked us if we
wanted to go swimming at the Thiripyitsaya Hotel. It seemed that
the pool was open to non-residents, of the hotel and the country,
but the thought did not appeal. We were tired from our travels and
I paid him. 'The first money that I earn,' he said, slapping the notes
on the cart and on the horse itself. 'This bring me luck. It is my
good fortune that you have come to Pagan. Please sir, tomorrow we
go to buy souvenirs?'

'No souvenirs,' I said. 'No thank you.'

'I take you to quality lacquerware shop. My cousin working there.
He give you good price.'

'We don't want to buy any lacquerware. We are trying to find a
basket.'

'In Pagan?' he asked.

'Yes.' Katrin extracted the photograph from the bottom of her
bag. 'We were told that it might have been made here.'

Soe Htun held the picture at an angle, catching it in the amber
glow of a street lamp. 'Not Pagan style,' he said with finality. Our
spirits plummeted. Unwilling to see us disappointed, he added, 'But
I do know a woman who will help you.'

'Here in Pagan?' Katrin asked. 'Can we meet her?'

'She is an educated woman,' said Soe Htun with approval, 'and
my friend. But her husband, he is a drunkard and a criminal. They
say that he swings from a bamboo pole brushed with cess in England.'

'I beg your pardon?'

'He is a bad man. He fills the sky with lies.'

FOUR

Unpicking the Weave

STATIC. HISS AND WHISTLE. Distant voices strained through the crackle; Chinese martial music, a blast of rapidfire Morse code. A Baptist preacher ranted in the ether, his all-American twang drowning in a scream of heterodynes, then yielded to rock and roll. 'Maybe I'm tuned to your wavelength.' In the darkness of her room Ma Swe adjusted the shortwave radio, reached over borders, searched for clarity. Hiss and static, 9725 kilohertz 31-metre band, the bark of Burmese jamming. Another music station drifted across her signal. 'The world is collapsing round our ears, I turn up the radio.' Too loud, less volume, the walls were thin. More static. She needed new batteries. There wasn't the money. It was mad to keep the radio. She had to sell it. Then she heard 'This is London.' Diddly-dee. 'Lillibulero', absurd and frivolous in the Asian dark. Another growl of interference. She retuned to another frequency, quickly, 11850 kHz 25-metre. Would it be him? Please be him. Crackle and static. Turn it down, turn it right down. She leaned her ear against the receiver, listening as if to a dreaming child, and heard his voice. Half a world away he sat alone in a studio, in front of a microphone, speaking to her. To her alone. Ma Swe hadn't seen her husband, or received a letter from him, in over eight years, but she had heard him almost every night. Every night she listened to him, and remembered.

*　　*　　*

It had been through her ears, and not as other women through her hands and eyes, that Ma Swe had come to know the four loves. She had been born a frail child, at once fearful and curious, obedient yet independent, with an intense aversion to the sun. As a baby she had wailed through the hot season, crying to her mother to be taken into the leafy tamarind shade, cooing at her through the cool monsoon rains. Warm weather did not agree with her. So almost as soon as her legs would carry her she had retreated out of the smothering heat and into her own world. In the unlit recesses of the Ananda Pahto she had chased cold-blooded lizards and mythical tales, spinning herself into the *jatakas*, or Buddha birth stories, singing old love epics about the *kinnayas*, lovers half-bird and half-human who wept for seven hundred years after being separated for one night. Ma Swe loved the legends because her mother had been a poet. In the cool of evening she had been meshed into the passages of poems. 'Listen, my lovely,' her mother had said as they sat beneath the rhyming tree which grew in the temple precinct. Ma Swe had obeyed, hearing the song in her words, gaining a kernel of truth from each story. 'Into every poem goes my only life,' her mother had told her, and after each recital they had wound around and around the tree, repeating a line from here or a stanza from there, before collapsing in a heap to drink sweetened lime juice to the music of language. The gentle, loving childhood had set the pattern of Ma Swe's life; to attend to others, to cherish the finite, to accept her insignificance. It also taught her the art of listening.

It was as a child that Ma Swe had been drawn to the first love. There were caves near the temple, and she had often played alone in their dim shadows. She was not afraid of the dark, but rather of that which she could not hear, and one day she overheard the soft sound of whispers. She squeezed herself into a dim alcove and, above the beating of her heart, overheard the rustle of clothing. Beyond a stone lattice a man sighed, murmuring eternal promises in a moment's passion, and a woman laughed in the blackness. Ma Swe lay as still as a reclining Buddha, almost near enough to the lovers to have been taken into their entwining arms, and listened. The thrill of their intimacy stirred her and she trembled beside them for hours, hidden in the alcove until nightfall. She hung onto the silence long after the unseen couple had regathered both their clothes and their modesty, and departed.

The wonder of the second and third loves had come to her five years later with the wails, pain and push of labour. She had been an adolescent lying on her sleeping mat in the family house, listening through a moonless night and thin bamboo walls. Late in life her mother had borne a last child and first son, but within twelve months the family's whirl of joy had tangled into taut sorrow. The boy died from cerebral malaria. As they washed the little corpse from head to toe, then closely swathed it in new white cotton cloth, Ma Swe wept alongside the women. She shared the aching emptiness of her mother's arms, but grieved alone for the loss of a brother.

Another decade later, as a wife herself, Ma Swe had understood the fourth love. Every night in her dark solitude she had reached out to grasp it. She tuned the radio to hear the voice of the man who had been gone for too long ever again to be her lover, whose child she would never bear, who would always remain her companion. The carnal and the maternal, platonic and filial love; all her life Ma Swe had learned by listening. At school, at the side of her mother's cooking pot, even when walking alone in the arid, brick-littered fields between the *payas* of Pagan, she had always been quiet and intent, observant yet somehow distanced from experience. It had seemed such an obvious concept to her, to listen and to learn. But as she grew older the people around her had seemed to lack both the patience and the inclination to pay attention to anyone other than themselves.

The family that had embraced her could not alone contain her, and she had to reach beyond its confines. In time it was in the unpicking of the poems that she had come to understand her need to leave Pagan. Her mother's words helped her to decide to train as an editor. There was so much noise and static in the world. Both deafness and verbosity muddled the search for clarity, and Ma Swe had learned of the importance of succinct expression. She had an ear for the leanness of good writing, as well as the good fortune to have a teacher who was a member of the Burma Socialist Programme Party. Ability had always played a large part in a child's education, but with the military controlling the country a parent's connections were more important. Ma Swe's teacher was her uncle and he arranged for her a scholarship from the Ministry of Home and Religious Affairs. The condition attached to it would not become apparent until later.

In her three years at college Ma Swe never missed a lecture. She also never lingered outside. Her pale, translucent skin gave the impression of fragility, as if a bout of fever might be fatal. Her tutors, who were cowed newsmen and imported East German advisors adept at ideological journalism, worried for her health. They singled her out for special treatment, though not only because of her delicate constitution. They saw that Ma Swe observed and absorbed, but kept her opinions to herself. She was a good listener and therefore a suitable journalist. In early 1988 she graduated near the top of her class. But she had no ambition to write editorials for the *Working People's Daily*. Instead she hoped only to return to Pagan, or at least to nearby Meiktila, and to find herself a quiet position as a regional correspondent, or better still a district editor. The ministry which had supported her education had other plans. They offered her a junior position at the Press Scrutiny Board, the government censor, in Rangoon. Ma Swe was free to refuse the post, of course, but if she turned it down she would be required to repay the full cost of her scholarship – plus interest.

The pages rustled in the fan's languid breeze. Piles of manuscripts waited on a dozen dark wooden desks, beside Bakelite telephones which only received incoming calls, and carousels of rubber stamps: 'Approved', 'Rejected', 'Refer to MI'. The reams of paper were stacked like sheaves of yellowed tobacco leaves around the old plaster walls. A single typed sheet was caught by the breeze and blown free from its binding, sailing across the office, over the bowed Monday morning heads before crumpling to the floor below a barred window. Beneath the slowly turning fans the censors read and yawned and sauntered out for coffee, idling past anxious authors and publishers who waited on the hard bench by the door. Ma Swe found her way to her seat, a ministry crest on its shoulder. She had been issued with a grey civil service uniform and a red pencil. She sat down at her desk and vanished behind the mountain of paper. The telephone rang and she picked up the receiver. The Board's chairman, a major on secondment from Military Intelligence, barked a curt welcome then counted off the Eleven Principles.

'In scrutinising literature and the media no publication may contain:

> 1. anything detrimental to the Burmese Socialist Program;
>
> 2. anything detrimental to the ideology of the state;
>
> 3. anything detrimental to the socialist economy . . .'

As he spoke Ma Swe scrabbled in the empty drawer to find a pen. She tried to note the guidelines with her red pencil on the back of a collection of short stories. In her confusion she missed Principle Number Five, but lacked the courage to interrupt the Major.

> '6. any incorrect ideas and opinions which do not accord with the times;
>
> 7. any descriptions which, though factually correct, are unsuitable because of the time or circumstances of their writing;
>
> 8. any obscene or pornographic . . .'

Ma Swe broke her pencil lead in the midst of Principle Number Nine.

> '10. any criticism of a non-constructive type of the work of government departments;
>
> 11. any libel or slander of any individual.

Is this quite clear?'

'Yes, *saya*,' she answered.

'The Principles are listed on the wall behind your head. Refer to them at each opportunity,' he instructed and hung up.

Every newspaper and novel, comic and calendar, magazine and religious manual intended for publication in Burma had to pass through the PSB office. Works were submitted either in triplicate at manuscript stage or after printing, when five copies were required. The Board then read and approved – or forbade – distribution. Because of the costs involved in editing text after a book had been printed and bound, most writers tended to censor themselves. They wrote either bland *pyei-thu akyo-pyu*, that is 'works beneficial to the people', or allegories, veiled enough to pass the inspection yet not so disguised that readers overlooked their true meaning. A misjudgement meant non-publication; honesty guaranteed imprisonment. The restrictions did little to encourage clarity of thought.

Burma's press had once been the most dynamic and free in Asia. The country's first newspaper had been published in 1836. The colonial *Rangoon Gazette*, founded in 1861, had survived until the Second World War. For decades the nationalist cause had been served by Aung San's *Oway*, the *Dagon* magazine and the *Myanma Alin*, or 'New Light of Burma'. By the 1950s the country boasted more than thirty daily papers, including six in Chinese and three in English. But in 1962 the situation changed. The country was in chaos, rebel armies threatened to tear apart the union, and the military saw free thought as a threat to national stability. Irresponsible journalists – that is writers who expressed independent views – were perceived as troublemakers, capable of lobbying opinion against the *Tatmadaw*. So, for the sake of national unity editors and publishers were arrested, their newspapers closed or nationalised. To silence the voices of dissent the government banned all private dailies, and the press was placed under the direct control of the Ministry of Information.

At college Ma Swe and her classmates had learned of their responsibility to promote the ideology of the state. They were taught that the media needed to explain official policies, to inform the people of relevant facts and to exhort the virtues of hard work and sacrifice. Their role as editors and journalists was to help to strengthen the unity of the country, not to undermine it with criticism. The Burmese constitution granted every citizen freedom of speech, expression and publication 'to the extent that such freedom is not contrary to the interests of the working people and socialism'. There was little room for interpretation and imagination.

But at the PSB Ma Swe was not yet responsible for imposing the Eleven Principles. She was a clerk, and too junior to be in charge of the dissemination of information. Her job was simply to look for spelling mistakes. On her carousel there hung a single rubber stamp: 'Fee Payable due to Errors of Spelling'. For every mistake that she found an author was required to pay ten pyas to the Board. There were one hundred pyas to the kyat. This charge was in addition to the reading fee, paid in advance, of fifty pyas per page.

Ma Swe had hoped that she might be able to learn from the work, but when the Major left his office and went out a few minutes later, she didn't have time to read. The other clerks and the deputy supervisor gathered around her desk, bringing with them cups of tea and conversation. One clerk was from Meiktila and knew her uncle. Many of the others had, like her, studied journalism. The supervisor outlined for Ma Swe the daily routine of trimming words and unweaving thought. It was her work that had led to the recent banning of a series of articles recounting the legends and myths of famous pagodas. The articles, she recalled with pride, were censored because 'there was no proof that any of the legends were true'.

'Did they tell the story of the days when it rained gold and silver?' Ma Swe asked her. 'That is why there are so many pagodas in Pagan; after the rains even widows became rich enough to build them.'

'I believe that the legend was mentioned.'

'And the story of the Shwezigon? Where men and celestials laid the rows of bricks in turn?' The temple's bronze Buddhas were cast with their right hands held palm outward, fingers extended, to portray the *abhaya* gesture, which means 'no fear'.

'I don't know about gold in Pagan,' said the supervisor, 'but it does occasionally rain silver here in Rangoon.' She and her workmates went on to outline the correct procedure for sharing out the cash bribes that were received by the Board. Ma Swe listened in silence, wary of speaking her mind again. In her hesitant voice she indicated that it was time to begin her reading, but the supervisor laughed and said, 'Not until after your lunch appointment.'

'You are being taken out to lunch,' explained the woman from Meiktila, her face breaking into a grin. 'It is your first "present".'

'We have told him that you are in charge of issuing licences to new magazines.'

'You have told whom?' asked Ma Swe, now worried.

'Ko Lin.'

'But I do not know anyone named Ko Lin, and I have nothing to do with licensing.' Ma Swe held up her broken red pencil. 'I correct spelling mistakes.'

'Don't worry, little sister; Ko Lin is a gentleman,' the supervisor told her, hoping that her smirk went unnoticed. 'It will be very pleasant.'

'And amusing,' said another.

'He's a photographer who has decided to become a publisher,' added the woman from Meiktila, not wishing to prolong Ma Swe's anxiety. 'It is only a little joke that we are playing on him. He tries to get his own way, and we don't wish him to become too confident with his requests to us. You don't mind, do you? Please.'

It was common practice for a publisher, or a writer if he could scrape together the cash, to entertain his censor to a meal. The favour tended to expedite approval, though not of course if a work was unsuitable for ideological reasons. It followed that the better the meal, the sooner the permission to publish would be forthcoming. A plate of sour-hot fish and noodles at the Palace Restaurant might reduce waiting time from a month to a week. A slap-up mixed grill at the Strand, the best hotel in Rangoon, would guarantee authorisation by the next morning, even sooner if the evening was rounded off with karaoke or a dinner show. The practice was rather like endearing oneself to a wealthy relative, who controlled one's inheritance and paid an allowance only if it pleased him.

Early 1988 was a period of new hope in Burma. In the spring of that year the first wave of pro-democracy demonstrations, though ending in bloodshed, unleashed a sequence of events which seemed to promise an easing of repression. The spirit of optimism was reinforced by the government's grudging admission that students had died in police custody. As a result of the confession both the Home Minister and the Rangoon Chief of Police resigned. A civilian lawyer, Dr Maung Maung, was appointed President. The government reopened the universities, which had been closed after the first demonstrations to disperse the students, and lifted the curfew.

At the Press Scrutiny Board the changes were reflected in a measure of leniency. The censors began to permit the publication of controversial articles. Writers found the courage to be bolder as the likelihood of arrest receded. Their allegories became less veiled. In addition licences began to be issued to publishers wishing to start up the popular new monthly magazines. By the middle of the year over ninety different titles had appeared, printed on poor-quality paper, offering the public a bounty of original stories, foreign news reports, scientific articles and gossip columns. The periodicals became the most animated forum for literary activity, because of both their topical nature and the economic circumstances. A complete novel, or, when available, foreign news magazines such as *Time* or *Newsweek*, were beyond the reach of most Burmese. They also took a long time to read. So neighbourhood lending shops sprang up, fulfilling the role of local libraries, loaning well-thumbed reading material to the public for a few kyat a day. Magazines were popular because they could be hired, read and returned within an economical twenty-four hours. It was with the intention of starting up a new monthly that the publisher-photographer Ko Lin asked to meet the Board's Head of Licensing, and offered to take her to lunch.

Ma Swe stepped with care aboard the Karaweik, a gaudy, ostentatious replica of a traditional Burmese floating palace, feeling apprehensive both of the meeting and of sailing on central Kandawgyi Lake. She needn't have worried. The floating restaurant was cast in concrete around reinforced pillars, and Ko Lin was too fond of the sound of his own voice to let her speak a word. He sat at a table beside the water, drinking a bottle of ABC Stout, looking as though he would rather be in a toddy shop.

Ko Lin was not a young man, nor particularly old, and like many Burmese there was an agelessness in his features. A fondness for alcohol had left him puffy-eyed and overweight. His ruffled, inky hair was unwashed. The tail of a faded tennis shirt hung out from his *longyi*. As an overdressed singer buzzed around his table like a bejewelled mosquito, crooning an unidentified pop song into his ear, Ma Swe felt an inexplicable pang of irritation.

Ko Lin looked up to meet her eye. 'I'm sorry,' he apologised, struggling to his feet to greet her, 'I didn't see you come in.' He shouted for the menu and asked if she would like beer or whisky. She quietly requested a glass of Sparkling Lemon. The singer withdrew and Ko Lin began to talk. He was not, like Ma Swe, a listener.

'There is complicity in silence,' he said, sitting down sharply, wasting no time on pleasantries, not even asking her name. 'Words are useless fancies unless they lead to action. Don't you agree?' Her soft drink arrived and saved her from having to answer him. She looked at the menu, at a loss for anything else to do. He leaned forward and glared at her over the top of it. 'You see, I believe that our actions can improve the present situation. That's why it is important to publish a new monthly, to give today's events a voice. Don't have the fish. The seafood here isn't fresh.'

Ma Swe took an immediate dislike to Ko Lin. His directness made her uneasy, and he tended towards self-aggrandisement. He was also no gentleman, as the supervisor had lead her to believe. 'There are guidelines,' she said simply.

'Things can be changed. Things *are* changing, within the parameters of the Eleven Principles, of course.'

'I don't know if it is possible,' she answered in all honesty.

'If I didn't believe that it could be done, we wouldn't be talking. Time is too precious to fritter away on matters of no consequence. What will you eat?' They ordered a few dishes and, so that a single minute wasn't lost while waiting, he told her about himself.

Ko Lin's life had been distinguished by frustrated expression. He had squandered years training as a film-maker, cajoling his friends and neighbours into helping him make a movie, only to have it refused distribution by the video parlours. So he had turned to writing, churning out in a year a dozen short stories and two novellas, but his work was rejected by every publisher in Burma, whether for reasons of politics or quality Ma Swe chose not to ask. He had then dabbled in painting, but decided instead to become a photographer, although he owned no equipment. With a borrowed camera he had travelled around the country taking pictures of 'the true Burma'. Ma Swe looked startled, and as he ordered another stout he explained, 'Whenever the authorities challenged me my defence was simply to say that I was recording events. If they found fault in that then they were admitting their own responsibility and failure.' His high principles had earned him five years in prison. The friend who had loaned him the camera was also jailed. 'That is why I value time, why I never sleep for more than four or five hours a night. They kept me locked up for so long that I don't want to waste another minute of my life.'

On his release Ko Lin had tried to sell the photographs and his accompanying text, but without success. The PSB always blocked their publication. It was then that he began to see himself in another role, as one who documented facts, rather than interpreted them. He accepted that his role was to publish the work of others. 'I'm a late bloomer,' he said, digging in his breast pocket to look at his watch. Its strap was broken. 'It's another reason for me to get a move on.'

Throughout his monologue, from the chicken satay to the fried bananas, Ma Swe did not speak at all. But as she listened she began to sense that for all his haste Ko Lin was a man who never finished what he had started. She also felt that she had eaten too much.

At the end of the meal Ko Lin presented her with a list of writers and, in triplicate, a handful of stories. He proposed that the first issue of the magazine would run news items about the March demonstrations and an article about how democratic elections are conducted in the West. 'For the general education of the public,' he explained. 'You do understand,' he stressed, 'that without your licence the Paper and Printing Corporation will not release me an allocation of paper.' There was urgency in his voice. 'Without your approval I cannot proceed.'

Ma Swe's head spun. She had not yet been a day with the Board, had not corrected a single spelling mistake, and now a difficult, assertive man, who knew nothing about her, was depending on her support. Ko Lin on the other hand was satisfied with the meeting. He cared little about the personal life of the censor who had to be bribed. She had spared him the bother of making small talk. He suggested that they meet the following week to discuss her decision.

'This is a terrible place,' he said when the singer came back. 'I think your colleagues only suggested it because of the expense. Next time let's meet somewhere else.' It was the one point on which they could both agree.

They did meet the following week, and the week after that too. The supervisor issued Ko Lin with a temporary licence, which required him to report to Ma Swe every Wednesday at noon. Ostensibly the arrangement was to enable the PSB to rein back improprieties, to ensure that restrictions still bound the press at a time when all rules seemed to be unravelling. For her part Ma Swe assumed that the supervisor only wished to prolong her entertainment. But in truth there was evil intent in the Board's game, and Ma Swe was its pawn. Leniency was being used to flush out free-thinkers like Ko Lin. Their meetings were not isolated incidents. All around the country people were losing their fear, following their hearts, speaking their minds, while in secret their names were being added to long, detailed lists.

Ma Swe, unaware of the broader game, continued to listen to Ko Lin, letting her silence draw him out. The public optimism convinced her that her gentle efforts and softly-spoken reports could never be used against him. She had also begun to enjoy their lunches together.

Over Peking duck at the Bamboo House Restaurant, Ko Lin updated Ma Swe on the commissioning of new writers. As he spoke of investing the last of his savings to buy ink and paper, she considered his sagging, scruffy features and ironic smile. She recalled that her mother had once advised her, on meeting a person, to discover their face, and to like it. Ma Swe looked at Ko Lin's knotted brow, watched him drain another glass and detected hope in his heavy eyes. Then, her mother had advised her, imagine the person as a child. In her mind's eye Ma Swe wanted to picture Ko Lin as a boy, his skin taut and unblemished, his breath sweet not bitter, standing up against a bully, demanding that some small injustice be put right. Finally, her mother had said, see the spirit within the person. Ma Swe stared and tried, and the thought made her suddenly smile.

The smile, which was beautiful, surprised Ko Lin, for it made him notice the quiet young woman who ate with him, listened to him, week after week. He asked her where she was from, and when she told him he recalled the Ananda Temple, which he had photographed years earlier, and the two statues of courtly dancers which flanked the golden south-facing Buddha. Ma Swe knew them well, having chased lizards over their painted toes and dozed against their plinths. She had stared at them the evening after listening to the lovers in the hidden cave, hoping that their arrested beauty might help her to understand the overheard intimacy. Ko Lin spoke of the frozen grace of the temple dancers, one arm stretched down to accentuate their slender figures and the long fine fingers of the other hand lifted up in the traditional movement. The gesture pulled the spectator's gaze across their narrow waists, over the small breasts, up to the downcast eyes, humble in expression yet with the confidence of women who fit well in their bodies. Ma Swe listened to Ko Lin and heard the animation in his voice. She saw his eyes glint, as they often did after a third can of stout. The beads of sweat stuck to his face like seed pearls.

'I am a poor dancer,' she told him, 'but I like to listen to poetry.'

He proposed including verse in the magazine – as well as an article on King Kyanzittha, whose devotion to Buddha and whose lithe, nubile dancers had been perpetuated in the Ananda – and asked Ma Swe if she had a favourite poem.

'I know a story,' she said, clasping her hands in her lap.

'Tell me,' said Ko Lin, listening.

'It is about the *kinnayas*,' she said, her words all but lost in the clamour of the restaurant, and he nodded. His description of the dancers had reminded her of the graceful creatures, half-bird, half-human, who inhabited the green forests of Burmese legend. As a child Ma Swe had imagined them dipping in the shallows of the Irrawaddy like elegant, long-limbed egrets.

'Long ago there lived a prince named Bhanlatiya who was fond of hunting,' Ma Swe began, then added, 'But excuse me, you know the story.'

'I would like to hear it again,' he replied, 'from you.'

'One day while wandering far from home Bhanlatiya came upon two *kinnayas*, weeping by a shallow stream.' Her manner shed something of its hesitance, her voice warmed like polished teak. 'You know that *kinnayas* are always seen in pairs?' she asked with a tilt of the head. Ko Lin nodded, sipping on his beer. 'Well, the prince thought it wrong that such fine, beautiful lovers should be crying, and asked them what had happened.

'"We were dancing together here in the shallows," explained the young male, pointing at the water's rippled mirror, crystal blue and polished bright, "when the skies suddenly turned dark and a great storm blew up out of nowhere."

'"The stream swelled into rapids," said the female, "and we were cast onto opposite banks. We could hardly see through the rain."

'"It was only when lightning flashed that we spotted each other."

'"The storm lasted all night long," said the female, "and we were apart the whole time. We were only reunited in the morning when the river reverted to a stream."

'"But when did this happen?" asked Bhanlatiya. "I have been hunting in these woods for over a week and have seen no rain at all."

'"It happened seven hundred years ago" – more than half the lifespan of a *kinnaya* – "and we have been crying every day since the storm," they replied, and started again to weep.'

Ko Lin laughed, and Ma Swe explained, 'Their story brought Bhanlatiya to his senses. It helped him to realise that he should not be wandering so far away from home and his family.' It was hot at the Bamboo House, and for a moment she wished that they had taken a table away from the window, in one of the restaurant's darker rooms. 'I love the rains,' she said.

Ko Lin accepted Ma Swe's story for publication, even though Buddhist legends were not to his taste, in the hope that the gesture would help to sustain official approval, or at least to stave off a ban. He was not suspicious that the PSB had demanded no concessions, and as public opinion forced the government to admit more and more of its mistakes, he was encouraged to take an even bolder editorial line.

To deepen Ma Swe's involvement he invited her to visit his office. In a tiny alcove behind a bookshop on 32nd Street she was introduced to the typesetter, a cheery Indian with good teeth and toffee-coloured skin, and the student illustrator. Ko Lin was determined to enhance both the magazine's appearance and its contents. His professional attention to detail impressed Ma Swe, even though so many matters remained undone that it was difficult to imagine that the magazine's first issue would be ready on time. She took pleasure in hearing him read his editorial aloud, especially its candid sincerity. He asked for her opinion, and to her surprise incorporated her comments. She decided not to ask him for a copy for the Board.

At the end of August, in response to the killings at Maha Bandoola Park, the country went on strike. Hundreds of thousands of demonstrators demanded the government's resignation. No newspapers were printed for three days, as the journalists too had taken to the streets, and after the break the publications were much changed. At the same time dozens of unofficial, independent news sheets suddenly appeared, spread out on the pavement in front of the town hall like a mosaic of truth, which spurred the established press on to even greater openness.

To a people deprived for twenty-six years of a free press, the factual reporting of news was a wonder. The greater miracle though was that lucid, intelligent voices had remained alive to be heard. Over the decades the tentacles of state repression had silenced those men and women brave enough to speak out. Writers were entwined in the official line, turned with literary prizes and favour, twisted to serve the government. Those who broke free of the cosy web were persecuted. Fear became a habit, a sinister harness that tethered sincerity.

But at the Shwedagon Pagoda, Maugham's 'sudden hope in the dark night of the soul', a young mother broke the habit. Beneath a huge portrait of her father, Aung San Suu Kyi called for 'democracy through unity and discipline'. She spoke of her love and devotion for the country. 'The present crisis is the concern of the entire nation,' she said, speaking from the heart, not looking at her text. 'I could not, as my father's daughter, remain indifferent to all that is going on. This national crisis could, in fact, be called the second struggle for national independence.'

Her short, concise sentences appealed to Ma Swe's sense of clarity. Her bold sincerity won deafening applause. The audience of half a million hopeful, heroic Burmese cheered her demand for free and fair elections.

'Our strength should be used for the cause of what is right,' she called out. 'May the people be free from all harm.'

The day that Ma Swe joined the march was sunny and fine. She walked out of the shadows with Ko Lin, holding hands with strangers, under an upside-down socialist flag. The government appeared to have collapsed under the weight of protest. Its inaction had been misconstrued as weakness and its ribbon of control, the *Tatmadaw*, had been withdrawn from the streets. Local citizens' committees had emerged to fill the administrative vacuum. That morning the opposition had demanded that the regime concede to their demands or face an indefinite strike. The rapidly unfolding events had encour aged Ko Lin to bring forward his publication date. He and two senior journalists had put their names to a bold article calling for the toppling of the regime. Ma Swe was aware of the risks, both to themselves and to her job, but the defence of truth was at stake. The euphoria of the final editorial meeting committed – and condemned – her. The marchers carried them forward under the multi-coloured banners. Students walked with their faces undisguised by handker-chiefs. Customs officials found the courage to shout out their griev-ances. There were Palaung pilgrims, dressed in traditional velvet caps and heavy hoods, and a band of ethnic Chinese who had travelled down from the Shan State. Christian clergymen shouted, 'Jesus loves democracy.' No one paid much attention to the innocuous clerks taking notes or the uniformed photographers on rooftops. The tide of protest drove the people together. Then, in the thick of the crowd, surrounded by cheering students and a chanting detachment of the People's Railway Police, Ko Lin asked Ma Swe to marry him.

It was partnership rather than passion which had brought them together; a meeting of minds, not bodies. Ko Lin liked to speak out, and Ma Swe loved to listen. As a wedding gift he bought her a little shortwave radio, and the batteries to go with it. She gave him a fountain pen. Unfortunately none of her friends could attend the brief ceremony because of the strike. No trains or buses were running. Even her mother was not able to reach Rangoon. The magazine staff and a handful of writers did join them for a celebratory drink, but they were at work in the office anyway. Of her colleagues from the Board only the woman from Meiktila attended the simple reception. She stood alone at the back of the room by the printing press, appalled at how the game had unravelled itself. Ko Lin and Ma Swe spent their nuptial night in his room above the bookshop, sur-rounded by reams of newsprint and empty stout bottles, listening to the clunk-clunk-slap of the old press and the hopeful cries of the demonstrators on the street outside. In the morning they rose early, he to bind the loose-leaf pages of the first edition, she to go to the Board which was preparing to tear them apart.

*   *   *

The suppression of the first August uprising had been a wild and ill-disciplined affair. The government had been unprepared and its soldiers had butchered the demonstrators out of fear, and with a brutal arbitrariness. By contrast the second massacre in the following month was calculated and clinical.

On 18 September the military reasserted control over the country. The Council of State was dissolved and the State Law and Order Restoration Council erected in its place. The army's Chief of Staff, General Saw Maung, became Prime Minister, Foreign Minister and Defence Minister. On the streets gatherings of more than four people were banned and troops fell into orderly ranks to fire at the demonstrators. The soldiers were village boys trucked in from up country 'to free the capital', as they had been told, 'from insurgents'. They were paid in advance. Their officers, fearful of revenge for past excesses, ordered the shooting of 'communist' children and housewives. Any change of government would undermine their privileged positions. Hit squads went from door to door, with detailed lists and files of photographs in hand, arresting the student leaders, journalists and monks who had spoken out. They were taken away in trucks. Most were never heard from again. On 21 September the old-style *Working People's Daily* alone reappeared on the news-stands, its pages as before devoid of real news and objective comment. The operation to silence the Burmese had been executed with steely precision.

Ko Lin's press was seized. The printed and bound magazines were collected by the PSB, counted and destroyed. Not a single copy was allowed to remain in existence. The toffee-skinned typesetter was arrested. When his wife pleaded that he had not been a spokesman, and merely set the words of others in type, she was shot on the spot, dying among romantic novellas and picture postcards. But Ko Lin himself was not arrested. Every time the hammering came on the door – and it came often in the first days – he stood up expectant and prepared, a small gripsack packed with biscuits and cash for bribes in his hand; but the soldiers always pushed past him, taking instead his records and the student illustrator. Ma Swe too waited for the inevitable, surprised each morning to be woken by the dawn and not by the sound of boots on the stairs, relieved every evening to find Ko Lin still at home, slouched over the desk, drunk.

Ma Swe did not understand why he was not arrested, or why she herself remained at liberty. She, like all employees, had been ordered back to her job. 'Anyone who prevents, obstructs or interferes with workers returning to work,' the government warned in radio and television announcements, 'will be dealt with sternly.' The general strike collapsed and a fearful normality returned, now heightened by a sense of despair. The feral reek of terror again dominated lives. At each new checkpoint, every time her identity document was inspected, Ma Swe closed her eyes, listening to the rough unfolding of paper, hearing the cold tap of rifle strap against gun metal, waiting for the short intake of breath and urgent shouts of discovery. 'Move on, little sister,' the soldiers said instead, shoving the document back into her hand. 'I don't have all day. Move along.'

It seemed inconceivable that the PSB, which had destroyed Ko Lin's magazine, could be protecting them. Yet there was no other explanation. Civil servants were not above suspicion, but some escaped reproach. At the Board it was as if the whole office had slept through the eight-week general strike. There was no mention of the demonstrations or killings. The Eleven Principles were taken down from the wall, every reference to socialism was removed, then they were rehung behind Ma Swe's head. To create the impression of reform, the SLORC had replaced the Socialist Programme Party and embraced capitalism. But the same soldiers remained in control. The censors, like the generals, fabricated a world of illusion. Nothing changed. The Major telephoned Ma Swe at her desk and said only, 'So you are there; good.' Throughout the first afternoon she checked one short article for spelling mistakes, reading the same sentences over and over again, terrified of letting a single error slip through her fingers. She stayed late in the office to complete her work.

Ko Lin on the other hand, believing himself to be shielded by his wife's position, became reckless. Rather than wait to surrender himself he borrowed a camera and began to photograph the street-corner arrests, the steel-helmeted *Lon Htein* armed with clubs, the civilians press-ganged to serve as human minesweepers in rebel areas. He recorded events, rather than commenting on them. Ma Swe tried to caution him but Ko Lin would not listen. He met foreign journalists and passed his rolls of film to students on the run to Thailand. He wrote letters to the Board demanding the return of his printing press.

Then one evening Ma Swe returned to their room to find him gone. A cup of Chinese tea, still warm to the touch, was on his desk. His toothbrush lay by their washbasin. Her shortwave radio was in its hiding place, wrapped in a coloured cloth and slipped like a plinth beneath the small Buddha shrine. There was no note or sign of struggle. Only his wedding present fountain pen appeared to be missing.

All night Ma Swe slept fitfully, the radio tucked under her pillow, starting herself awake with imaginings of Ko Lin's drunken footfalls on the stairs, knowing even then that he would never return to her. The next morning she was dismissed from the Board. The guard told her simply that she could no longer enter the building. Her desk had been cleared and its contents discarded. There was no redundancy payment or explanation for her dismissal, as if one were necessary. 'Reason for Discharge,' the official rubber stamp might have read, 'Married to Free-Thinker.' She wandered the streets for the rest of the day, aimlessly looking for Ko Lin in the tea shops and toddy bars. On the bus she overheard his voice and pushed through the jam of commuters to come face-to-face with a startled monk. Twice more she imagined seeing him, disappearing behind a vegetable stall at the market and drinking at a restaurant where they had once eaten. On both occasions she gave chase, knocking over baskets of cabbages and upsetting self-important waiters, but it was not him. He had gone.

At the end of the week Ma Swe was arrested without fuss or drama. She was not, like countless others, beaten by a squad of soldiers or raped in the back of a lorry. Instead a young officer in a new uniform simply asked her to come with him and she obeyed. He took her to Insein Jail and locked her in a cell where she waited with forty other women. After a week she found the courage to complain to the guards, pointing out that she had not been charged with any offence, and they put her in solitary confinement. Her chamber was too low to stand up in and too narrow for her to lie down. Muffled sobs echoed through the dank walls. She crouched in the corner, afraid, an unknown fate awaiting her.

In the cell Ma Swe remembered her first meeting with Ko Lin. He had told her how imprisonment had taught him to value time. The memory directed her disordered thoughts to their unreleased magazine and she held it in her mind, turned its pages, recollected its articles. It was a good issue, she judged, too good to remain incomplete. She decided to finish it in her imagination. She composed an article about the killings at Rangoon General Hospital and another on Aung San Suu Kyi's speech at the Shwedagon. She edited them both, and although the magazine was a little short, she was just in time for their Thursday publication date. 'Whatever happens,' she told herself, while reviewing each column and story, 'the magazine must come out without fail on the first Thursday of every month. It must always be published on time.'

Ma Swe set to work on the second issue, deciding that it would be larger than the first. She acted as writer, publisher and editor, composing and cutting, soliciting imaginary advertising and laying out the wished-for pages. She introduced regular pieces on politics, wrote features on the drug trade, about prostitution, on how the wealthiest country in Asia had been impoverished and vandalised by its rulers. To keep her mind occupied she worked as librarian too, training herself to remember the contents of every issue, so that when she wrote a letter to the editor – that is, to herself – she could refer back to earlier editions: 'Madam: with reference to your editorial on the religious interpretations of love and charity in issue no. 1, I wish to correct etc. etc.' Alone in her cell she tried to encourage discussion and debate.

In many ways her fanciful work was less difficult than it had been trying to publish the real magazine. She didn't need paper and ink. There were no writers to chase up, no bills to pay, no PSB to satisfy. As money wasn't a concern she began to commission articles from famous people: the Dalai Lama wrote about China's occupation of Tibet, Desmond Tutu penned a piece on economic sanctions. Even General Ne Win agreed to write her an editorial on humility, but in the end he was too busy, missed the publication date and never paid back the advance.

When after two months Ma Swe was moved back into a shared cell, she stayed in her inner world. There were no books to read in Insein, nothing to distract the mind but the mournful cries of its inmates, so she continued with the magazine. She introduced a poetry corner and encouraged readers to send in their work. Her mother submitted three pieces, as did, surprisingly, the supervisor from the Board. Ma Swe had not known that the woman was a poet. She also ran a small ads section – For sale: Festive fans and monk's utensils; Cassette tapes for hire; Lost: One green Triumph bicycle – and through a personal column a number of friends who had been separated during the September killings were reunited. Tripple Mountain Brand Super Tonic placed an advertisement with her every month: Look Young, Regain Your Youthful Energy, Lack of Appetite, Sleeplessness, Sexual Impotency, For Female Menstrual Troubles and for Skinny Persons (Directions Included). Ma Swe concentrated on the magazine, noting the coming and going of prisoners in her cell only in relation to her publication date.

In the third issue she decided to have Ko Lin's photographs printed, big and bold and on the front page. Robert Frank, the American photographer, wrote her a review on them. It was very satisfying to see them in print, though maybe a little indulgent. She also published a number of cartoons, and remembered her husband's tendency to laugh at his own jokes. Sometimes, of course, her imagination failed her. In the fourth edition, which was eight pages long, there were too many articles on prison routine.

One day, Ma Swe told herself, I will share the magazine with Ko Lin. I will read him every issue, every article. It will be ours to keep, together, for ever. Throughout her incarceration, in the face of brutal repression, the magazine kept her sane. It also helped her to find her voice. Over the year of her imprisonment she produced eleven issues, missing only one month after a difficult period of 're-education'. Her body might have been worn down but her mind had remained intact. One hot Thursday morning, half an hour before the magazine was due to go to press, she was released without explanation into the sunlight.

The sky was high and the sun so bright. Ma Swe stumbled out of Insein dazzled by the light, blinking, stretching, laughing because of her trust in the words now woven inside her. There was nothing to keep her in Rangoon. She would return home. Her only possession was the little radio, which a neighbour had kept safe for her. Ma Swe retrieved it and tied it to her inner thigh, hoping that the soldiers at the checkpoints would not be brazen in their searches. She was lucky. The Pagan line-bus was stopped only once, by a yawning new recruit near Prome. He was willing to let the vehicle pass for the price of a pack of cigarettes, and afterwards the passengers travelled in silence, unmolested through the rest of the night.

It was dawn when the driver dropped her near the Ananda Temple. Ma Swe followed the route by memory. She turned off the main road, hurrying along the familiar footpath into her lane, skirting the caves where she had once played. She hoped to be in time for breakfast, to hear the family's news, but the lack of sound caught her attention. She stopped and listened. No cockerels crowed, no children laughed, no farmers called from the fields. She did not hear the monks as they went on their morning rounds with alms bowls and blessings. The unexpected silence disoriented her, jolting her back to Insein. She panicked, taking her bearings from the temples. She recognised the range of hills, placed herself, and then in the half-light saw the outline of the rhyming tree. It was wilted and downcast, dying as if from a lack of love. Ma Swe stepped beneath it. A scorpion scuttled in the dust. The garden fence which had once surrounded the tree was gone. She could not see her bamboo gate. There was no family home, no village hall, no neighbours' houses. She stood at the edge of a dark, barren field, once the site of old Pagan village, alone.

Suffering is an unavoidable aspect of existence, the Buddha teaches, and life is *dukkha*, or unsatisfactoriness. The world is characterised by *anicca*, that is impermanence, and *anatta*, which translates as insubstantiality. Buddhism helped its people to cope with their disappointment. It was no wonder that the government promoted public adherence to its principles. A religion based on the acceptance of the status quo posed no real threat to its power. Happiness, Ma Swe reminded herself as she turned away from the tree, is a temporary state.

She crossed the bare field and retreated into the corridors of the Ananda. She stole into its lightless recesses, hid herself in her secluded corner and listened. In the darkness a bat fluttered back to its perch. Outside day broke with the buzz of cicadas. The dull ring of a brass gong echoed from the small temple monastery. She heard the flat slap of feet on the inner stone floor and a worshipper's whispered devotions. 'I take refuge in the Buddha, I take refuge in his teachings.' A single broom swept away the night's dust from steps and stairs. Somewhere a child cried. An hour passed in silence, then another, and Ma Swe made no sound. The squeak of a pony-cart's wheels reached her ears and she heard the cool swish of new silk. Coins dropped into a donation box and camera shutters snapped. A foreign voice guffawed, its haw-haw too harsh for the temple's soft peace, and heavy footsteps idled away. At midday the sounds became hushed again, the intense heat of the sun drawing the coolness out of the dark alcoves, like breath from a body, like life from the soul. Ma Swe tucked herself deeper into the dark embrace and felt the building exhale around her. Its old walls sighed, its tongue of bricks clicked and a wordless draft whispered through the cool interior and past her ears. She listened to a heartbeat, whether hers or the temple's own she could not tell, and felt a numb comfort encircle her. Her hearing stretched to the edges of the Ananda, as if encompassing the whole building within her, her ears hearing everything, missing nothing. She listened to the rustle of unfolding prayer mats, felt the scratchings of beetles, sensed evening crickets chirp around her walls. She dozed and strained and half-heard again soft whispers and the rustle of clothing. Through the long night she listened for lovers' sighs. She overheard eternal promises murmured in a moment's passion. Day came and passed and came upon her again, no inkling of light penetrating her retreat, the passage of time measured only by changes in sound. Temple bells chimed easily in the breeze at dusk. Tired labourers dragged themselves to work in another dawn's dusty shuffle. Stray dogs panted in the muffled exhaustion of mid-afternoon. At night she remembered the two statues of courtly dancers and the frozen grace of the dance which Ko Lin had loved. She listened for the sound of their finger cymbals, heard the banging of the drum and in her mind felt them spin around and around the rhyming tree, repeating her mother's poems, swaying to the music of words.

An old monk found Ma Swe a week later. In exhaustion she had slumped over, switching on the radio which had remained lashed to her thigh. Its batteries had retained a last spark of charge. Distant voices and cheerful jingles had blared through the ancient corridors. The monk had followed the scream of static down the maze of darkened passageways, through the child-size openings into her tiny alcove. When the man had spoken she had called out in her delirium, then wept in the blackness.

The monastery took her in, giving her a quiet haven, allowing her to live by herself but not alone, sheltering her within the bamboo walls with a dozen other women who had been widowed or orphaned by the elimination of the village. In return for sanctuary the women cared for the last, chaste monks, sweeping, cleaning and preparing their meals. Ma Swe spent her hours in the company of the elder who had found her. His eyes were bad but he liked to keep up with events, as much as precepts and censorship allowed, so every day she read aloud for him articles from the *Working People's Daily* and stories from the copies of *Asiaweek* left by passing tourists. She once found a back-issue of the *Economist* and so learned of Aung San Suu Kyi's house-arrest, of her party contesting and winning the election, of the SLORC's annulment of the results. Sometimes, when the monk's concentration drifted away, Ma Swe was tempted to recite from memory a passage or poem from her magazine. But she never did. There was no one with whom the eleven imaginary issues would ever be shared. The past was past and she tried to look forward, giving what she could as deeds of merit. She learned to be content with her lot, and rarely left the environs of the Ananda, except when she tuned her radio.

On the wavelengths she travelled the world. At night alone in the dark she listened to the news from Moscow and heard poetry readings from Bangladesh. Over the airwaves came the music of Zakir Hussain's tabla and Cape Breton Island fiddles. She turned the dial around and around, reaching out beyond the borders, drawing the precious strands of dialogue towards her. The Soviet Union collapsed, Nelson Mandela was released and Winnie Mandela appeared before the Truth and Reconciliation Commission. Seasons and events slipped away without touching timeless Pagan. Nothing changed until one evening when, as she dozed, she heard his voice.

Over the intervening years Ma Swe had imagined Ko Lin in the muffled half-sleep of dreams. He had often drifted into her thoughts, laughing at his own jokes, repeating his disdain for the complicity of silence, asking her again to marry him. But now his words were fresh and new and their clarity shook her awake. It was not a fantasy, rather it was as if his ghost had come back to life, as if he had laid his head down on the pillow beside her. He was talking to her from another world. He was reading her the news. Ma Swe sat up holding the radio, gripping her husband in her hands. The movement knocked it out of tune. A growl of interference, hiss and whistle, quickly, 11850 kHz 25-metre band. She retuned her receiver. Again she heard him, finishing the bulletin, then conducting a short discussion on recent political arrests and finally, when the news was done, starting to tell a story. 'Long ago there lived a prince named Bhanlatiya who was fond of hunting,' he said over the airwaves. 'One day while wandering far from home he came upon two *kinnayas*, weeping by a shallow stream.' Ma Swe heard her words, carried in her husband's heart to safety beyond Burma, read back to her from another world. 'A great storm blew up out of nowhere and the river swelled into rapids and the *kinnayas* were cast onto opposite banks, unable to reach each other across the angry water, hardly able even to see through the rain.' The temple bells of Ananda chimed above the monastery walls and Ma Swe no longer felt afraid. She wanted to speak out, to tell Ko Lin about herself, to recite to him every issue and article and story in their wished-for magazine. But he could not hear her. He was with her, yet he would for ever be too far away, out of hearing. 'We spent one night apart,' said the wanderer across the ether, 'and we have been crying every day remembering our loss for over seven hundred years.' He finished her story and wished his wife – and the rest of their poor, golden country – goodnight from London.

FIVE

Heart Strings

MA SWE SERVED US EACH a bottle of Pepsi, though she would drink only weak Chinese tea herself, and sat talking in a beam of dusty sunlight which filtered through the open shutters of the cool teak monastery. The shortwave radio lay on the smooth floor at her side. There was no one else to overhear her recollections, apart from the old monk who leaned against a wooden pillar eating rice and beans. The stray cat circling his low table probably had better hearing.

'My house was very old,' Ma Swe remembered, her features serious, her inflection light. A Citizen 'Electronic Big Ben' quartz clock chimed the quarter hour. The year in prison had marked her, yet her voice remained polished and thoughtful. 'It was Grandmother's Grandfather's house.'

'Your family had lived there so long?' asked Katrin. We were still dismayed that a whole village and its people could vanish.

Ma Swe dipped her head in a nod. 'When I returned to Pagan the house – and my mother – were gone.'

Immediately after the 1988 uprising the government had begun to promote tourism, in part to resurrect its tarnished image abroad, but primarily to earn itself hard currency. The generals and their allies had confiscated hotels, requisitioned bus franchises and built airlines with the profits from opium sales. Rangoon, Mandalay and Pagan were chosen as the three destinations to be opened to tourists. To make way for the visitors the 5,200 residents of Pagan were evicted from their homes around the ancient temples. The number was small when compared to expulsions elsewhere in the country: a million civilians were relocated within the capital, according to the International Confederation of Free Trade Unions. But the method employed was similar. The army simply announced through loudspeakers that the village was to be resettled. The residents, many of whom had lived in the same house for generations, were told to pack their belongings. Compensation of only 250 kyat – about $2 – was to be paid per property. No money was given for the buildings themselves. The owners of the Mother Hotel received nothing. Two weeks later the lorries and bulldozers arrived. The people were taken away and two hundred homes destroyed. The old village was replaced by a tourist enclave of modern hotels catering for dollar-bearing foreigners. The dispossessed residents were given plots of barren land three miles away in 'New Pagan'.

'There were no trees in New Pagan,' said Ma Swe. 'It was very hot and, when rains came, very wet. Some people, their land wash away. Three four five old people die every day. My mother given land but she sick and with no family cannot work. She die the first monsoon.' There was dignity, even grace in her controlled, direct speech. 'The old monk save me and I meditate every night – to Buddha, to the monk – and if I forget I cannot sleep. I am happy here but now I must leave.'

'To live on your mother's land?' I asked.

Ma Swe nodded. 'I have no choice. It is forbidden for women to stay on in the monastery.'

'But why?'

'Because tourists come, and we are not photogenic for them.'

In the seven years since the resettlement, New Pagan had found an identity of sorts, expanding to supply old Pagan with waiters and souvenirs, tour guides and pony-carts. The palm-frond huts were replaced by breeze-block guest houses. Migrants moved in from Meiktila and Thazi to profit from the growing tourist business. The receptionist at our hotel came from Taunggyi. She had trained as an archaeologist but earned more money working on the front desk than she would restoring temples. The old community had been destroyed.

'I will build my house,' Ma Swe said, tucking a stray tendril of hair behind her ear. Her mother's small lot lay behind the modern Paradise Guest House. 'My friends will help and we build in five days. But first I have to save enough money to buy the bamboo. The matting and walls cost twelve thousand kyat.' Our four nights in the cheapest room at the Thante Hotel had cost us $100, the equivalent of twelve thousand kyat at the black-market rate. Foreigners were allowed only to stay at 'dollar' hotels. 'So I must try to sell my radio.'

'You cannot sell your radio,' said Katrin, appalled by the thought. To give up the radio was to lose her hearing, as well as her sanity.

'You like it?' Ma Swe asked, hesitant.

'It is very nice,' replied Katrin.

'It is good one, but you are right, I cannot sell it. In Rangoon I could get two thousand kyat but here no one will buy it. Everyone is too busy with tourist-working to worry about the outside world.' She picked up the little radio. 'So maybe you would like to have it?'

'I can't accept it, Ma Swe,' said Katrin, startled by the offer.

'But I would like you to have it.'

'It is more important that you keep the radio.'

'We met a boy who believes that your husband fills the sky with lies,' I told her. 'Is that true?'

'Even in a small place you have to – I do not want to use the word – you have to be brave. You have to stand up. The boys say wrong things. I tell them right, but they do not listen.' She pushed the radio into Katrin's hands. 'Please, it is for you.'

It was wrong that Ma Swe should have to sell the radio; even worse that she should try to give it to us. We managed to persuade her to keep it, then offered to help her finance her house. At first she refused, but we insisted. She would build herself a house for the same cost as a good lunch in London.

Ma Swe then began showering us with gifts of local *yun* lacquerware: two trays, a miniature chest, a matching pair of vases and an octagonal-topped folding table. 'To remember me by,' she explained. We tried to decline her gifts, explaining that we had only one small rucksack, but she could not be dissuaded. The giving seemed necessary; to refuse would be to deny her her deed of good merit.

'You do not like lacquerware?' she asked, her tired eyes protruding in her thin, bony face. 'Pagan lacquerware good quality.' To demonstrate she squeezed together the rims of a bowl. It suffered no damage. 'All tourists like.'

I explained that although the lacquerware was beautiful, we were searching for a specific basket. A maker in Rangoon had directed us to Pagan, where we hoped to find it. We had been told that she might be able to help us.

Katrin showed her the photograph. Ma Swe shook her head. 'Sorry, not Pagan style,' she apologised. 'But you go to Mandalay. Maybe you find in Zegyo market. Then afterwards you come back,' she insisted, pressing two small lacquer betel boxes into our hands, 'and stay in my house, not hotel.'

'Has the post gone yet?' demanded the tanned, middle-aged German couple at the hotel reception desk. A thin boy, his head bowed, loaded their monogrammed suitcases into the Air Mandalay minibus. 'It is not good if our cards arrive home late.'

'The postman will pick them up this afternoon,' promised the receptionist. She chose not to point out that the censor's inspection would delay their cards in any event. 'Have a good trip. Goodbye.'

'*Auf wiedersehen*,' replied the wife. 'Try to say it in German, not just English. Next time we come you will say it in German.'

The Ministry of Hotels and Tourism – under the direction of Lieutenant General Kyaw Ba – ensures that all independent and package travellers are catalogued, controlled and contained. Each evening every hotel and guest house in the country is required to produce thirteen copies of their guest register, to be distributed to:

> External Passenger Control Unit (one copy)
> Immigration Office (one copy)

Township Law and Order Restoration Council (four copies)
Ward Law and Order Restoration Council (one copy)
Police Station (five copies)
Navy Intelligence Unit (one copy).

The thirteen copies have to be submitted by seven o'clock every evening. If a guest arrives at a hotel after that time, thirteen amended lists have to be prepared and delivered to the authorities before midnight. In addition, once a week a full roster of visiting foreigners needs to be lodged with both the Military Office and the Ministry of Hotels and Tourism. In this regard alone tourists are treated in a similar manner to residents. Every Burmese household also has to register with the Ward Law and Order Restoration Council, and no guest – family or friend – is allowed to spend the night in another place without obtaining permission from the local chairman. Ma Swe's invitation to us had been sincere, but foreigners are forbidden from staying in private homes. The intrusive system ensures that every journey is made under surveillance. Tourists alone retain the luxury of itinerancy. The Burmese travel only out of necessity.

We could have flown to Mandalay, of course. We could have dropped our knapsack into the thin boy's arms and joined the German couple on the back seat of the minibus to trade stories of plum-size cockroaches and egg-on-sugared-toast hotel breakfasts. We could have confused landscape and historical remains with the living country. Our credit card could have been debited and a round of drinks ordered. Peanuts and crispies would have been served in the departure lounge. We could have checked in, taken off, touched down and still had time to take in Mandalay Hill before lunch at the Novotel. But instead we decided not to luxuriate on the ATR 72-210 *Hintha* Golden Flight. It wasn't a question of saving the cost of the airfare, or even our response to the rumours that the airline had been financed by the profits of arms trading. It was for a greater reason than that. We had the freedom to choose.

The next morning, at the hour when – as the Burmese say – 'one first sees the veins on one's hands', we sat in an Isuzu bus beside the Irrawaddy, yawning. In the cool dawn a drowsy mother lit her breakfast fire. The match hissed, kindling crackled and her child called out in its sleep. Waking sparrows chattered. The ebony sky turned to ash grey, tinged itself with rose then burst into morning bloom. Voices warmed in the sun, growing excited with the heat. Our driver detached himself from a circle of conversation and slipped behind the wheel. He was a cut above the usual line-bus driver, wearing a dusty tailored blazer with his *longyi*. His ticket collector sported a flutter of banknotes around his fingers and a T-shirt which read 'Top of the Heap'. The engine shook itself awake and, with an alarming shriek of gears, the bus eased forward along the low, muddy riverbank.

The Irrawaddy rises in the southern Himalayas, winds its way through the Kachin Hills, curls around the rice paddies of the Shan Plateau and crosses the arid central plains before uncoiling, like the frayed end of a rope, into the Andaman Sea. In an earlier age our dashing driver might have captained one of the forty steamers of the Irrawaddy Flotilla Company. At the height of British rule its ships carried nine million passengers a year along the river. But instead of sounding a polished brass whistle, he tooted his horn to encourage a bullock-cart out of our path, and startled a heron fishing in the shallows.

The bus gathered speed, racing along the single-lane carriageway and swaying onto the cinder shoulder to pass oncoming lorries or local pick-ups with live pigs lashed to their roofs. The wild motion shook us with such violence that our vision soon became blurred. Our bodies bounced out of contact with the hard bench seat. Within thirty minutes our brains felt as bruised within the bone of our heads as were we inside the metal box of the bus. The appalling road was a long, weaving Morse-code line of contact and non-contact, and after an hour our comfortable Pagan hotel seemed a lifetime away. A stone punctured the muffler, releasing a deafening blast of exhaust. The wearying movement created an impression of great distances travelled, but after four hours we had covered only forty miles. 'I think I need a new bra,' Katrin groaned as we shivered and jolted into Myingyan, our lunch stop.

The Burmese passengers scrambled out of the bus and into the café to wolf down plates of curry. We took longer to collect ourselves, and were besieged by a clamour of street vendors, balancing on their heads trays of plastic-wrapped quail eggs, bunches of grapes and fierce ruby-red sausages. Katrin ate a tiny boiled egg and I managed to stomach a *samosa*, its fried pastry stuffed with pigeon peas. We drank three bottles of purified water ('UV Treated for your Good Health and Extra Comfort') while our driver finished his second 'brain sweet' bread pudding. Across the road a gang of villagers thatched a house with toddy fronds, and we remembered Ma Swe.

The journey after lunch was no more comfortable, but because the morning had numbed our senses, it became easier to think. I noticed again that, as on the Meiktila line-bus, children slept on their parents' laps undisturbed by the vicious motion. Their calm reminded me of the words of Major Grant Allen, as quoted by Scott in *The Burman*. 'Unlike the generality of Asiatics,' Allen had declared with a Victorian's certainty, 'the Burmese are not a fawning race. They are cheerful, and singularly alive to the ridiculous; buoyant, elastic, soon recovering from personal or domestic disaster.'

Allen's assertion that the Burmese were 'not individually cruel', yet were 'indifferent to the shedding of blood on the part of their rulers' intrigued me. Watching the children, dozing innocents in a harsh environment, I began to wonder if the tolerance of tyranny could be a legacy of the past. Was the present military dictatorship simply a modern version of the old despotic monarchy? If this was the case, then could the 1988 uprising, with all its hopes for democracy, have been more the result of Western influences than a response to an intrinsic Burmese need for freedom? Neither Allen's nor Scott's words could explain the central dichotomy of Burma: that the gentle generosity of the people – the constant offers to share food, to give us presents and pay our bus fare – was at odds with the grasping brutality of authority.

Beyond the bus's dust-caked windows the scorched plains gradually yielded to tilled land. Against a backdrop of sunflower fields a goatherd leaned on a bush and lowered juicy new shoots to within his herd's reach. Chalk-white egrets fed in emerald-green rice paddies. Beneath a stern but imperfect red and white sign – 'Anyone who Gets Riotustive and Unruly is our Enemy' – we entered Mandalay on sore, bruised bottoms.

'This city is at the centre of things,' insisted Michael, dislodging the familiar downpour of dandruff onto the car's upholstery. 'It is the heart of the country.'

I had decided to meet him again, despite Katrin's objections. We knew no one else in the city, and needed someone to translate for us at the Zegyo market. Katrin had not enjoyed our night with him on the Leo Express, and had agreed to see him only on condition that we didn't visit his shopping malls.

'Did you know that 60 per cent of all the country's monks live in this area?' Michael enthused, as his chauffeur cut a straight path through the weaving traffic. The self-help paperback, *The Leader in You*, was tucked into his pocket. 'That makes for good karma. Makes it a prosperous place to live, too.'

Mandalay was booming. Its broad, dusty streets bustled with new Nissans, old bicycles and packs of stray dogs. But good karma alone did not explain the profusion of high-rise office blocks. In 1990 the government had granted a four-month tax amnesty. Individuals were permitted to declare their unexplained assets by paying a 25 per cent profit tax. This legal method of money-laundering earned $66 million for the SLORC. It also allowed illegal earnings to be invested, which resulted in a boom that increased property prices tenfold. Trade in the 'red, green and white lines' – rubies, jade and heroin – lay behind the dramatic growth.

'Then why does it feel so foreign?' I asked. Mandalay had once been the most Burmese of the country's cities. It was the last pre-colonial capital. Its residents were said to speak the finest Burmese. Yet in spite of its history and central location the sprawling city seemed to be teetering on an edge. It felt like a border town.

'Mandalay is a crossroads, not only for Burma but between China and the members of ASEAN – the Association of South-East Asian Nations,' said Michael. 'It is a centre for all of Asia. Now, shall we see my shopping mall?'

'I just want to go to the market,' stated Katrin, who was not in good humour. The chauffeur wheeled the car around and swept up to its entrance.

'Scruffy old place,' Michael complained, kicking the dust from his shoes. 'My mall has marble flooring and air-conditioning.' He guided us across a barren lot where a straggle of boys played football, towards a nest of low wooden stalls. There were trees here, and it was cooler in the shade. He eased his squat, suited frame along the narrow passageway between the sheds, past jumbled clothing stands and neat Chinese jewellers, a disdainful grin on his lips. Our search entertained him. He saw that there was no profit in it, but in spite of himself and like all Burmese, he enjoyed being of assistance to strangers. 'I made some enquiries on your behalf,' he explained, then stopped at a jam-packed stall and said, 'And here we are.'

Crammed together were sieves, waste bins and brooms, cradles and fans, bicycle baskets and food carriers. Wok whisks nestled in fruit-picking baskets. Fish traps enclosed canary cages. Stacks of bamboo hats, woven in two different plaits, towered above *thin-byu* sleeping mats. Strapping-tape carry-alls hung with cane shoppers. There were rolled walls, partitions, even woven doors and floors. We had never seen a shop like it, stuffed from hard earth to stitched ceiling with baskets made from bamboo, plaited in palm and plastic, multi-coloured or monotone, produced in Monywa and Amarapura. Every imaginable shape and variety seemed to be available to us, except a basket that resembled Scott's.

The stallkeeper and Michael pored over our photograph. The stallkeeper's wife left a customer to voice her opinion. The daughter of the jaggery stand owner opposite came over to help us out. Together they decided that Scott's basket was not from Rangoon, Pagan or Mandalay. It was not even, Michael translated for us, pure Burmese.

'It is Palaung,' he informed us.

The Palaung are one of the country's smallest ethnic minorities. They live about two hundred miles to the north-east in the Shan Hills, a fertile region renowned for its tea plantations, teak forests and poppy fields. They are a gentle people, once unfavoured by the British because they made poor soldiers. Their women wear remarkable turquoise and midnight-blue coats, velvet caps adorned with silver and heavy scarlet hoods.

'For sure, it is Palaung-style. You can tell here,' Michael said, pointing at the fine, narrow shaped stakes and slim, contoured waist. The stallkeeper, his wife, their customer and the daughter of the jaggery stand owner nodded in unison. 'You must take a train to get there, to Lashio and Hsipaw.'

'Lashio,' repeated the stallkeeper.

'Hsipaw,' insisted his wife.

'Oh oh,' said Katrin.

'Lashio or Hsipaw?' I asked, wearied by the prospect of more travel to uncertain destinations. The muddled run-around and heat were beginning to wear us down.

'Both,' answered Michael, then added, 'Or maybe neither. On reflection I am not certain that you are permitted to travel there. It was until very recently an area of much insurgent fighting.' For almost fifty years the Rangoon government had been at war with the country's minorities, trying to subjugate small national and ethnic factions fighting for independence, driving the peaceable Palaung to violence. In recent months truces had been signed to end the hostilities. 'I will make some enquiries,' promised Michael, flourishing his kyat-thickened wallet. 'Now will you allow me the pleasure of buying you a selection of baskets before we go on to see my mall?'

Mandalay is a city whose reputation outshines its reality. It disappoints in the same manner as Shanghai, Casablanca and Timbuktu. The resonance of an exotic name is let down by the mediocrity of the streets. Khartoum and John O'Groats are far more interesting places to think about than to visit. What, one wonders on arrival in Blarney, was all the fuss about? A century ago Scott wrote: 'Mandalay is a vastly less interesting place than it used to be. A siding from the railway cuts its way through the city wall ... a carriage drive goes around Mandalay Hill; the pigs have all been eaten up and the pariah dogs are poisoned periodically by municipal order. A, B and C roads testify to the unromantic stolidity of the Military Intelligence Department; electric trams make it easier for the Burman to move to the suburbs and leave the town to the hustling foreigner. There are no agreeable scallywags. There are Cook's tourists instead.' The modern snap-happy tour buses, the frenzied construction projects, even the gun-carrying drug barons in the city's discos would not have surprised Scott.

We decided to get out of Mandalay. There was nothing to hold us there. We even managed, with little grace, to talk ourselves out of the visit to Michael's mall. The Pagan bus ride had exhausted us and I asked his driver to return us to our hotel. Michael for his part looked into our onward travel into the Shan Hills. I felt no compunction in taking advantage of his help. He found that we were allowed to visit Lashio, but by train only. In a perverse twist of Burmese officialdom, bus travel along the same route required a permit from the military authorities. Michael kindly booked us two Upper Class seats on the next morning's train. We would have caught it, if not for an unexpected visitor.

Our hotel room, which had once been painted green, was lit by a single neon tube. Two bedside lights dangled on their wires from the wall, which had lost much of its plaster. The grimy window was barred and its curtains were stained with suspect black marks. The towel rail was a rusty length of pipe and the sink took two minutes to drain. 'In this Hotel most of the rooms are comfortable and up to the standard of the Western type,' claimed the promotional brochure. 'Hot showers are also available.'

Katrin sat with her head between her knees in the dark, then lay on the sagging bed and moaned. I tried to cool her with a bamboo fan until the onset of the first bout of diarrhoea. I rubbed Tiger Balm into her temples after she vomited with candid, colourful violence. Our Myingyan lunch was the likely culprit, but the illness could simply have been brought on by the conspiracy of heat, travel and poor hygiene. About midnight my gut too began to churn. Over the next two days our usual sparing use of medicines went out the grimy window. Instead of food we nourished each other on drugs alone: Nurofen to soothe aching heads, Diorolyte to replace lost salts, Dextrosol to try to restore energy. We swallowed Valium, bought over the counter in Bangkok, to induce sleep. To ward off malaria we tried to keep down our Paludrine and Nivaquine. Our bodies were doused in medicated talcum powder and 'Neat Deet' (100 per cent Diethlytolumide) mosquito-guard. Our posteriors – rubbed raw by the bouncing bus journey – were soothed by pots of camomile lotion. By the third day my state of mind became delirious. I convinced myself that I'd contracted hepatitis. As I swung from diarrhoea to constipation and back again, I began a course of Ceporex to dislodge my florid amoebic travelling companion. Katrin battled on without antibiotics and, on the fourth morning, woke with the taste for something other than pharmaceuticals and flat 7-Up.

When the stomach cramps abated, I volunteered to venture out to find food. The hotel had advised us that it could 'provide us with our petty requirements on the ground floor', but when I stumbled downstairs there was no one at reception. I stepped out into the scorching sunlight to hail a taxi but only succeeded in attracting the attention of a passing cycle trishaw. I didn't feel that I had the strength to travel in an open vehicle.

'Where you go?' asked the driver, spouting the usual patter. 'Mandalay Hill? Golden Palace Monastery? I know good restaurant. You want girl?'

'Food,' I groaned, still scanning the street for a cab. 'My wife is sick.'

'Sick?' said the driver, with sudden, sincere concern. 'Is she with child?'

'No,' I replied. 'No, I don't think so.'

'If she is with child then sesame seed is very good. She will have strong, big baby. My wife like sesame. We make six healthy babies together.'

'Okay,' I said, looking into the fine-featured Indian face. 'I need soup too. A clear broth.'

'No problem, sir,' the driver smiled, his black eyes sparkling with a child's optimism. 'Sesame and soup. I help you.'

I collapsed onto the seat and tried to shield myself from the sun's glare. The Indian strained to push the trishaw into the traffic. I had lost weight – more than a stone – but the oven heat still made me a heavy load. We cut in front of a clutch of other cyclists and my head began to ache. 'Six children,' I managed to repeat.

'Yes sir, four good girls and two better boys. I am proud father.'

'Children here seem to be so well behaved. My wife and I haven't heard a single child misbehaving since we arrived.'

'I think it is because in Burma many generations of a family live together.'

'I suppose because of Buddhism too,' I heard myself add. 'I mean, teaching children to obey their elders.'

'Buddhism?' laughed the Indian. 'It is a luxury, sir. If you are wealthy enough you give money to a pagoda, then it is very comfortable. I say this as a Muslim, of course. But every ordinary man must live hand-in-mouth.'

'Hand-to-mouth?' I suggested.

'Yes, sir. Day-to-day we survive with bribery and black market. It used to be that a bribe was called tea money. Now we pay so much it is called beer money. I am very blessed with my family but, *insh'allah*, I wish for no more children.'

'Because of the expense?' I asked.

'In times before there were three kinds of people in Burma: poor, middle and rich class. Today there is only poor and rich class.' He turned onto 26th Street and swung his trishaw away from the other traffic out into the middle of the road. 'Chinese and Singapore men come to Mandalay, build new enterprise, we must move to "new pastures".' His black eyes flashed with anger as he gestured at the New Great Wall Hotel. 'This is a brutal repressive regime,' he hissed, his passion and an oncoming bus alike startling me. 'You must understand this.'

'I do.' I felt weak, the blood pounded in my ears, yet once again I appreciated the private courage of individual Burmese.

'The Lady understands,' he whispered.

I almost said Aung San Suu Kyi's name out loud, but the Indian put his finger to his lips. 'Aren't we a little far away from the kerb?' I asked instead.

'Walls have ears, trees have eyes,' he warned as we wheeled past the New Land Souvenir & Money Changer Shop. 'In next days we have water festival, sir.' *Thingyan* marked the start of the Burmese new year. At the height of the dry season in every city and village buckets of water are thrown at passers-by in celebration. 'The people become excited, and then you must be careful. The police turn blind eyes to many things and it becomes an outlet for people's grievances. The government encourages this bad behaviour.' He pedalled in silence across an inter-section. 'Our leaders are very arrogant; they wish us ill. They are like another people, like men from Mars.' His mouth tightened into a red razor-cut of rage. 'To change this we will have to sacrifice ourselves for the country,' he hissed, 'or the country will be damned.'

We shuddered to a stop at the Nylon Ice Cream Bar and the shadows lifted from his face. His black eyes sparkled. The need to talk was contained. 'Here very clean food,' he announced, like any other benign tour guide.

It seemed to be the least likely place in Mandalay to buy a bowl of soup. 'Do they sell broth here?'

'Oh no, sir. You eat pineapple ice cream here and I find sesame seeds.'

'And soup.'

'Yes sir. And soup.'

The Indian slipped across the road to the Min Min Restaurant. I waited, drank a cup of stewed, sweet, umber-coloured tea and turned down three offers of ice cream. The girls at the next table giggled and pretended to look away. A stranger, who introduced himself as a retired ophthalmologist, stopped at my table to ask if he could be of assistance. Even in my delicate state I was struck, once again, by the stark contrast between the rulers and the ruled.

Ten minutes later the Indian returned with sesame bars and clear chicken broth, carried in small plastic bags. I held them on my lap like bloated bladders on the ride back to the hotel. Along the way he said, 'A word of advice, sir. Do not eat Burmese food in the evening, eat Chinese or Indian. Burmese food is cooked for lunchtime only.' I would have told him that it was a light lunch which had poisoned us, but the rocking trishaw and the bubbling balloons of broth conspired to turn my stomach. The Indian looked away while I was sick in the gutter.

At the front door of the hotel he wished us health, happiness and at least six children. 'A big family is good,' he reminded me. 'With all the generations living together.'

I thanked him for his kindness, and promised to pass his suggestion on to Katrin. 'I'm grateful for the advice on sesame too.'

'Sesame will help, but you must take it upon yourself, sir,' he insisted. I went upstairs and lay down on the bed. Katrin ate the soup and sesame with pleasure. By the next day we were both well enough to rebook the tickets to Lashio.

Our train, the 131 Up, was scheduled to depart at 0445. Its unlit wooden carriages sat waiting on the grassy rails. Its silent passengers were crammed six to a bench in Ordinary Class. Candle wax covered the carriage dividers, evidence of the long night spent on the siding. Around the station other travellers slept under tarpaulin or in box-like mosquito nets erected on the platform. There were no timetables posted, no announcements made. There was no sign of a locomotive.

As we picked our way by torchlight towards the Upper Class carriage, the strange anthropomorphic shapes began to stir. Whole families unwound themselves from their sheets and possessions. Women folded away the insect nets. Bedding was bundled into baskets. Water sellers decanted brimming beakers, for the travellers to wash themselves over the tracks. Mothers rucked their babies up onto their backs in *longyi* slings knotted across a shoulder. Old women squatted and chatted, smoking morning cheroots rolled in maize leaves. The bare, dozing heads of five ragged urchins lolled off the edge of their mat on the buckled concrete. Their weary father had overslept. He pummelled the children awake. A pregnant mongrel with swinging, swollen teats idled past them. There was still no sign of a locomotive.

The deep, upholstered armchair seats and private booths made the Upper Class carriage look like a cross between a threadbare gentlemen's club and a filthy American diner on wheels. Its petite Burmese passengers dozed within the arms of the moth-eaten thrones. Clouds of mosquitoes swarmed out of the fermenting drains as we sat down to wait. Our travels – like Burma's transportation system – had begun to seem haphazard. The search for Scott's basket was unfolding by chance, not design. My frustration made me anxious to shape our journey, to give it form. The waiting increased my irritation and I began pacing up and down the carriage, as if my activity might speed our departure. The Lashio Express was a public conveyance without any sense of urgency or obligation of service. Its passengers remained patient and uncomplaining. Their low expectations made me angry. I marched along the platform looking for the conductor, taking matters into my own hands. But I could find no one in authority. There were no officials willing to offer an explanation for the disordered delay. I sat back down in the armchair and tried by force of will to move our shapeless, ragged trip forward. We remained unmoving and uninformed for two more hours.

Then a cleanly-groomed Lieutenant boarded our carriage. His features were well proportioned and his perfect teeth sparkling white. A whistle sounded as soon as he took the seat opposite us. The locomotive had arrived.

At once everyone awoke. A cry went down the train. The carriage's heavy glass windows were slammed shut as we started to move. Water suddenly slapped against the shutters, splashed into doors, poured through the vents in the ceiling. Passengers who didn't close their windows in time were drenched by the buckets and hoses. Some shutters were jammed open. Those travellers laughed in helplessness as the trackside deluge soaked them to the skin. The water streamed down the aisles and sloshed under our seats. It was the start of the water festival and only the Lieutenant didn't smile.

'Like sailing ship,' joked the conductor as we rocked north-east from Mandalay, the carriage lunging forward then jerking back on the ill-aligned rails, water dripping off the ceiling.

'Why are we so late leaving?' I asked, hoping that my example might encourage others to complain, wishing that their private courage might become public. I should have saved my breath. Our fellow travellers looked away. The Burmese have a saying: 'You can't make oil from one grain of sesame seed.'

The conductor shrugged. He said nothing. The Lieutenant was watching him. He inspected our tickets and took note of our visa numbers. Then he retreated as the train approached its first stop, his sandals squeaking on the saturated floor. Again the cry went up, the shutters came down and the *thingyan* water-throwers splashed the carriages. Our soaking would be repeated in every town and village throughout the journey.

It had only been in the last few weeks that tourists had been allowed to travel to Lashio again. There had been a real danger of attack from insurgent groups before the recent ceasefire agreements. A grinning woman offered us damp crispies while gazing at Katrin's pale skin. Two brothers asked to look at our passports and held them in their hands in wonder.

'You have seen Alaska?' asked the older man. He shook his head in awe. 'I have always wished to see snow.'

But the Lieutenant paid us no heed, dividing his attention between a comic book and the bored boy soldier who wandered into the carriage to report to him. The young man carried his rifle like a cricket bat. He never met our eyes.

An hour into the journey the train began to climb a switchback zig-zag of track, snaking back and forth up into the Shan Hills. Marco Polo described these uplands as 'vast jungles teeming with elephants, unicorns and other beasts'. We saw no animals, but did catch sight of the Burma Road and the heavy trucks nearing the end of their journey from western Yunnan in China. The isolated Shan

State occupies a quarter of Burma's geographic area, and for thirty years its high forests provided a safe haven for the world's greatest variety of ethnic militias. But since 1988 a thousand villages have been relocated or destroyed by the *Tatmadaw*, and over half a million people are estimated to have been forced to leave their homes. The Shans call themselves *Tai*, meaning 'free', and their passion for independence has kept them disunited from their Thai relations, and allowed them to be subjugated by Rangoon.

Above Maymyo, the hill station built by the British as a cool retreat from the heat of the central plains, thick jungle foliage pressed in along the narrow rail corridor. The boughs of trees whipped into the open windows. The carriage swung hard to the left and a branch slapped me in the face.

Every few miles the jungle opened out onto lush clearings of clean houses and orderly fields. Fat water-buffaloes wallowed in mud pools and villagers planted neat rows of rice. Farmers tended to smallholdings with handmade watering cans fashioned from old oil canisters. We caught sight of wheat fields and orange groves across the uplands. The train stopped often, waiting at stations for a longer time than it took to run between them. Townspeople strolled up and down the carriages looking for passing friends. Hawkers balanced on their heads trays of tiny strawberries, thin roast chicken legs and squat bunches of bananas. The Lieutenant stepped away to speak to another soldier and the brothers leaned forward to whisper to us, 'And have you met the Lady?' They fell silent when he returned, armed with a pink plastic water-pistol. He proceeded along the length of the carriage, spraying each passenger with squirts of water. His was a private, sinister New Year's celebration. When he reached us he hesitated for a moment, then sprayed us too. After an eternity the locomotive's whistle sounded, the train shuddered forward and the wild vegetation closed in again around the line, cutting us off from the white-hot light.

The future for Burma ended on 19 July 1947. The Burmese had been calling for independence from British rule since the start of the century, and a young law student named Aung San rose to become the leader of the movement. He and twenty-nine fellow nationalists, known as the Thirty Comrades, underwent military training in Japan and accompanied the Japanese invasion of Burma in 1941. They saw British misfortune as their opportunity, until the Japanese broke their promise of Burmese autonomy. Aung San switched allegiance to support the Allies in expelling the invaders. A devastating conflict followed. Sixty per cent of all Japanese soldiers who died in the Second World War died in Burma. The country's infrastructure was ruined, and would remain unmodernised – as was proved by our rickety railway – for more than half a century. But Aung San and his comrades survived the war, and he alone was considered capable of leading the nation. Then, on 19 July 1947, not long after he had negotiated independence from Britain, he was assassinated.

The Burmese can be classified into four major linguistic groups – the Burmans, the Shan, the Karen and the Mon-Khmer. This kaleidoscope of peoples have clashed over the centuries, usually at times of Burman expansion. During the colonial era the British ruled in part by exploiting ethnic differences. Aung San, a member of the country's majority, was able to transcend the minorities' historical mistrust of Burman politicians. That trust – and the ethnic leaders' faith in a just union – died with him.

In 1948 the new Union of Burma attained independence without the leadership or vision to sustain it. Civil war erupted within months. Mandalay fell to Karen rebels and communist insurgents laid siege to Rangoon. As many as thirty-five guerrilla armies declared war on the new administration. Railway tracks and riverboats were attacked daily, bridges were demolished, the economy floundered. Government forces fought to drive the rebels back into the hills, and despite the violence, a tenuous democracy survived in those parts of the country under central control. Regular elections were held. A free press flourished. Until 1962, when General Ne Win, the chief of the army, seized control.

Ne Win's Revolutionary Council suspended the constitution. All basic human rights were usurped. The *Tatmadaw* was instructed to eliminate insurgent groups. Striking students were shot. The army took control of the civil administration and doubled its size. The Council's xenophobic, inept ideology, 'the Burmese Way to Socialism', ruined the country, cutting it off from the outside world until the dictator came to realise that trade and tourism could further enrich him. It was Ne Win's sham resignation which had given the people hope in 1988, and his calculated orders which had led to their massacre.

After thirty-five years of military misrule, Ne Win's only achievement had been to end the civil war with the rebel armies. 'The *Tatmadaw* crushes the enemies of the Union,' declared the *New Light of Myanmar*, 'and promotes unity and friendship among national brethren.' The government-controlled press claimed that the insurgent groups had entered 'the legal fold'. Yet the ceasefires had not come about because of conclusive peace talks or a crushing military defeat, rather because of the wish of the former adversaries to cooperate in more profitable ventures. Between 1989 and 1995 the SLORC increased its military stranglehold over the country through $1.4 billion worth of arms deals with China. As well as through soft loans, the contracts were believed to have been financed by the profits of opium and heroin trafficking.

By nightfall we were still not halfway to Lashio. The train drowsed for an hour or two in a beggarly village without electricity. The carriage lights failed and candles were lit. The conductor wandered off into the night. Katrin slept and woke and fell asleep again.

In time the Express shuffled on. Across the valleys slash-and-burn scrub fires ran crimson lines up the steep hills, casting the railside banana groves into dancing, blood-red silhouettes. The brothers asked again to see our passports. At the next town the mosquitoes returned. It was near midnight when we arrived in Lashio. It had taken us eighteen hours to travel the 150 miles from Mandalay. I collected our bag from the overhead rack. The Lieutenant stood up and pointed at me. 'You have the look of a journalist,' he said in impeccable English. He left the carriage before I could find the words to express my anger.

As the other travellers fought for seats on the town bus we hired a whole pick-up. For one dollar it raced us through the unlit streets to the modern Lashio Motel. Twenty more dollars bought us a cool room, hot water and a firm double bed. There was a spittoon in the corner and *Baywatch* on Star TV. I felt drained. Katrin cried in the shower, washing the stench of the journey out of her hair. Ni Ni was dead, Ma Swe homeless, the trishaw Indian ate a bowl of plain rice for supper and the brothers on the train would never see snow. It was unjust and selfish, but I wanted the comfort and ease that money could afford. I did not want us too to suffer from the despotic evil. On the state-controlled BBS news a graduate class of officer cadets dressed in crisp white uniforms paraded around a mock-up of a golden pagoda. Then a Burmese fashion model skipped across a dirty beach to advertise Feeling Beverly Hills deodorant spray. We ate imported Laughing Cow processed cheese for supper and fell asleep expecting the Lieutenant's knock on the door.

If Mandalay had felt like a border town, then Lashio seemed to be deep in the next country. It wasn't a Burmese city, or for that matter Shan. It had the atmosphere of a highland trading bazaar in western Yunnan, even though the Chinese frontier lay over a hundred miles away to the north. We awoke not to the chants of Pali formulas but to the sound of canned 'Canto-pop'. The roar of heavy Hino transports, down-gearing on their long drive south from China, rather than the chime of bicycle bells disturbed our breakfast. The restaurant's laser karaoke bar was a popular destination for businessmen from Kunming. On its wide-screen television our Yunnanese waiter watched Pekingese performers act out a Ming Dynasty melodrama, *In Search of the West*. A Black & White whisky box lay discarded on the stage. More than half of Lashio's residents were Han Chinese. Ten years before they had numbered fewer than 10 per cent of the city's population. Lashio had always been one of the great trading posts on the Burma Road. The newcomers had flooded in to take advantage of its strategic position – and the political opportunity.

We set out to find our basket and, instead of the morning market, stumbled onto a building site. Clouds of cement dust billowed over the town. Builders swarmed up scaffolding and along walls, carrying bricks and pallets of plaster. All around us was the racket of hammering and sifting soil, chipping rocks and crying birds. The old Shan town hall had been demolished. The Anglican church seemed to have vanished. The marketplace was being replaced by a concrete emporium.

We skirted the piles of gravel, watching browbeaten Burmans scurry through the site with heads bowed. None of them paused to splash us with water. The confident Chinese residents stocked the shelves of their stores and did deals in noodle shops. They alone seemed to appreciate the town's rush to modernity. For our part, we became aware of a paradox. I had returned to Burma in the hope of discovering why my first visit had moved me. I had not expected to find the country living in the past, as Ne Win's naïve isolationist policies had been discarded, yet I had hoped that certain traditions and standards would still remain at the heart of the society. It shocked us to discover that, starting in Lashio, Burma was selling its future to finance the present. In the process, it was becoming a Chinese colony.

In the Chinese mini-markets we found Crest toothpaste, Californian prunes and Cadbury's Fruit & Nut bars. There were bottles of Veuve Clicquot and Unipart oil filters. No one with dollars went without in Lashio, except for us. We could find no bamboo baskets for sale, only garish plastic carrier bags.

Our search had begun to obsess me. It had become heightened by frustration, as well as infected with the indigenous, jumbled madness. Katrin tried to soothe my disappointment, suggesting that we take in the Quan Yin San Temple, the largest Chinese shrine in Burma. We climbed up through the heat and noise of the town to its dragon-peaked entrance arch. Women in trousers lit joss-sticks and kowtowed to snarling, wrathful Buddhas. Girls wearing frilly Western dresses chased each other around the heavy, sweep-roofed building. The shrine's brash, busy activity seemed to have little in common with the contemplative peace of Burmese Theravada Buddhist temples.

In the temple forecourt the faithful crowded around a pair of ceremonial furnaces. They jostled each other aside to throw into the flames miniature houses, furniture and televisions fashioned from folded paper. A serious young man dropped a perfect, tiny, cardboard Mercedes Benz into the fire and watched its smoke rise into the sky. It was believed that ancestors rewarded their living relatives' offerings with real houses, televisions and cars.

'We should make a paper basket,' suggested Katrin, ripping three pages out of my notebook. She tore them into strips and wove a simple base. Then she bent the elements into an upright position and, working from left to right, twisted them around to fashion a crude border. 'Now we can have our own *kong tek* ceremony,' she said, and threw her handiwork into the furnace.

I decided to make more practical use of the flames. I write notes when travelling which, at the end of every day, are transcribed into my journal. In most countries the original jottings are then dropped into a wastepaper bin. But where does one dispose of honesty in a dictatorship? Certainly not in a public place or in a hotel room. The notes could easily have been retrieved and read. Toilets had seemed the obvious answer, but the Burmese are discouraged from discarding any paper in such a manner. The country's drains were in such a state of disrepair that I had imagined my scribblings bringing Rangoon – and me – to an unpleasant, incriminating standstill. So since the beginning of our trip the scraps of paper had been stuffed into my pockets. In Pagan I had tried tearing each leaf into minute scraps and dropping them off the back of the horse-cart, only to find myself leaving a Hansel and Gretel trail in the dust. Next I attempted throwing them out of bus and train windows, but no matter how isolated the chosen spot, children appeared out of nowhere to gather them. In the Quan Yin San Temple I recognised a rare opportunity. In one movement I emptied the old notes out of my pockets and dumped them into the furnace. A great whoosh of flames caught them and carried their smoky thoughts towards the heavens.

We left the temple and drifted back down into the town. I was at a loss whether to wander around the dusty market again, to book a seat on the next train or to return to the hotel for an evening of *thingyan* karaoke. Every option seemed pointless. Then, ahead of us in the crowd, we saw two elderly Chinese women walking in step, wearing identical apricot tunics, arguing. They were twin sisters, and each carried a basket in her right hand. One was made of plastic and moulded into the shape of Mickey Mouse's head. It declared 'I love Disneyland.' The other was a perfect, delicate bamboo shopper.

SIX

Within, Without

HER ROOM WAS BARE. Its bald white walls retained no history. It was a place without a past, where games began but life could not be contained. The windowless recess held only a stool and an atlas. In the dim evening light May sat on the stool. Kwan stood before her, the atlas held flat between her hands. 'I hope that you enjoyed your luncheon, madam?' she asked, anxious to please.

May mimicked the sipping of tea before setting her imaginary cup back on the atlas. The Tristar's engines droned in her ears. 'The duck was tender, stewardess, but it could have had more *hoi sin*.'

'One hundred pardons,' apologised Kwan, bowing as deeply as her rheumatism allowed. 'I will advise the head chef in time for your return journey.'

May looked out of her daydream window and pictured the sunlight touching the clouds high over the Pacific. She imagined feeling its warmth on her face. The shimmering jetstream of another aircraft caught her eye. She inspected again her tattered boarding pass, turning it over and over in her hand. It must be pleasant to fly first class. Downstairs the tailor Ch'ien was drilling his nephew in his multiplication tables. On the dark street below a pack of dogs howled at the moon. 'I do not think that I'll be returning to Asia,' she said, disturbed by the interruption.

'But you always return, madam,' Kwan replied, puzzled. 'Every Sunday evening. It is our custom.'

'My son may insist on me remaining in America. He has always wanted me to live with him there. He has a degree in mathematics from the University of California, you know.' May's empty smile quivered, then she lost hold of the sense of warmth on her face. She shivered as dusk's mist rolled down from the hills. Lashio's mountain damp had always irritated the sisters' joints. She thought of the wide world that might have been hers, and for the first time in her long life felt old. 'Stewardess, the cabin has turned chilly,' she fussed, gathering up the strands of fancy. 'Pass me my coat.'

Kwan lay the atlas down on the floor and reached up as if to an overhead locker. She unfolded a make-believe coat and lay it on her sister's lap. The twins' hands touched. Kwan's fingers felt rough and callused, while May's had retained the smooth, soft skin of a young girl.

'You stink of cloves again,' said May in irritation, jerking her hand away. 'What is the in-flight movie today?' she demanded.

'*Dream of the Red Chamber*,' said Kwan, while arranging a fanciful footrest for May.

'I'd prefer to see a Hollywood film, like the ones shown at the video parlour.'

As neither sister had ever been on board an aircraft, their knowledge of air travel was at best uncertain. Their single visit to the Mansu video shop had done little to enhance the accuracy of their make-believe.

'*Rambo* would suit me very well. Ch'ien's nephew tells me that it is popular with young people. Please arrange it.'

'Yes, madam,' Kwan said, and tried to recall how to load a videocassette player.

'I can't see the screen, stewardess. Move aside. You are blocking my view.'

Kwan hesitated while miming the action of tuning a television. Her voice slipped out of character, becoming softer and doubtful. 'You always go home, sister,' she repeated. 'You must come home. You live here.'

'My parents and husband are dead. My son is in California. I have no family in China, and only a forgetful old sister in Burma.'

'I am no older than you.'

'But you do forget.' May stood up, straining her back with the sudden movement, and cursed her age. The stool toppled over.

'Be careful not to step on the luncheon tray,' cautioned Kwan, pointing at the atlas.

'I'm finished with this game,' May complained, sweeping their play-acting away with a sharp gesture. Her room did not order the world within, rather it tried to exclude the chaotic disorder without. 'It's late and time for bed.'

'Look, madam,' said Kwan, resuming her role in the hope of pacifying her sister. 'You can see the coast through your window now. We will soon be arriving in California. You will see your son. Would you please be so kind as to fasten your safety belt and extinguish all cigarettes?'

'I cannot see my son,' May bristled, displeased and impatient. 'I cannot go there because I must care for you, in the memory of parents you don't even remember.'

'I wish that you would show me a little human-heartedness,' sighed Kwan, her eyes downcast, her spirit subdued.

'I am tired of you, old woman. I have had enough of this place.'

The twins were as old as the century, or at least that is what their parents had said of Kwan. May, they used to say, was as young as the century. The girls had been born in the year 1900, in the age before the aeroplane's invention, while the dowager Empress Tz'u Hsi still occupied Beijing's peacock throne and Mao Tse-tung wore a topknot. Their father had been a herbalist, a dispenser of cures and spices in Lashio's clay-tiled Chinese quarter. In a paper-lined sleeping chamber his first daughter had emerged from the womb with reluctance, carrying with her the burden of past lives. Her eyes had been closed as if in reflection. It had taken two firm slaps to start her breathing. Her father had named her Kwan, which means 'together', because she had not entered the world alone.

The second twin, on the other hand, had begun her life as she would continue it, wailing and kicking. The child had fixed her eyes on the open window and uttered a deafening, demanding cry. 'This one will travel far,' the midwife had predicted. Her father had called her May, which translates as 'beautiful', not only because she was the prettier of the two. When spoken aloud the name also suggested 'the very last one', or 'enough': a suitable pun for the father of twins. Within the first hour of their birth May had pushed her elder sister away from the more generous nipple. For the rest of their lives she would claim the better part of all things from Kwan.

Their father and mother had been trying for over a decade to have children. He was a methodical man and had tended to their infertility with dandelion tonic and lenitives of eucalyptus. Litres of ginseng infusion had been supped in tender anticipation each evening, only to be thrown out in the morning with the night water. They had applied pepper balms and poultices of almond. In one spendthrift moment he had even prepared himself a draught of ground tiger whiskers. But the remedies, like the prayers to their ancestors, had seemed to be wasted. It was only when they had stopped worrying about conception that his wife found she was with child. He had wanted a single son, but did not admonish her for bearing him two daughters instead. In truth he suspected that his over-generous dose of gingko leaf had been to blame.

It was the necessity of the time to put children to work almost as soon as they could walk. In the storeroom there was cardamom to weigh and acacia leaves to package. Small hands were suited to removing the tiny stones from the big, aromatic sacks of cloves. Kwan enjoyed being beside her father, and began her work with him at the age of four. As they sized and sorted chillies, she listened to him tell how he had come to Lashio. She never tired of hearing the tale of his escape over the Nan Ling Mountains and across the Yunnan Plateau. He had wished to travel without baggage, but Kwan's mother had insisted on bringing the family portraits. To him the old photographs were an unnecessary burden. He did not want his wife to strain herself and had advised leaving them behind. The young couple had argued for the first and only time, and it shamed him to admit that he had raised his voice at her. But in the end it had made no difference. She had refused to leave China without the portraits.

'And now I'm glad of it, my daughter,' he confessed to Kwan, pausing to look up at the four pictures, 'because they have brought good fortune. Their presence gives me the strength to work harder, and has blessed me with you and May. It was wrong of me to want to abandon them.'

Kwan felt their forebears' sepia gaze upon her back as she sorted and cleaned. She kept her young head bowed, only looking up from her labours when dusk had gathered around the storeroom's front door.

For her part May managed to ensure that an unjust proportion of her work fell to her sister. She avoided preparing ginger remedies, because the syrup was bad for her skin, and never bundled *fu ling* mushrooms, as the spores always seemed to irritate her eyes. It wasn't that May was lazy, but that she simply wished to be somewhere else. Every Friday morning she hurried ahead of her father down to the marketplace. While he met the herb traders from Hsipaw and Siakwan, she stared away beyond the lime groves, reaching out along the trade road towards another place. Her steps were always heavy on the return journey home. She had a restless spirit that would not be contained.

The twins had been born, as the Confucians say, into interesting times. Their century had begun in an age of waning Chinese influence. The Middle Kingdom had yielded to foreign territorial demands and lost Ili to Russia, the Ryukyu Islands to Japan and control of Korea. France had made Annam its protectorate and the Manchu Dynasty was enfeebled by rebellion. For the ordinary Hunanese peasant, life was hard and cruel. Men toiled or starved, women were sold like slaves into wedlock. The twins' father had brought his wife out of China to escape servitude and injustice. He had settled within Lashio's city gate, willing to integrate himself into Burmese society. But the community had excluded him, though not to the extent of exempting him from the arbitrary tax imposed on immigrants by the Assistant Township Officer. If he failed to pay tribute in this way his trading licence and residence permit might be rescinded. It was bad luck to be both Chinese and poor. The young family was forced to live apart from their neighbours. They had nothing to do with the British colonists. Yet, in spite of having left their mother country, events over the border continued to shape their lives more than decisions made in Rangoon.

Before Kwan and May reached their twelfth year, China – and two thousand years of Ch'ing monarchy – were overthrown by Sun Yat-sen's revolution. The turbulent decades that followed were marked by famine, invasion and war. Fear and uncertainty dominated people's lives. The twins' aunt in Anhwei province was killed in rioting. An uncle died when the Kuomintang seized Beijing. Survival came to depend to an even greater extent on self-reliance. Their father impressed upon Kwan that money alone ensured security. To earn it she devoted herself to helping him. The same events led May to realise that, with the advent of modern modes of transportation, people were more able to travel to places which offered greater opportunities for success.

In the year that Mao lead the disastrous 'Autumn Harvest Uprising' the twins' mother passed away. She lay down one evening complaining of a headache. Their father lit a burner by her bedside and ministered a smudge of moxa leaves. The remedy induced a sleep from which she never awoke. As the Communists and the Nationalist Kuomintang swept in on each other in civil war, their father too turned in on himself. In all his life he had never missed a day of work. His regulated schedule had given him a sense of control. But with the death of his wife, he no longer reserved the week's first day for the sorting of medicinal herbs, the second and third days for pounding cardamom and preparing volatile oils. His discipline faltered and the tight structure of his hours began to unravel. Age came on him as a deep tiredness, with a sudden confusion over dates. The absurdities of his failing memory both irritated and amused him.

'Never in my life have I seen so much *ku sheng*,' he raged, considering three costly packets of bitter root. 'Who told you to buy it, first daughter?' He himself was responsible, so he added in a softer tone, 'Please take pity on your old father.'

He began to repeat himself, to mix poppy seeds with sweet *gan cao* liquorice, to prescribe hot chilli compresses instead of soothing camphor rubs to arthritic widows. He cursed his forgetfulness, growing fearful of his waning faculties. All day long he shuffled the order papers around and around his desk like *mah-jong* tiles or playing cards, lost in a losing game of Patience.

'My daughter,' he told Kwan during the sleepless nights, 'you must remember to order the swallows under the eaves. Do not pay more than two rupees.' Then he cried, 'Are all the baskets becoming unwound?'

As his concentration deserted him, his conversation slipped into an irrational babble. At first Kwan assumed that he was talking sense – he had been lucid and informed before their mother's death. She tried to make logical connections. But none existed outside his mind. 'When did you come back?' he would ask her, even though she had not been away. 'I never asked for coriander.'

'Please let him die so his pain may end,' Kwan wished to herself.

'Please let him die so my imprisonment can end,' begged May aloud. The second daughter felt trapped by her father's illness. She imagined the days of her youth slipping through her fingers like the bushels of sesame and soya, measured but unsavoured. His age seemed to deny her her youth.

Kwan held their father's hand and felt it as cold as stone. Using his herbal textbook, she diagnosed a deficiency of *qi* and blood. His movements became slow and he began to have difficulty with his speech. There was a puffiness under his eyes. Camomile infusions did not relieve his headaches. The neighbourhood doctor could not cure the scarlet rash which appeared on his neck and face. One week later he was dead.

May married in the spring of the year that Chiang Kai-shek's Nationalists encircled the Red Army in Kiangsi province. As Mao broke through the siege and began the *ch'ang cheng*, or long march, she tried to extend her own horizons by taking Liu Wei, son of the railway booking agent, as her husband. Wei was a bachelor with good prospects, and with a seductive knowledge. He knew by heart the times of the Mandalay trains, the schedule of Irrawaddy ferries, even the date of the next sailing of the *Canadian Pacific Empress* from Hong Kong to Vancouver. The arrival time of the London mail plane and the ports of call of Japanese freighters slipped off his tongue. During their engagement May was allowed to sit with him in the booking office, which acted as a sort of travel agency for the town. It was there, while Wei consigned bales of cotton and sacks of rice to the morning train, that she first began to conjure up her fanciful journeys. She pored over his timetables and freight-rate guides, travelling in her mind from Mu-sé to Kunming, then on to Kowloon, Saigon and Colombo. Wei saw no harm in his fiancée's imaginary travels, and it flattered him to be able to impress her with his grasp of the routes of Indian Ocean steamers and European railways. But he had no desire to travel to the exotic destinations himself. His interest in transportation was that it made good business. He was due to inherit his father's position, and the web of land and sea routes that wrapped itself around the world comforted him with an illusion of certainties.

The morning after the wedding Wei made an offering to his ancestors' shrine and wished for a son. May lay in their bed unclothed, planning a trip to Shanghai, dreaming of taking a honeymoon across the Pacific to America. She drew her fine black hair back from her face, exposing her slender neck, and laughed. Her heart was free. She felt herself no longer tethered to Lashio by duty and convention. She hoped that marriage would thrust her out into the unknown, but instead it tied her back to the familiar. Nine months later she gave birth to a baby boy.

The world war came and went, taking away first the British and then the Japanese, razing Mandalay and driving the Shan into their fight for independence. But the conflicts did not touch May. Over the years, whenever a stranger arrived on the station platform, waiting for a bus or train, she would appear beside him, her son on her hip, and without shame quiz him on the details of his home city. In such a manner she came to know the names of the good hotels of Tokyo and the dosshouses of Taipei. She learned to be wary of the crafty rickshaw drivers of Soochow and, without ever leaving the landlocked Shan State, became an authority on ocean-going steamship lines. Neighbours who were considering fleeing sought her advice on the comparative advantages of life in Malaya and Siam. Her knowledge grew to include an understanding of trade routes, exchange rates and tariffs. She entertained her son with elaborate adventure stories of air travel by Empire flying boat and German Zeppelin, even though the only aircraft she had ever seen had passed high over the town as a distant, silver speck. She became an authority on international travel, containing the globe with railroad schedules, though like her sister she never ventured further afield than the town gate.

Kwan did not marry; she mourned. To come to terms with her loss she tried to forget her parents, unpicking their memory and casting them out of her mind. She gave away their clothes and burnt their bedding. The few mementoes of their lives – her father's abridged *Beng Cao Gang Mu* text, her mother's tortoiseshell comb, the handful of family photographs – were consigned to a tightly lidded basket at the back of the godown. Her waking hours were filled with work alone. She coped with the vagaries of business: the disruption of the kaoliang supply due to fighting in Honan, the plague of frogs which devastated the Szechwan tung-oil harvest. Her labour kept her distress at bay, and ensured the continuing prosperity of the family's spice business. But because she feared the pain of remembering, because of her refusal to acknowledge the memorial that death had erected in her heart, she felt only emptiness.

The hard work took its toll. Time and profit margins smothered the spark of youth. The years of industry in the dim storehouse dulled Kwan's clear brown eyes. A walnut virus affected her hearing. Her lustrous skin turned paper dry as if withered by the barrels of sea salt that aired in the yard. She became anxious about her dependency on smell, even though it, alone of all her senses, remained unaffected by age. She feared that if her nose failed her, unscrupulous dealers would sell her bitter tamarind and scentless saffron. She worried that her customers would desert her and that the business would fail, making a farce of her father's devotion, leaving her with nothing. Her fears affected her sleep and, in the toss and turn of her nights, she became aware of dreams.

One morning on the edge of dawn a sweet perfume wafted through her mind. In her dream she rose up to chase after it, running barefoot through her mother's old lavender garden, following the fragrance towards the storehouse. The aroma inside the building was so heady that at first she did not notice she was not alone. Then Kwan saw her parents standing in the dark room, throwing up into the air the precious stocks of vanilla and roselle leaf.

'Within,' her father shouted, digging his hands into a basket of jasmine, 'and without.' He cast the white petals out of the door.

'Within,' said her mother, opening a container of galangal root.

'And without,' cried her father, tossing it away with the turmeric.

Even in her sleep Kwan knew that her parents were dead, or at least for ever apart from her. Denial had been the only way in which she could cope with the loss. Yet in her dream they stood before her, scattering spices and herbs on the hard earth floor, emptying out all that was contained.

'Within and without,' repeated her father as they passed through the door, a balmy trail suspended in the air behind them. Kwan called out their names. She asked them to stay with her. But they could not, or would not, hear. Her father spread the flowers and leaves to the wind. Her mother turned and waved. Her parents vanished down the lane. Kwan awoke to the sound of her own crying.

She was too distraught to go to her desk that morning. Instead she left the storehouse locked and hurried out to find her sister. May was not at home, and Wei directed her to the station. 'Where else would she be at this time?' he sighed over his breakfast *bao-sii* bun.

'What, if not the family,' Kwan asked herself as she rushed along the Namtu Road, 'entwines the ties of the heart? To whom does the child owe her birth?' By the time she reached the station, she had worked herself into an agitated state.

'I've seen them,' Kwan cried out, breathless, across the rails. May stood across the platform waiting for the departure of the Mandalay No. 132 Down train. 'I dreamed of them.' Kwan skirted the last carriage and led May towards a bench. 'Our parents came to me, talked to me.' She wept again as she recounted her dream. 'Do you understand, sister?'

'What are you talking about?' said May, trying to stem the flood of Kwan's tears. The train's departure had distracted her.

'We owe everything to them.'

'Within, without?' repeated May, catching the story between the gasps of breath. 'Those are the words you heard?'

'Yes. They were telling me to remember that they are within us, even when we are without them.'

May shook her head. 'It means that we should leave this place. It's a warning.'

'No, sister.' Kwan had a habit of looking doubtful when she did not understand, but now there was wild certainty in her eyes. 'We are contained by their love.'

'They're telling us that we are *not* contained,' insisted May. 'We have always been outside this place.'

'I was wrong to deny their memory.'

'Sister, you spend too much time alone.'

'We have never honoured our parents,' said Kwan. 'The man and woman who gave us life.'

'Take a husband and have children. It is not too late.'

'I have no need.'

'Our need is to leave Lashio. You must look forward, or for ever be an old maid.'

According to Confucianism, man is in essence a social creature, bound to his fellows by *jen* – that is sympathy, or human-heartedness. *Jen* is expressed through the five relationships: sovereign and subject, parent and child, elder and younger sibling, husband and wife, friend and friend. To many Confucians the filial relationship is the most virtuous bond. Kwan had had suitors, bachelors who had taken an interest in her modest manner and lucrative business. She had understood that marriage would enable her labour to be shared. But her devotion to her parents outweighed her wish for a partner. It was not that she had no feelings for the living, but that those emotions were overpowered by the debt of birth. Her parents remained her deepest love, even in death. They bound her to life, even after their memory was beaten out of her during the Red Badge riots.

It had long been believed in China that, with correct conduct and a sense of virtue, the millennial 'great commonwealth', or union of mankind under ethical rules, would be attained in time. But after twenty centuries of autocracy and thirty years of civil war, the Communists had lost patience with waiting for an ethical Utopia. Their commonwealth, or People's Republic, aimed to unite men by imposing upon them a central vision. In pursuit of a classless society private property was seized. Labour was organised. Agriculture became owned by all for the benefit of all. Work was performed in the service of the state, not for the advancement of the individual. Food and land distribution was made more equitable. The natural obligation to be virtuous that had rested upon all men was supplanted by the demand for adherence to a pragmatic interpretation of the common good. Mao's 'Great Leap Forward' was intended to speed the attainment of this ideal by imbuing the people with revolutionary vigour. In the process it devastated China's small entrepreneurs. Local businesses were replaced by labour-intensive industries. Family control was surrendered to peasant groups. Wealth shifted from the people who had made it to those whose labour had produced it. Tens of millions died of starvation on the road to Utopia.

In Burma too an attempt was made to redress the imbalances and injustices of the past. After the 1962 coup, all shops were nationalised and tenancy rights abolished. People's Councils took control of land use. But they were packed with soldiers who had no experience of paddy production. The result was inefficiency and corruption. By 1967 there were acute shortages of food throughout the country. Farmers had to buy rice on the black market to fulfil the obligatory quotas. To deflect public anger the government incited anti-Chinese riots. Their excuse was the refusal of some Sino-Burmans to remove their Mao badges. It was put about that the Cultural Revolution was causing Burma's destitution. Furthermore, Chinese traders were rumoured to be hoarding rice.

The zealous young men who arrived at Lashio's railway station did not wear uniforms, but no one doubted where their allegiance lay. They took possession of food stalls and seed stores. They ordered the Chinese proprietors out of their shops. Zhang Chow, the manager of the textile firm, was driven from his home. His cousin's rice mill passed into the hands of a workers' cooperative. The soldiers advanced under the clay-tiled roofs from the cotton spinners to the dye house, the employees of each pressing them forward. A crowd gathered behind them, driven by hunger and ready to vent their frustration. The Chinese were scapegoats, Burma's Jews or gypsies. No one wanted to miss out on the redistribution of their 'secret' stocks.

It was not until late morning that the mob reached the herbalist's shop. Even though the town was small there had been many enterprises to search. Fear opened all doors before them, and the Shans and Burmans looted as they pleased. But the failure to discover any hoard had enraged the crowd.

Kwan stood on her threshold, blocking their path, halting the advance. She explained, with good grace, that she had nothing to hide. 'My father came to Lashio because he believed in the uprightness of the Burmese people,' she said. 'It is unjust to submit his house to a search.'

The leading soldier shoved her aside. She held her ground and took hold of his cuff. He shook it and her, sneering at the spectacle of the petite, powerless woman gripping onto his clothing. The crowd laughed with him, mocking Kwan and goading Liu Wei, who had followed them up from the station. He confronted the soldier and demanded to know if he made a habit of beating old women. He provoked the mob by telling them he was hungry too. In truth his first concern was not for his sister-in-law. It was terror which made him speak out. Wei was defending the twins' property more than

Kwan's honour. May, who had chased after her husband, apologised for him. She called him a fool. She tried to pull him and her sister away. But the soldier turned his fury on the man. In the scuffle baskets and jars were overturned. Wei was seized by a dozen hands. Kwan was knocked to the floor. As she fell her head hit a chest of fresh herbs. She lay unconscious among the crushed mint and dust.

Wei fared less well. Beneath the open window on which May had first fixed her eyes, his life was beaten out of him. She uttered a deafening, impatient scream.

The next morning May's son ran away, a railway timetable tucked under his arm, chased by his mother's plea, 'Watch out for the rickshaw drivers of Soochow,' and a promise, 'I will follow you.' Armed with her knowledge of transportation systems, he rode lorries and trains, evaded Burmese border police and the Red Guards to reach Hong Kong and then, after waiting for three months for her to arrive, sailed on to America. He did not know that May could never follow him. The winding lines of road and rail, so often travelled in her mind, would remain unexplored. For Kwan had been wounded. She had lost hold of the threads of memory, as well as her sense of smell.

In her dark room, above tailor Ch'ien's shop, Kwan stared at the photographs of the family. Six matching faces glared back at her. Two sepia patriarchs wore pigtails and stern expressions. A silvered woman in embroidered robes gazed out of a daguerreotype. A bride and groom ventured a smile in their wedding portrait. There was also a snapshot of a small boy playing outside a booking office. Kwan knew the pictures and noted the sitters' similar features: the high family forehead, the rounded shoulders, the pinched nose. But she no longer recognised the faces. Her ancestors were strangers to her.

On the street below the dogs howled. In the bare room next door May tossed and turned. She always slept poorly after playing the airline game. No amount of *fu ling* could calm her spirit. It was not simply that the game reminded her of her son. She slept no better when their imagined journeys avoided America altogether, venturing instead out on Yangtze ferries or into the Mandarin Oriental Hotel at Macau. The fantasies that diverted and amused May always left her with a sense of dissatisfaction. She often cursed them, stopping in mid-flight and swearing never to play again. Yet less than a week would pass before she insisted on resurrecting the entertainment. Kwan obliged her not so much because she enjoyed the game, but because she was dependent on her twin. All her knowledge of the past came to her through the sister who didn't honour it. She remembered nothing of her life before the riot, except for the smell of mint and dust.

Burma and China are ancient adversaries. The Burmese have long been suspicious of the intentions of their powerful neighbour. But in 1988 and 1989 the two countries were drawn together by their respective massacres; first in Burma and then at Tiananmen Square. The governments found mutual solidarity in the face of Western outrage. And when Beijing ended its support of the Burmese Communist Party, political expediency smoothed the old animosities. History books were rewritten to overlook the numerous Sino–Burmese wars. State agriculture agencies were instructed to purchase Chinese hoes and shovels, not home-produced tools. Schoolchildren were taught that linguistics linked the two nations, both Burmese and Chinese being Sino-Tibetan tonal languages. Textbooks failed to mention the Red Badge affair. The old enemies became new friends; and the SLORC generals had a dependable source of weapons.

The official cross-border trade, which swapped teak and jade for bullets and mortars, also enticed new entrepreneurs from Yunnan and Szechwan. As soon as Chinese law permitted it, migrants poured across the border to settle in Lashio, which straddled the only road between Yunnan and the sea. They set up shops and hotels, trucking lines and import-export agencies. To them Burma was a land of opportunity. Its isolation and poverty had left it backward, with resources unexploited and locals vulnerable to fast deals and flashy tat. It was a good place for the Chinese to get rich quick.

After the attack May had buried her husband. She then carried her sister into their parents' sleeping chamber and waited at her bedside. Kwan had not fully recovered consciousness and May fed her like a delirious child, changing her bedding and explaining over and over how they would leave Lashio as soon as her health improved. For the first twelve months she rarely left the house. She avoided the station and never talked to strangers. The Burmese neighbours, the strangers who had watched Wei being killed, now brought food and medicine. Offerings of rice and curry were left on the table inside the storehouse door. Every morning for four years fresh limes appeared in her kitchen. The doctor called by every third week and never once asked for a fee. May did not thank her neighbours, but she held no grudge against them. No one in Burma who valued their life stood up against soldiers.

The postman stopped demanding payment for the letters that reached her from California. Her son described a new world of rapid-transit systems and jumbo jets. He worked nights as a baggage handler at LAX, enrolled at UCLA, bought a beige Ford Pinto. He graduated with a degree in mathematics and became an air traffic controller. As she watched her sister sleep, May fantasised about her own escape to America. She imagined her flight on its final approach. Over the cockpit radio she listened to her son talking down the aircraft. 'Roger, Pan Am 002. You are on course for touchdown on runway two-niner. Have a nice day.' After the landing he took off his headset, strolled down from the control tower and drove her home to his house in Long Beach. He had written that each room had its own television set. In another letter he wrote that forty-two different airlines flew into Los Angeles International and then listed the name of each one, from Aeroflot to Varig Brazilian. He marked with an asterisk each carrier that served South-East Asia. Yet as desperate as May became, as much as she missed her son, she never considered going to America alone. Kwan was her twin, half of a whole, and she could not imagine them ever being parted.

In time Kwan regained her health. She walked from room to room, moving with unfamiliarity through the familiar house, fingering unknown objects which she had always known. May, who preferred to talk about the future, told her little about their past.

As they had lost the family business, Kwan suggested they open a small market stall with the money sent every month by May's son. It was a sensible proposal. Their savings would buy herbs and a simple weighing scale, with a few kyat spare to bribe the appropriate official. They could build on their father's reputation, and with luck one day expand into a little shop on Lashio's main street. Kwan stood beside the market's only herb vendor and whispered to her sister. 'Do you see?' she asked, speaking in Chinese so that the Burman would not understand. 'Poor quality. And he has neither *gan cao* or ginger. None of the new Chinese will buy here. We could do very well.' She had already chosen a fine spot in the shade of a tamarind. 'We can lay out our herbs in baskets here.'

'Baskets,' interrupted May. 'Now that is something to consider.'

'You want to sell baskets?' asked Kwan, disappointed but not surprised by her sister's dismissal of her idea.

'Not old bamboo baskets, no,' said May, shaking her head. She wanted to break with the old ways. She saw the new possibilities. 'I think these newcomers want something different.'

'Different baskets?'

'Wouldn't they rather walk through the market carrying their shopping in a bright plastic bag? Something colourful, with words on it?'

On the dusty lanes around them every woman carried a bamboo basket. Every man had a woven Shan bag with a broad shoulderstrap. There was probably not a single plastic carrier in Lashio. Those found elsewhere in Burma had been imported by tourists or business travellers, and were considered status symbols, especially if emblazoned with English or American advertising slogans. They were prized even after their handles had ripped, their bottoms had torn and their colours had faded.

'You want to make them?' asked Kwan.

'I want to import them. They will fetch a healthy premium.' Plastic bags could make May's dream of travel come true, if she could raise sufficient capital to begin the venture.

'But no one is unhappy with bamboo,' said Kwan, shaking her head. 'And they don't need plastic bags.'

'It isn't a question of need.'

'I would prefer to sell spices.'

'Then you'll do it without me.'

May could risk being dismissive, even though she needed Kwan's help, for she knew that her sister would never set up the stall alone. Kwan needed to feel contained, either by the family or by tradition. She had always lacked the confidence to step out into the unknown. May felt a new sense of urgency with the passing years. Day by day age was diminishing her future. She had to seize the chance to earn enough money to buy their passage to the United States.

Glacé fruit and citrus preserves were popular delicacies in Burma. But local factories, having been starved of investment for forty years, were unable to produce a consistent supply, so the luxury was expensive. Limes, on the other hand, were cheap. They grew in the hills around Lashio. It was in this discrepancy that May saw her opportunity.

She knew of a cousin over the border in Kunming who would be willing to buy the fruit for its juice. She had heard too of a synthetic sugar mill in Kwantung that was in need of business. With the last of their savings the sisters bought a truckload of fresh limes. Kwan paid twenty-five pyas – a quarter of a kyat – for each. The price pleased the farmers, for in the past the People's Council had often allowed the fruit to rot on the trees. The truck drove to Kunming, where the limes were squeezed to produce juice for the Chinese market, then carried the skins on to Kwantung to be conserved in syrup. With the money from the sale of the juice, May paid for the printing of catchpenny wrappings to package the preserves. The lavish sleeves of dehydrated Burmese limes were then returned to Lashio as imports, and sold for twelve kyat apiece. The locals bought back their fruit at forty-eight times its original cost. May's knowledge of trade had served her well.

The profit enabled her to place an order with a plastic works in Yunnan. Five thousand plastic carrier bags were delivered one month later. May opened each bundle with care, smoothing the sleek surfaces, tracing the slogans of Lifebuoy soap ('Protect the Ones You Love') and Montana cigarettes ('Your taste, baby'). She compared the logos of Aviation batteries, Kosmo lubricant and Jesus's Cream Crackers. She was excited by the brash colours and bold lettering and held one carrier at her side. It read 'Flour Power'.

'What do you think?' she asked her sister.

Kwan didn't answer at first. She was too startled. Her nose, which had sensed nothing for years, was filled with the keen stink of new plastic. She didn't like the smell. It percolated through their rooms and into her clothes. She gestured as if to sweep it out of her hair. Kwan wanted to breathe in sweet honeysuckle, or even the earthy aroma of *ku sheng*, instead she smelt only plastic. But she didn't want to disappoint May, and nodded in approval.

'One day every woman in Burma will carry one of our plastic bags,' May crowed. 'By which time you and I will have left this place for ever.'

May had decided not to sell the carriers directly to the public. If anyone with a few kyat could buy a Coca-Cola bag, their rarity value would soon be lost. Instead she chose to sell them only to the new Chinese electronic stores, charging a premium that prevented the shopkeepers from giving the bags away with any but the most expensive purchases. The tactic hindered her sales at first, but it established the carriers as luxuries by association, and earned them increased status. She took the same approach with shops in nearby Mu-sé and Bhamo, and started to build up the business in calculated steps.

In a handful of months Lashio's streets, which had been unaltered for generations, began to change. The brightest colours in the markets were no longer the crimson mounds of ground chilli or the morning-green dresses of the Palaung. Levi's denim blue had become more popular than traditional Pa-o turquoise. Yamaha yellow turned more heads than did the golden plaid of a Kachin *longyi*. 'Have a Good

Taste for your Life', proclaimed one azure carrier. The brazen, synthetic glare of Pepsi and Sony transformed the look – and the aspirations – of the town. The vast majority of locals would never be able to afford the expensive Western goods, but they all wanted the plastic bags that were linked to them. There were fewer and fewer bamboo baskets to be seen.

Success invigorated May. She was ninety years old, but moved like a woman half her age. Money won her respect in the swelling Chinese community. It lightened her step, so that she always appeared to be about to break into a brisk run. Her mornings were spent in the market visiting her outlets, discussing current designs with the young shopkeepers. The importers of Walkmans and whiskies guided her selection and became the town's arbiters of taste. They suggested dropping Brut aftershave for Chanel, replacing Mandalay beer ('The only local choice') with Heineken ('Refreshes the parts other beers cannot reach'). May's afternoons were reserved for planning, not for the business but for her travels. She pored over the *ABC Airline Guide*, shipped at considerable expense from an agent in Kunming, working out again and again her route out of Asia. Should she fly by way of Guangzhou or Bangkok? Air Mandalay had daily flights to Rangoon. Would it be better to travel with Thai International to Chiang Mai? Air China had the most competitive fares across the Pacific. May sat in the bare, white room and planned to travel the world.

But success brought little richness to Kwan's life. Her days lacked variety, both in their pattern and in her imagination. She rarely ventured far from the low table which served as her desk. There was a sameness to her work, a steady march of time from dawn until dusk. She was responsible for checking deliveries, paying suppliers and maintaining the accounts. She worked hard because there was nothing to distract her, no memory of past lives, no fantasy of future travel. She did not share her sister's dream of going to a better place. Her step lacked May's lightness, and her nose crinkled in disgust at the stink of plastic.

It seemed unfair that the sisters' undoing should come by air, but it did. The Chinese were not alone in seeking out business opportunities in Burma. After 1988 the country's borders had opened to admit French oil companies and Korean industrial groups. British engineers arrived on Biman Bangladesh. Japanese traders flew up country on Air Mandalay. May could have traced the route of the Taiwanese-American salesman who landed one morning on their doorstep: Singapore Airlines from San Francisco, Silk Air on to Rangoon, Myanma Airways to Lashio. He wore a cream linen suit, and when he reached for his card a boarding pass fell out of his pocket. It fluttered to the ground, and he did not bother to pick it up.

'You're from California?' gushed May, having never before met an American. His Chinese had an odd nasal twang. 'But my son lives in California. Maybe you know him?'

'It's a pretty big place,' replied the salesman, not bothering to ask her son's name. It was too hot and he was too jet-lagged to make polite conversation.

'He's an air traffic controller there. He may have given your aircraft its departure clearance.'

'You never know.'

While Kwan prepared the tea, May invited him into the front room and asked if he preferred the Airbus or the new Boeing. He admitted that he hardly noticed the difference. 'Boeing, I reckon,' he said.

'My son always favours Boeing too,' said May in delight. 'He lives in Los Angeles, you know.'

'Small world,' he sighed, uninterested. He had two more calls to make before his afternoon flight back to Mandalay, followed by another half dozen in Rangoon. He already knew that this was a wasted visit. The two old women did not fit into his company's profile.

The salesman was a representative of a large advertising firm coordinating trademark protection for its clients in South-East Asia. The agency, he explained, wished to establish itself as the market leader by centralising marketing strategy for branded products. His assignment was to contact established small traders and to offer them the chance to buy a local distribution franchise. Out of habit, he gave the sisters a glossy brochure. He told them that his firm's T-shirts and plastic bags, which were printed in Thailand, were of superior quality to their Chinese imports.

May was confused by the offer. She did not understand why she should have to pay for the franchise. She and Kwan had built up their business themselves. It was the agency that should pay them for it, not the other way round. 'Thank you for your compliment,' she said. It pleased her that he had called on them. 'You may have heard that we are outsiders here.' She assumed that the salesman knew of her intention to emigrate. 'And it is true that we plan to leave Lashio.'

'My sister wishes to join her son,' explained Kwan, pouring out three small cups of Namhsan tea. It was first quality, grown in the Shan State and served to their rare guests.

May added with pride, 'In less than one more year we will have earned sufficient money to make it possible.'

'Great,' said the salesman, and yawned. As the twins tried to decipher the brochure, he looked at his watch. 'My car is waiting,' he apologised, closing his briefcase and rising to his feet. He hadn't touched his tea.

'You must not think us ungrateful,' said May, standing too.

'Look,' he said, with as much sensitivity as he could muster, 'this isn't my concern, but I don't think that this really suits you.'

May hardly heard him. She calculated only that the visitor might help them to leave Lashio sooner. 'It is this matter of our purchasing something that we already own that disturbs me. Please understand that we have no aversion to *selling* our business to you.'

The salesman laughed, and enquired if the sisters were aware of the laws concerning copyright infringement. They were not. He said, 'There are other traders in town who are interested in the proposal.'

'The fragrance of our good name is known by all in Lashio,' said Kwan. His comment had upset her, and she reminded her sister that their father had advised them to depend on the family alone.

'We have worked hard and are proud of our achievement,' said May, a sudden sense of loss emptying her heart.

The salesman took back his business card. Anxious that he might reclaim the boarding pass too, May asked if she could keep it. He laughed again and said that she could. 'No charge,' he added.

In the windowless recess of her bare white room, May sat on the stool and watched the activity of arrival. The ground crew directed the Tristar towards the bright terminal, their orange torches glinting in the evening light. Landing strobes flashed off metal fuselages and flightdeck windscreens. A yellow Follow Me van sped along the tarmac. Her aircraft taxied across the concrete apron then swung wide into its bay. The engines wound down, the throaty whine of a shrunken world dying away. Catering crews and baggage handlers snapped hatches and holds open. In minutes they offloaded suitcases and restocked the galley with tin-foil chicken for the return flight to Asia. The passenger walkway craned out to meet the opening forward door, and May tried to catch sight of her unseen son's face, cloning in her mind the features of a child onto a man's body. But the observation deck was too crowded. She saw only other families, other lives, not her own flesh and blood.

Kwan stood before her sister, miming the action of collecting her belongings, anxious to please. 'Welcome to Los Angeles, where the correct time is eight o'clock. I hope you have enjoyed your flight, madam.'

'Yes, thank you,' May answered, straining to spot his forgotten face.

'Can you see your son?'

'Isn't that him there? In the blue jacket? No, he was never that tall.' She turned to Kwan, seeking reassurance, the tenuous hold of her hope shaken by the finality of their imprisonment. 'But he will be waiting for me. I know that he is waiting.'

'I am sure of it, madam.'

The new plastic bags had appeared in the shops a few months after the salesman's visit, and, as the twins had been assured, their quality was superior to the Chinese imports. Storekeepers had sold off the twins' carriers and replaced them with Thai-made stock. Anyone with two spare kyat had become able to buy a Chinese bag, but as soon as they had them, as soon as their bamboo baskets had been consigned to the bin, they wanted the finer Thai versions. The deficiencies of Kwan and May's imports became obvious. Their bags had a tendency to tear and stain their contents with cheap dye. They had also often been printed with misspellings of Toshibi, Gorgon's Gin and Yum Yum Nooodles. The town's merchants had understood the value of the new, superior product. Once again, they only gave them away with purchases of Alpine car stereos and bottles of Chivas Regal. The certainties of Marxism had been swept away, as had the confidence in the Confucian Utopia before it, by the vagaries of the market.

The twins' business had been lost. Their savings had been squandered on a fruitless attempt to improve the standard of their imports. There wasn't enough money left to buy air tickets, even if they had been granted an American visa. The letters too no longer arrived from California. They never knew if May's son had stopped writing or if the postman had simply taken to withholding his correspondence. The harsh economic reality had changed attitudes in Lashio. The sisters couldn't afford to pay the bribes, so there was no reason to deliver their letters.

In the end they had opened a small market stall to sell herbs and spices under the tamarind tree. There hadn't been the money to undertake anything more ambitious. Kwan had retrieved their father's texts from the godown and rediscovered lost satisfaction in grinding cloves, preparing pepper balms and weighing out doses of *mu li* oyster shell. The week's first day was set aside for sorting medicinal herbs, the second and third days were reserved for pounding cardamom and distilling volatile oils. The fine remedies won the devotion of the old families and new customers alike. No one suspected that Kwan's sense of smell had not returned. Neither the familiar herbs nor the old routines had restored her memory. All she could smell was the stink of plastic.

Kwan and May cut an unusual image in Lashio, squatting beside jars of ginseng infusion, lighting incense in honour of their parents, arguing on their slow walk home from the temple. They were a part of the town and they would never leave it. Their lives had become contained again, as in truth they had always been, with only May's fantasies reaching out beyond the lime groves, travelling along the Burma Road towards her ever-distant somewhere else.

SEVEN

The Long and Winding Road

'THIS IS PURE PALAUNG, SIR,' confirmed the old Chinese herbalist. 'The Pa-O people make a similar basket, but it has no lid.' She tapped the photograph. 'This one has a lid.' She turned the picture over in her hand. 'The style used to be common here.'

'It's very similar to your basket,' I said, gesturing at her delicate bamboo shopper.

'Ten US dollars,' interrupted her sister, her voice snapping out from the back of the stall. Then she added, 'So when were you last in California?'

'Your basket isn't quite the same,' pointed out Katrin, as much for my benefit as for that of the herbalist.

'It is not for sale,' she said, and bowed her head as if to brace herself against a series of blows. Her sister hissed at her in Chinese.

We had followed the twins down from the Quan Yin San temple and through the market to their stall beneath the tamarind tree. They had opened the shutters, pulled the covers from the jars and filled the market with the smell of cinnamon. Its pungent aroma had masked the stink of pig meat, putrefying in the sun at the adjacent stall. We had bought a few handfuls of spices, and when Katrin admitted to knowing San Francisco, had been invited to sit with them. A spot was cleared on their mat and the younger-looking twin had poured out their story, along with Namhsan tea from a flask. Her sister, whose hands were rough and callused, had stayed silent, except to confirm the odd detail or date. She only spoke when I asked her about the basket. I had hoped that she would send us across the road to a vast antique emporium and so conclude our search. Instead she told us that the basket had belonged to her mother, and its Palaung makers had long since deserted Lashio. She directed us back down the Burma Road.

'Many Palaung now live around Hsipaw,' said her sister, with a tight smile. She would rather have told us about airport transfer times or the rickshaw drivers of Soochow. 'Would you like to go there?' I sighed and nodded. I would have preferred to go to bed. 'Then you will need a taxi.' I guessed that she had a neighbour who would give her a finder's commission. 'I find very cheap one. For you five thousand kyat.'

The price was steep, more than double the usual rate. 'But it's only a forty-five-mile drive,' said Katrin.

'We'll take the bus,' I said. Our slow, snail-slide journey to Lashio had put me off Burmese trains for good. Its memory was also more recent than our last bus bruising.

'The line-bus is bad for sophisticated travellers like you. I always travel first class myself. I recommend it to foreigners also.'

But it was not possible to travel to Hsipaw by bus, in any class. The agent would not sell us a ticket without a permit from the Immigration Department, and the office was shut for *thingyan*. The local military commander was willing to issue the appropriate pass, but only if his superior in Mandalay had approved our preceding journey. Without it we were not officially in Lashio, even though we were standing in front of his desk. I explained that we didn't have a pass because travel to Lashio by train required no special permission. He in turn apologised that authorisation could not be applied for by telephone. The local exchange only took incoming calls. He then advised us – off the record – to go back to Mandalay, obtain his superior's approval and return to Lashio. He assured us that our permit would then be issued promptly, or certainly within three working days. I considered offering him a bottle of whisky but, noticing his new gold Rolex, decided that my bribe might be more effective at the Myanmar Tourist Office. I was right. The supervisor there was grateful for the gift. He tried to help us by booking two seats on the afternoon flight to Rangoon, even though we had no intention of going there. 'You are lucky to get any reservation at such short notice,' he assured us. Our mounting frustration reminded me of a comment made by Stalin. When vetoing a plan to extend Russia's telephone network he said, 'I can think of no better instrument of counter-revolution.' The free flow of people and information breaks the grip of tyrants. Few countries have been more successful than Burma in hindering communication.

It was a paradox that, had we wished it, we would have been free to travel in the opposite direction, north from Lashio. In the fly-infested tea shop by the bus gate Yunnanese girls in white plastic stilettos slurped cool cans of 7-Up. Three smug Chinese traders, returning home after offloading cheap nylons and brassieres, unscrewed brimming jars of bitter green tea, to be topped up with boiling water through the long journey. Nearby money-changers sucked on chicken feet and rooster heads while waiting to meet the Kunming bus. Between Lashio and China there was no frontier. No Burmese customs post stood on the bridge over the Shweli River. People and goods passed between the two countries without documentation, as if between English counties or American states. We were 112 miles south of the border, yet beyond Lashio one was to all intents and purposes inside China.

There had never been any attempt to disguise Han ambitions in Burma. In the 1960s Beijing had sponsored the outlawed Burmese Communist Party, supplying it with recoilless rifles, anti-aircraft guns and political commissars. At the height of the military campaign, twenty thousand square kilometres of the Shan State fell under Communist control. Then the *Tatmadaw* mounted a counter-offensive to halt the invader's advance. As the expense in lives and ammunition swelled, it became apparent that conquest could be achieved by more economic means. China turned its back on the insurgents and began to arm the Burmese government. Beijing recognised that Rangoon's greed could be exploited. The leaders of the regime were so insecure, and so obsessed with lining their own pockets, that they alone failed to see the triumph of their long-feared neighbour.

By the time I finally accepted that we had no option but to catch the train to Hsipaw, the booking office was shut. We rushed back to the market, only to find that the twins had vanished, and so we were also unable to follow up on their overpriced taxi. All the stallholders had closed early to prepare for the New Year celebration, gathering at a temporary *pandal* stage equipped with buckets and high-pressure hoses to soak passers-by. Katrin and I avoided the main square, dragging ourselves back through the crippling heat to our hotel. A bold Burmese child dogged us, a rusty tin of stagnant water in his hand. He wanted to douse Katrin but accepted me instead, pouring the murky liquid down my neck.

The exceptional ugliness of the hotel had gone unappreciated the evening before. It glowered at the head of a sweeping drive, an uncompromising concrete box that celebrated the triumph of rigid authority over sympathetic design.

'Important visitors stay tonight,' said the manager, with a proud smile. At his feet a cleaner squatted on her hands and knees scrubbing the grouting between the slabs of marble. It had taken all day for her to work her way across the vast expanse of floor. 'They come from nearby.'

'Nearby?'

'Yes. Please you eat in restaurant?' he asked. Behind him three clocks noted the time in Rangoon, London and Beijing. 'There will be special entertainment. You very welcome.'

We lay down for an hour and then, rather than brave a *thingyan* drenching or watch satellite reruns of American sitcoms, decided to take ourselves down to the dining hall. We had to eat, and the prospect of another evening of Laughing Cow cheese on crumbled water-biscuits did not excite us. I also hoped that 'nearby' might mean Hsipaw and that, over a quiet dinner, we would be offered a lift to our destination. But as we approached the noisy hall I realised once again that my hopes were misplaced.

The door swung open and the music stopped. Our breakfast waiter, now dressed in a clean and pressed linen jacket, led us across the room towards the central table. The local band, who had been warned of our arrival by the receptionist, struck up a clanging fanfare sort of welcome. It reminded me of 'Jailhouse Rock'. The hundred-odd Chinese guests straightened their ties. All eyes were on us, or at least on Katrin. She was the only woman in the room.

No sooner had we sat beneath the heavy perspex chandelier than a jug of beer was placed on our table. 'We didn't order this,' I said.

'It is a gift from the gentleman opposite, sir,' said the waiter with a deferential gesture.

The well-groomed executive at the next table raised his glass and said, 'Chin-chin.'

Katrin smiled but did not drink. 'I think we should have settled for *Baywatch*,' she whispered.

With a twang of the guitar the executive then stood up and mounted the stage. The band broke into a mellow refrain and, right on queue, he began to sing. 'The wrong and winding road . . .' Katrin took my hand under the table. His voice was terrible. 'That leads to Yunnan . . .' The other diners did not move or meet our eyes. 'Will never disappear . . .' Their sombre looks were as expressionless as their grey suits. 'I've walked that road before . . .' Then the song's chorus began and, without warning, the hundred Chinese account-ants joined in like a massed corporate choir. 'Many times I've been at home and many times I've drived, anyway you never know the many ways I've died . . .'

'But still they leak me back,' the executive sang on in solo, 'to the wrong, winding road.' I glanced towards the exit and wondered if we would ever get out of Lashio. Theravada Buddhists believe that our past conscious and unconscious actions determine both our current lot and our spiritual position in the next life. The law of causation suggested that if our day of judgement was to be in this fiercely bleak hotel, we had clocked up a bumper crop of past wrongs. 'Don't leave me standing, dear,' crooned the executive with feeling. 'I've walked that road before . . .' The corporate chorus joined in for another whine before leaving the final refrain for the soloist alone: '. . . that leads me to Yunnan.'

His last note hung in the air like a mosquito in a bedroom after midnight. Then there was silence. Sweet silence.

'I think we'd better applaud,' I hissed, reluctant to cause offence. So we did, and in delight of our approval as much as for their performance itself, the others clapped too. The executive was pleased with the response. He bowed and left the stage. 'Thank goodness that's over,' I said, and looked around for a menu, failing to notice that a second accountant was mounting the stage. He nodded to the band and, in a swirl of discordant chords, began to jiggle to an approximation of 'Crocodile Rock'.

'I remember when rock was young,' he wailed in a toneless serenade, 'me and Suzy had so much fun . . .' His superior's singing had been mellifluous in comparison. '. . . holding hands and spitting stones, had a pair of wellies and a place of my own . . .' As he howled I wondered if the accountant, who had lived through the Cultural Revolution, had ever had the chance to have fun. He certainly would never have had a place of his own, let alone Wellington boots. '. . . while the other kids were rocking round Bangkok . . .' We had become hapless, honoured guests at a conference karaoke evening. It was too late to escape from the revelry but, I reasoned, at least we could eat. I managed to catch the waiter's attention. '. . . we were hopping bopping to the crocodile rock oh . . .'

I asked to see the menu, but before it arrived plates of spare ribs and stir-fried rice appeared on our table. The well-groomed executive broke off from the 'I-never-knew-me-a-better-time' chorus to smile. I tried to make myself heard above the clamour, making the usual, embarrassed English excuses.

'Please,' he insisted, 'You are our guests tonight. Enjoy the meal.'

'. . . Suzy went and left me for some foreign guy,' they sang on, 'long nights crying by the record machine, dreaming of my wellies and my old blue jeans . . .'

We managed to grab the odd mouthful of food between the medley of Beatles numbers, after 'Yesterday' and before 'Help!', but in their tipsy excitement the initially reserved accountants began to crowd around our table. They nodded at the stage, encouraging our enjoyment of the proceedings.

'I can't get no, no satisfaction ...' The musical murder of the Rolling Stones was followed by the slaying of the Spice Girls. 'I'll tell you what I want what I really really want ...' One trader, who had been drinking alone at a small corner table, subjected us to Abba's 'Money Money Money'. 'I work all night I work all day to pay the bills I have to pay ...' His more idealistic neighbour tried to hum 'Imagine'. Then, after all the senior officials in the room had sung their party pieces and we thought we could take no more entertainment, the well-dressed executive appeared at my side and asked to dance with Katrin.

'It's up to her,' I said.

Katrin's instinct was to refuse the invitation. But the nature of the country was to be hospitable, and opportunities to reciprocate were rare. 'Well, maybe just a short one,' she said, somewhat grimly.

As soon as Katrin had left the table the knot of accountants closed around me. 'Your wife is very beautiful,' said one, taking her chair.

'Thank you.'

'I will give you two hundred grams of jade for her.'

'Three hundred,' offered another with a laugh.

'I'm afraid she's not for sale,' I replied, shrugging off the offers but irritated at their liberty.

'One kilo; my best price.'

'I'm sorry.'

'A new Mercedes, then,' smiled a little man at the back, taking a different tack. 'With CD player and air conditioning.'

I shook my head.

'Her weight in gold,' shouted the 'Money Money Money' drunk, who was then admonished by his peers for mocking their negotiating technique.

The first dance finished and Katrin reclaimed her chair. It was then that the queue began to form. One by one the officials and managers lined up at our table for the chance to dance with her. The attention made her feel anxious, even threatened, but she treated them all equally although, because of their number, she soon had to ration her time.

'I wonder if any of you are travelling to Hsipaw in the morning?' I shouted above the chorus of 'Saturday Night Fever'.

'Kunming is a more beautiful city,' replied one functionary. 'Maybe your wife would prefer to see it?'

Katrin danced for a minute each with half a dozen men, smiled for every flash photograph, and then began to protest. She had had enough. The accountants wanted more dancing, insisting on it in good humour but with unpleasant undertones, so I reinforced her refusal.

When the band took a break, a raffle was held. Katrin won a porcelain doll, even though she hadn't bought a ticket.

'So you will not forget our friendship,' said the well-groomed executive.

Then the whisky started to flow, and we seized our moment to escape from the hall. As the men became distracted we slipped into the night.

Outside the streets were dark. No lights glowed in Lashio. The town's electricity had been disconnected. Katrin breathed in the fresh air and shivered, as if to shake off the touch of many hands.

'We should have watched that rerun of *I Dream of Jeannie*,' I lamented, wishing we had stayed in our room.

'I felt like a commodity,' she said, furious at herself. 'I've had enough of Lashio.'

'We'll go tomorrow.'

We walked for a few minutes, but beyond the glare of our floodlit hotel we risked stumbling into an unseen pothole. I took Katrin by the arm. She – and I – had encouraged our hosts' arrogance by embracing Burmese politeness. The accountants had taken advantage of our affable courtesy.

'I didn't like pandering to their assumptions,' she said. 'They thought they could do with me what they wanted, because women in the West are free.'

'I don't think it's a matter of national stereotypes.'

'It would be the same for any woman,' she said with a shudder, maybe thinking of Ni Ni. 'And the paradox is that with them I lost my liberty.' Katrin's freedom, Ni Ni's innocence, Kwan's respect for the past and May's hope for the future; unless one defends that which is most cherished, it is stolen away. 'I'm worn out. Can we go back to the room?'

As we turned back towards the Lashio Motel the muffled revelry of the water festival rose up from the darkened town. But we were not about to be drawn into more celebrations. Then a distant glimmering caught our eyes.

Away in the dark there glowed a low-lying line of stars, like fireflies marching in regimental rank. We stepped with care down the black lane towards them, unable to see our feet, unable to judge our progress, drawn by the flickering lights. After a few moments we found ourselves on a broad avenue. Bamboo scaffolding had been erected along the length of a long billboard, and painters, working by candlelight, were updating the sign. In the half-light we could make out the familiar official propaganda: 'Burmese land – our land, Burmese language – our language. Love your motherland.' As we watched, the patriotic catchphrase was blocked out and replaced by a slogan promoting solidarity with the Burmans' new brothers. 'We live like eggs in the same nest; break one shell and all our nests are torn down,' directed the new decree from the junta. Its sentiment reinforced my unease. The sign painters worked on in silence, their candles flickering in the night breeze.

The next morning we felt in need of sanctuary and so, after breakfast, we went to look again for St John's Anglican church. The church had been built before the last war by the then District Commissioner John Shaw. I had heard of its active congregation – a mixture of Shans, Chins, Karens and Wa hill tribe peoples – and of its minister, the Reverend John Michael Tay-maung. American Baptists and English missionaries had been active in the Shan State during the nineteenth century, but only about 4 per cent of Burmese citizens had remained Christian. I was interested to see how they coped in the Buddhist borderland.

It was a national holiday and most Burmese were still in bed, nursing hangovers, praying that the flash frenzy of *thingyan* water-throwing had washed away the old year's realities. The air was humid from the wet streets, as if the monsoon had arrived early, and our sandals squelched in the mud. A drunk, having been unable to find his way home in the dark, slept off the night's excess on the roof of a bus.

At first we could not find the church, even though it fronted onto the main street. We walked up and down the empty, sodden road, past the new town hall and the old No. 1 and No. 2 hospitals, around the Ko Nyi 'Beauty Adorner' Salon, searching for a steeple.

'My feet are killing me,' complained Katrin. 'I can't go much further.'

It was only after twenty minutes of wandering that we caught sight of the church, hidden behind the concrete pillars of another building site. Its exterior was the colour of dirty linen. The neglected walls were encrusted by a decade's grime and the filthy cross perched above the door was canted at a precarious angle. But the neat interior would not have been out of place in an English village, assuming that frangipani grew in the Home Counties. Katrin and I stepped into a lush hanging garden, under streamers of white *hkayayban* blossom and bursting trumpets of scarlet hibiscus. An exuberant jasmine encircled the altar. Luscious flowers sprouted from every nook and pew. A sparrow darted into the eucalyptus. The fabric of the church was adorned with unrestrained curtains of vegetation. At the centre of the pious plantings moved a dark figure holding a trowel.

'Reverend Tay-maung?' I called.

'I'm sorry, but John is away until Sunday,' replied the gardener, laying down his trowel. 'Can I help you?'

'Do you know how we can get to Hsipaw?' I said, more out of instinct than reason. The familiarity of a church, albeit one more floral than Kew Gardens, had eased my last remnants of reserve.

'We've asked everywhere,' said Katrin, anxious to put Lashio behind us.

'I can drive you.' The gardener's response was so spontaneous that I suspected he had misunderstood me.

'Hsipaw is forty miles down the Burma Road,' I said. 'It is a long way.'

'I know.'

'You have a car?'

'My uncle owns a fine car.' He stepped down the aisle towards us. 'But I would ask that you purchase the petrol, if you do not mind. It is rather expensive for me. Have you eaten breakfast?'

'At the hotel.'

'Then it will have been of questionable quality. Please, let me invite you to join me.' When we hesitated the gardener insisted. 'You are my guests. I will care for your journey.'

Throughout our travels in Burma – and in its Shan State – arrangements had a tendency to work out. Logistics didn't defeat us. We were never lost or stranded for long. It was not because of forward planning or the persuasive power of dollar bills. It was because of the generosity of the peoples of Burma. Someone always, eventually, turned up to help us – as now. Buddhism alone did not explain their behaviour. The Burmese value *bama hsan-chin*, a standard of good conduct that honours a knowledge of the scriptures, respect for elders, discretion and modesty. To the foreigner the word translates into a care for guests.

The gardener had false teeth and a thinning crown of short silver hair. A halo would not have looked out of place above his head. He introduced himself, but spoke so lightly that we didn't catch his name. In the vestry he prepared an unnecessary second breakfast of fried eggs, toast and a huge bunch of bananas. It is said that in Burma the hungry need only to ask and food will be provided, while in China it is not the custom to ask, so one waits for it to be offered. It seemed that in the Shan State one was fed without even being hungry. Our gentle host sat us by the font under a potted white jasmine and watched us eat, not touching any food himself.

'The church looks beautiful,' admired Katrin. 'I don't think I've ever seen so many flowers.'

'You are very kind,' said the gardener, lowering his voice even though we were alone. He drew his hands together as if in prayer. 'As you see, we have all retreated into smaller worlds. Please, have another piece of toast.'

I hadn't eaten my first piece. 'Smaller worlds?'

'Here,' he said, looking around at his ecclesiastical grove, 'I grow a few blooms. It is the only sensible choice. You must eat more,' he insisted. 'You are too thin. Here, have another egg.'

'I couldn't,' I apologised, straining to catch his meaning and unable to swallow a second banana. 'Has the Reverend Tay-maung retreated too?'

'The Reverend cares little for self-preservation. He has greater concerns,' replied the gardener. 'He is away on business.'

'Church business?'

'You might have noticed the building work outside. The Bishops of Mandalay and Rangoon sold our grounds to a Chinese entrepreneur in secret. They also sold Church land in Bhamo under similar conditions.' He shrugged in polite understanding. 'We each do what we must to survive.'

'But wasn't the congregation consulted?'

He shook his head. 'The Reverend supported the congregation's complaint, and so the bishops suspended his salary. Everyone with courage is mistreated. That is why it is better to live in a smaller world. Is it the hill-tribe market you wish to see in Hsipaw?'

Katrin explained about our search for the basket, producing the photograph for him to consider. The gardener nodded. 'Yes, this is Hsipaw Palaung. We had better get a move on if we're to arrive in time.'

'Are you sure?' I asked, concerned for his safety. 'We don't want to cause you difficulties.'

'It is the Buddhist New Year. Everyone will be too thick-headed to notice us. I hope only for your sake that it is the police, not the army, who stop us at the city gate.'

'Why?'

'Because the police charge a hundred kyat for permission to pass.

The army charge five hundred.' He gathered up the leftovers and said, 'Come, we will take this along for your picnic on the journey.'

In a lean-to behind the church was a large, rounded package. Three layers of tarpaulin were wrapped in braids of jute. The gardener uncoiled the cords one by one and with great care rolled back the covers. A flash of a chrome fender caught our eye, then two bug-eyed headlamps. The tyres gleamed with boot-black polish, even though they were worn down to their fibre core.

'It's an Austin 30,' I said, excited.

'It's very old,' worried Katrin.

'Not so old,' replied the gardener. '1954. My uncle bought it from an Englishman who worked for the Bombay Burma Trade Corporation. Unfortunately he could not take it with him when he returned home.'

'That was fortunate for your uncle,' I said, running a hand over the burnished badge and 'Flying A' hood ornament. The A30 was the spiritual successor to the original Austin 7, the post-war British family car. Its stubby body brought to mind the sort of shiny beetle that boys like to put in their pockets. It was two-door, two-tone and totally unsuited to the tropics. 'She's in perfect condition, apart from the tyres.'

'There's a worrying knocking from the front end,' said the gardener. 'But I believe it to be a design flaw.'

'Will it reach Hsipaw?' asked Katrin, not unreasonably.

'It was brought from a village near there; I am certain it will make it back.'

'Maybe we should just take the train,' she said.

The gardener wouldn't hear of it. 'It will be an easy journey,' he assured us, pulling back the 'Flying A' and opening the bonnet. The compact 803cc engine had an endearing quality, like a clockwork toy. 'See? It's no more than six months since it last ran.'

The car started first time, after we had changed the oil and borrowed a neighbour's battery. I would have preferred to replace the spark plugs but spares were only available for Willys Jeeps and Taulagy motorised wheelbarrows. Katrin and I squeezed onto the back seat and, with our knees up around our chins, puttered back to Lashio's leafy No. 1 Sector. We parked at the back of our hotel, behind the few colonial houses which hadn't surrendered their teak balconies and fanciful cupolas to woodworm and bulldozers.

'It will be better if you don't tell the hotel manager how you are travelling to Hsipaw,' suggested the gardener, his voice sloshing between his teeth. 'He's not a local fellow.'

But the manager took no interest in our departure. He sat on the sofa beside the desk with his young daughter, an inked brush in his hand. As I gathered our bags Katrin watched him help her to draw Chinese characters. 'Do you teach her alone?' she asked.

'Oh no,' he replied, shaking his head. 'She learns at school. But I try to share with her the little knowledge that I have.'

We managed to cram our knapsack into the boot of the Austin. The baskets and lacquerware which we had been given filled the front seat. There was barely room for the spare petrol tin. The gardener slipped the car into gear and drove slowly, very slowly, towards the city gate. He hoped there wouldn't be trouble there.

'They may say that we are smuggling goods from China,' he warned. Katrin pointed out that we hadn't been to China. 'It is no matter; they like to make money from you.'

The idea of a city gate struck us as medieval. A physical barrier to protect a settlement's inhabitants from bandits and rebels seemed archaic. Yet there was nothing old-fashioned about the barbed-wire barrier strung across the road. Nor did the immigration, customs, army and police posts on the high grassy bank seem interested in protecting their citizens. In the cool shade I discerned the flash of epaulettes. A white military police helmet rested on a stool. The gardener shifted down in a screech of grinding gears. The sentry must have detected his nervousness.

'Oh dear,' the gardener sighed. 'It is the army.'

Our passports were fingered, and each page inspected, before being taken off to the nearest hut. After a moment the gardener was ordered to follow them. It was hot in the bug-eyed little car, and we started to sweat. Ten, twenty, then thirty minutes ticked away. I worried about him, but we had been told to wait. Chinese lorries lumbered by the checkpoint, swaying around the bamboo barrier like wind-lashed sailing ships. Their vast cargoes were watched over by boys clinging to the top of the khaki tarpaulins. Ox-carts squeaked and squealed along the rutted verge, unmolested by the sleepy guards. An over-loaded line-bus thundered down the centre of the road, its exhaust long ago dislodged by a collision. A lizard stole across our bonnet to stalk a fly on the 'Flying A' hood ornament. The soldiers only jumped up once, to salute a passing black Mercedes. I wondered if it was the car I had been offered in exchange for Katrin.

'There is a compulsory transit tax,' the gardener told us when he returned, 'of five hundred kyat.' I passed the notes through the window to him. He moved to hand over the money but the soldier grimaced, stealing a quick look back towards the post. The gardener discreetly placed the bills between the pages of a document which he then surrendered.

The soldier seemed displeased. He fingered his automatic and unleashed a series of short, sharp, rapid-fire questions at the gardener. Like the officer in the train, he refused to meet our eyes. Our host backed up against the Austin and whispered over his shoulder, 'I think he wishes more money.'

'Please tell the soldier,' I said in as light a tone as I could muster, 'that everyone in Lashio has been very kind to us.'

'Such kind, generous people,' echoed Katrin, smiling at him.

'And that we have enjoyed our stay in his town.'

'Very much.'

The gardener translated, and the soldier looked startled. It seemed that compliments were as uncommon as foreigners at his checkpoint. The exercise of authority was at odds with his natural manner. He stepped back, straightened himself, glanced again at his peers dozing in the shade and nodded.

'You are very kind,' Katrin told him as he returned our papers.

'Bye bye,' he said under his breath.

The open road beckoned, assuming that we could negotiate a fair price for a few gallons of black-market petrol. We coasted downhill from the checkpoint to the first vendor. Burma has vast oil reserves but the military rations fuel, not only in an attempt to limit car imports. Every petrol shop knows a bureaucrat or soldier willing to sell on his ample official supply for profit.

A glass bottle of fuel was balanced on top of a brick at the side of the road. Scavenged oil filters and distributors filled a display case. Machetes were on sale for carving bypasses when trees blocked the road. Two thousand kyat – about a month's salary for an office clerk – bought us six gallons of petrol of unknown quality. The gardener watched the attendant measure and pour it through a tea strainer into the Austin. He twice asked him to shake the bottle so as not to waste a drop.

'Officials only pay twenty-five kyat for a gallon,' he explained as he slipped back behind the wheel. 'When they resell it we say that their cars are "milking cows".' He shook his head in quiet despair. 'Everyone has to make a living somehow.'

We pulled away from the pump and hit the first pothole. The Austin jumped out of gear. 'It needs a stronger synchro spring,' sighed the gardener.

The ragged strip of asphalt, its metalled edges like cliff-edge precipices, wove through banana groves and jungle. The Burma Road, along with the disused Ledo Road which once ran north and west to India, had been built by thirty-five thousand Burmese, Indian, British and Chinese troops under the direction of American engineers during the Second World War. The Bhamo arm had spanned ten major rivers and 155 smaller streams and had cost so many lives that it had been nick-named 'the man-a-mile road'. Yet despite the horrific human cost of construction, little had been done to improve or maintain it since the Allies withdrew in 1946. The Austin skirted the ruts and hesitated across 'temporary' US Army bridges. Along the roadside crippled lorries expired in the dust, bleeding black oil into plastic containers, their drivers lying beneath them in pools of brake fluid. The line-bus which had raced past us at the checkpoint lay wounded by a waterhole. Its patient passengers idled on the bank while one woman, familiar with travel delays, took the opportunity to wash her hair.

'We Burmese don't call it the Burma Road any more,' the gardener said, plunging aside to avoid a Chinese truck, its back groaning under the weight of imported diesel engines, tin teapots and coconut shampoo. 'It has nothing to do with us, apart from running through our country.' He reeled off a list of statistics – GNP, import tonnage, the number of local factory closures – then eased the Austin back onto a perforated length of metalled surface. 'It's called the Dragon Road now, because the Chinese use it for smuggling.'

'You've got quite a head for figures,' I said.

'I was once an economist in the Ministry of Finance,' he said, trying to find second gear. The revelation took us by surprise. He had given us the impression of being an uneducated man. 'But no more. No more.' He concentrated on the road ahead, slowing down to avoid a flock of scrawny chickens. 'The Chinese sell us their arms and pumps and ploughs. It is bad for Burmese industry, but even worse is the import of technical advisers. These people come with each delivery and they instruct us to follow their way, instead of using our own tools and methods.' We reduced our speed to such a cautious pace that a cyclist overtook us. 'Burma is becoming China's Baltic States. Government employees are leaving the civil service, creating vacancies for even more Chinese advisers.' A line-bus raced head-on towards us, its horn blaring. The gardener wrenched us off the tarmac to give way and the bus swerved at the last possible moment, just avoiding a collision. Our journey to Hsipaw would take hours. 'We cover our ears and eyes and, as I said in the church, retreat into smaller worlds.'

'But isn't it better to try to resist from within?' I asked.

'You must be an American.'

'Canadian.'

'It is very refreshing to hear your optimism,' he smiled, indulging me. 'But no, it is not possible. My associates have left the civil service and gone into tourism and hotel management. I too am looking after myself, and hiding from the loss of my country.'

'I'm sorry,' I said. 'I'm sorry.'

'When I become disheartened I compare our lot with the people of Cambodia or Stalin's Russia,' replied the gardener. 'Then I do not feel so bad. Would you care for an egg sandwich yet?'

Along the roadside women and children broke stones by hand to make gravel. We circumnavigated cavernous potholes, paused for bullock-carts and stopped when a puff of smoke from a burning field obscured our view. Twice we waited in the shade to let the engine cool. Cicadas buzzed in the trees above our heads. I ground grit between my teeth. The black Mercedes swept past us on its return journey to Lashio.

'Five years ago that man arrived from nearby with nothing,' said the gardener, nodding after the swirl of dust.

'"Nearby" is China?' asked Katrin.

He nodded. 'In the first year he opened a small shop, a year later a large store and now, just this past month, a hotel. Only the Chinese are rich.'

'In five years? How is that possible?'

'Because he was willing to trade anything, except his nationality. Please understand, the Shan and Burmans and local Chinese all got on well enough before all this . . . this invasion. Now it is too much. We are no longer at home in our own country.' We asked him about Burma's prospects. 'Do you mean the future? Oh, no hope,' he smiled.

It was nightfall by the time we crawled into Hsipaw, which means 'four corners' in Shan. In 1888 a plague had swept through the state and the Shan Prince, Sao Kya Kaine, had chosen the site for a new settlement, burying a pot of oil at each of its four corners to ward off evil spirits. It was said that the town would prosper as long as the pots remained full of oil. If they dried out the residents were fated to suffer. But it was no longer possible to inspect the pots. In 1988 the government had cemented over them.

The events of our evening suggested that, if not bone dry, the pots were all but empty. The road was not safe to use after dark – there were stories of rebels operating to the north and east – so we invited the gardener to stay with us overnight. He made enquiries on our behalf and discovered, first, that there would not be another market for two weeks and, second, that the basket wasn't from Hsipaw after all. We had not yet reached our destination.

'But I am told that these baskets are very common in Pan Chan Pan Cha,' reported the gardener, returning the photograph. 'There every Palaung woman wears one on her back.'

'Is it far away?'

'About eight miles.'

'Then we will go there.'

'It will not be good for you,' he advised, lowering his voice. We had stopped for supper at a sidestreet restaurant. Its yawning owner sliced slivers of boiled pork by candlelight. Two stocky Chinese skinheads drank and joked with off-duty soldiers. 'The area is under the control of the SSA – the Shan State Army – and they are cutting down teak to ship to China. They will not let you see.'

'But we have come so far,' I said.

The gardener hesitated. 'Maybe Namhsan is better. I understand that the baskets are common there too, and it is under government control. But it is far away.'

'How far?' I asked, opening up my Nelles map.

'Nine miles as the crow flies, but forty-five miles by road. At least a day's journey.'

I found Namhsan. It lay high in the hills, in a range of mountains dominated by the Loi Tawngkyaw peak. Few other places appeared to be as isolated. 'We can drive forty-five miles.'

'I'm afraid that the road is too poor for the Austin.'

'Then we'll go by bus.'

'A bus will be bad for you.'

'Why?'

'Because maybe the buses do not run, and even if they do, it is holiday and you cannot return. That would be bad.'

'We could rent another car.'

'The road is too poor for any car.'

My map classified the route as a cart track or path. I took a long, deep breath. The same map had categorised the appalling Burma Road as a National Highway. 'A four-wheel-drive, then?'

'Phahte has a jeep.'

'Paddy?' I said, encouraged by a familiar name. The skinheads glanced towards our table. 'There's a man called Paddy living here?' In my imagination I pictured a cheeky Irish rogue, fond of a glass, who had stayed on after the departure of the British. The heat must have affected my brain. 'Let's meet him,' I said, wishing I'd brought a couple of cans of duty-free Guinness.

'I am sorry, but I do not know him. I know only that he is an important man.'

'He must be if he owns a jeep,' pointed out Katrin.

'I understand that he owns eleven vehicles,' said the gardener. 'If you wish I can make more enquiries.'

We woke to the dawn chorus of monks calling for alms, but by the time we reached his compound Paddy had gone out. He was due back at noon. We idled away the morning on the banks of the Dokhtawaddy River. Bone-thin fishermen, stripped to the waist and wearing only baggy black Shan trousers, punted canoes as light as leaves across to the far shore. Naked children busied themselves around long poles stuck in the river mud. Cicadas were caught by the hundreds on their gummed, black lengths and little hands plucked them off one by one to be drowned in tin buckets. A mother washed clothes in the brown water, her youngest child dabbling in the shallows behind her.

At two o'clock Paddy was still not home, and in the white heat of the day we retreated to the cool shade under a river house to eat sweet sausages of glutinous rice. The rice had been steamed in lengths of bamboo, which were then shaved away until only a flower-petal skin remained to contain the meal. Paddy's driver was spotted at six o'clock, but he vanished before the gardener could speak to him. We returned to the sidestreet restaurant, where the skinheads still joked with the soldiers, and waited. Around sunset a message reached us, passed between envoys, that Paddy would meet us at midnight at the pagoda festival. 'Nice of him to turn up,' said Katrin. I thought her impatience was misplaced, especially as her grandmother had been Irish.

'I am told that he is a busy man,' translated the gardener.

The restaurant owner, who like everyone else in town watched our waiting, said in Shan, 'He is a generous man.' The words were spoken with a respect approaching awe. 'He is paying for the festival even though he is a Christian.'

'A Christian?' I repeated. My Paddy fantasy expanded to embrace damp sermons and timid confessions in a rain-soaked church in Donegal. His upbringing must have instilled a sense of charity in him.

'This man says that the festival has been organised to raise money for the monastery,' the gardener explained, then hesitated. 'These events usually occasion much drinking and gambling. I am told, please excuse me, that they are not suitable for ladies.'

Katrin did not object. She was in no hurry to be once again the only woman at an all-male gathering. 'I'll just curl up with a mug of hot cocoa and ring a friend for a chat,' she said, pining for home. As we walked her back to the darkened guest house she added, 'You know, they make beautiful *graticio* baskets in Tuscany. Next time, let's just go to Italy.'

The gardener and I carried on along pitch-black lanes, guided by the firefly flashes of torches carried by boys on bicycles. Shadows of people filled the sandy streets, spilling out of the cramped houses to catch a breath of evening breeze. The town's ration of electricity had been used up and young drunks wheeled through the dark towards the festival, singing American pop songs to the crickets and tree frogs. The night was filled with an outward air of celebration, but behind its mask I sensed a strained volatility, a ferment to be held in check only by the amnesia of alcohol.

The flickering oil lanterns cast a tarnished halo of light around the temple's perimeter. Tinny piped music crackled from a dozen loudspeakers. A diesel generator grumbled behind a Buddha. Beneath the canopies of a hundred bamboo stands, wild-eyed gamblers stepped forward crying out 'Dragon!' or 'Tiger!' They threw crumpled notes onto tilted tables marked with the symbols of animals, watched the dice roll, then slipped back into the crowd as long feather-dusters swept their money into a pot. The rare yelp of triumph brought an eager rush of new punters, a flurry of bets at the lucky table, then disappointment, always disappointment. The Shans' enthusiasm for drink was surpassed only by their love of gambling. The players, all of whom were men, roamed from game to game, their movements stealthy, their tired eyes charged with futile hope. When their money was lost they stole away, their tempers frayed, carrying with them the expectation of argument and despair. It was a place of extremes: of hope and delinquency, of sobriety and drunkenness, of grand future designs and denial of the present. The winking fairy lamps and pallid lanterns did nothing to alleviate the shadows cast by the darkness of spirit. A man could be murdered in the gloom. At least, I reasoned, Paddy would bring a measure of Catholic tolerance to the community.

We searched up and down the ugly aisles looking for him, looking too for some variation in the game but finding none. The gardener paused to speak to a noodle vendor and was directed towards a knot of gamblers. We pushed through the bodies, drawn towards the whiplash yelp of laughter, and found ourselves standing above a wiry spring of a man in green army fatigues. He squatted on a painted mat, across from a weary boy, snapping hundred-kyat notes onto the dragon symbol. He clicked his tongue and the dice were rolled. His eyes followed them with the quickness of a lizard. They landed on the elephant. He laughed again, a sound at once manic and cruel, then mussed the boy's hair.

'Phahte is like an angel to the children,' rumbled the stranger standing beside me, a whale of a man with minnow-like eyes. 'You should bet with him.'

The gardener took the hint. 'Yes, bet,' he whispered to me, pressing a five-kyat note into my hand, 'so he will like you.'

'This is Paddy?' I asked, too surprised to act.

'Lucky shrimp!' called the gardener, beginning to match Phahte's bets, losing alongside him, indicating that he was acting on my behalf. 'For my English friend.'

'"Phahte" means Honoured Uncle,' translated the stranger as they gambled. 'He is our guardian angel.'

'This man?' I laughed, but the stranger did not laugh with me. My Paddy was neither an Irish rogue nor a Burmese angel. He was very drunk. I looked again at the wiry gambler. My first thought was that it would be inadvisable to be disliked by him.

'Fish of fortune,' cried the gardener, casting another bet, emptying his wallet, 'bring our honoured uncle and welcome guest together.' He and Phahte lost their stakes, again.

Hsipaw's 'guardian' roared, springing to his feet to face me. Phahte was in his early fifties, though his taut, hairless skin made him appear younger. His hooded eyes were yellow and lustreless. His limbs were elastic and supple. He swayed, reached out a sinewy arm to catch his balance, and I saw the rubbery flange of his baby finger sticking out at right angles from his hand. 'Jesus loves little children,' he said to me in English, then resettled the pistol in the back of his trousers and swayed away.

An entourage of tall, unsmiling men shadowed his erratic steps from gaming stall to table, swinging left then right, ready to catch their protector if he fell to earth. Phahte slumped onto a stool and demanded beer. While it was being poured the gardener whispered to the minnow-eyed whale who, in turn, rumbled into Phahte's ear. I was led forward and pushed into the seat beside him. He did not look at me. The gardener indicated that I should talk. I began to explain about our search for the basket and our wish to reach Namhsan.

'I know, I know,' said Phahte absently, his vowels larger and longer than his attention span. 'But Namhsan road dangerous for gentle-man.' He spread out the word as if dissecting it, then swallowed the glass of lager placed before him. He demanded another and passed it to me. 'Drink,' he ordered, and I did. 'I am mountain man. But you are *gentle*-man.' He shrugged with disdain then told a joke in Shan which, for some reason, required him to jerk open his shirt and expose a lean, tattooed chest. His bodyguards responded with obsequious hoots.

'Laugh. Laugh,' hissed the gardener.

'I understand that you can help us get to Namhsan,' I said, as if asking for the time of the last coach to Cambridge.

'Namhsan my land,' Phahte insisted, slicing through the laughter by jamming the flange towards me. I had no intention of taking it away from him.

'Are you Shan?' I asked. His features seemed too rugged to be Palaung.

'I am Karen.' The Karen are a stoic people native to southern Burma and the Tenasserim Peninsula. He was a long way from home. 'And I am Christian.'

'I am Christian too,' I said, then added as an afterthought, 'And my great-grandfather was a church minister.'

'Church man?' Phahte roared with sinister laughter and revealed rotted, betel-stained teeth. 'My friend!' he proclaimed.

The nineteenth-century European missionaries had convinced themselves that the Karen's creation stories echoed the Book of Genesis. They had concluded that the Karen were a lost tribe of Israel and had converted them to Christianity.

'God loves you,' Phahte assured me and began to sing 'Onward, Christian Soldiers'. His entourage did not join in. 'I mountain man. You gentle-man.' He shrugged, casting away his initial disdain. 'Don't worry. I Christian. You Christian.'

'Two Christians together,' I said, adding up.

Then, in celebration of our bond, Phahte slapped his pistol on the table. He liked to make an impression. 'One day I die,' he said with hushed urgency. His voice was low and throaty. 'Never mind.'

'We will all die,' I pointed out, unnecessarily, wondering if death was a price worth paying to find the basket.

'I not frightened. Jesus in me. Thanks to God.' He downed another glass of Foster's and sang to the gathering of vassals, 'On a far hill is a lonely cross.'

How Phahte came to be in the Shan State was a mystery to me, especially as the Karen National Union was the single major ethnic group still fighting the Burmese government. During the Second World War the Karen had been the Allies' most effective guerrilla fighters. Their allegiance had been secured by a British promise of support for an independent Karen nation. But after liberation they were betrayed. Their autonomy was denied them, and since 1947 they had been at war with Rangoon. Human-rights groups estimate that half a million Karen have been killed in the five decades of fighting. In the first months of 1997 the SLORC army displaced one *third* of the entire population of the Karen State. Every month thousands of civilians escaped over the border to Thailand. Unlike them, it seemed that Phahte was aligned with the government – somehow.

'Here Chief of Police,' he said, concluding the hymn and gesturing towards the whale. The minnow eyes betrayed no emotion. 'And this inspector taxes.' The younger man, who wore a *Phantom of the Opera* T-shirt and an American baseball cap, broke off his conversation with Hsipaw's Chief Judicial Officer. 'Both go Namhsan.'

'Phahte speaks seven languages,' fawned the Chief of Police.

'Chinese, Burmese, Shan, Karen, Japanese, English and Palaung.' To confirm his ability he barked out a schoolboy's marching song, passed down from the days of the Japanese occupation, then crooned a Palaung love poem and followed it with the Taiwanese national anthem.

'I know it,' confirmed the judge. 'Phahte sings it perfect.'

'Yes, my friend; Chinese women are best cooks, English make finest housekeepers and Japanese are top for seeing to a man's needs.' He listed the womanly skills with neither warmth nor eroticism, without respect or ribaldry, as if reporting on breeds of horses or types of cars.

'Do you really speak Palaung?' I asked, thinking of the basket.

'What is Burma?' he barked at his retinue in Shan, uninterested by my enquiry. He repeated it in Burmese, and then in English to me. 'It is different people living together. It is a generous people who love our father – *our* father Aung San – but not his daughter Suu Kyi.' He spat blood-red betel between his legs. A droplet of phlegm caught in the thin wisps of beard that coiled down from his chin. 'I cannot come to your country.' I thanked God for His blessings, and prayed for the health and vigilance of all Home Office immigration officers. 'But you can visit Myanmar and I am happy.

I welcome you.' He shot out his hand and I shook it. 'Jesus loves you.'

'And you too,' I guessed.

But Jesus was not a favourite of the two Shan-Chinese traders who had been waiting in the crowd to speak to Phahte. It seemed that I had jumped the queue, and the traders, denied their audience, had begun to criticise me and our speaking of English.

'What you say?' snapped Phahte, a reptilian instinct alerting him to dissent. They complained in loud stage whispers, emboldened by their smart Thai suits. Phahte shouted in Shan, demanding an apology. When it didn't come, he seized the pistol and sprang to his feet, aiming it at the traders. Never in my life had I seen a man point a gun at another in anger. The judge, the inspector of taxes and the henchmen tried to restrain Phahte, to wrestle down his arm. But he was strong enough to resist them. The Chief of Police turned and looked the other way.

'You have been insulted,' bellowed Phahte, his dark anger inflamed by drink.

'Oh, don't worry about me,' I mumbled.

'My friend, I protect you like family.'

'No harm done,' I assured him, then added, 'Forgive them that trespass against us.'

Phahte let his men subdue him. He collapsed back down on the stool, smoothed his ruffled feathers and, while the Chief Judicial Officer poured him another glass of beer, tucked his pistol back in his belt. The incident seemed to strike no one as unusual, just as I imagined the shooting of one of the traders wouldn't have been considered extraordinary. 'God follows me,' Phahte announced. There seemed little sense in my correcting him. He then quoted from the scriptures and pulled from his breast pocket a cheap, tarnished crucifix. 'I will die,' he said. 'Don't worry. But when they find me dead they will know that I am not Buddhist. Oh yes. I not frightened.' Phahte laughed, spat at the ground again, and shook my hand. 'We go Namhsan together tomorrow. Never mind.'

'Thank you, Phahte,' I said.

'Don't thank me. Thank God.'

The gardener guided me back to the guest house. I woke Katrin and told her of the early start. She groaned and rolled back into the embrace of sleep. I lay in the dark pondering the last leg of our journey. With luck we would find Scott's Palaung basket by the next evening. Our trip would be complete. The momentum of our search, and its likely success, meant that I did not stop to consider the wisdom of my arrangements. In truth, I did not want to consider them. I had been assured that Phahte was a good man, and despite the drink and the gun, I chose to believe what I had been told.

Travel has always involved risk, but I had never thought of my journeys as endangering life. I had gone to the pagoda festival looking for a ride. I had found it. In the still Burmese night Katrin slept on beside me. A sliver of cool moonlight curled around a tendril of hair on the nape of her neck. I was willing to take risks. I was also capable of being very, very stupid.

The next morning we waited in the dust outside our guest house. Katrin brushed a mark off my shirt sleeve. The gardener brought us each a glass of sweet lime juice, and when I thanked him he gently laid his hand on my shoulder. It was the first time I had been touched by a Burman.

The two four-wheel-drive vehicles pulled into the lane, slicing through a saffron line of monks and causing a novice to drop his alms bowl. Phahte sat in the front of the leading Land Rover, sober and silent, a German G3 automatic resting on his knees. Behind him the tax inspector clutched the butt of a Colt assault rifle dating from the Vietnam War. 'Property of US Government' was engraved on its stock. Katrin and I were marshalled into the second Chinese-made Willys with the Chief of Police. We sat behind him next to a khaki-clad gun boy. Two Kalashnikovs were slung over his shoulder. On the floor pouches of ammunition were lodged in the hub of the spare tyre. The bristling display of weapons alarmed us; as far as we knew, there was no need for armed protection. Military ceasefires had been secured with all the northern rebel groups. The ruling junta posed no threat, judging from the previous evening's camaraderie. Yet Phahte's arsenal could not be carried for the sake of bravado alone. The drivers slipped the vehicles into gear, and I asked the gardener if we were safe.

'It is safe,' he whispered, smiling as if we were off for a jolly picnic by the river. And because of the quest, because of the impetus of our travels, because of my blind curiosity, I chose to believe him.

The tour by gunpoint headed north. Beyond the edge of town the broken highway climbed around lush plantations of wild banana trees, their broad leaves turning like windmills in the morning breeze. Gangs of farmers dug weeds from the steep fields of tobacco. Narrow tracks, trodden clay-hard by generations of feet, snaked up through the bush to hidden villages in the hills above us. Our Willys always kept fifty feet behind Phahte's Land Rover, slowing when it slowed, stopping when it stopped. We did not pause at any of the many standing earthenware pots which were always full of clean water, replenished by passers-by who wished to earn merit.

In the first hamlet, which nestled beneath plantations of dry hill rice, a woman pressed an offering of fresh betel *kunya* into our driver's hand, saying in Shan, 'For Phahte. For dear Phahte.' A girl gave him grilled cicadas from her roadside stall. In another one-street village our convoy paused and, without a word being spoken, a shopkeeper stowed a crate of beer under our feet. Every man we passed smiled or waved at the Land Rover in a mark of respect, though I could not make out the expression in their eyes. Phahte seemed not to notice his well-wishers. He ignored their greetings and stared ahead, hanging onto the automatic and the windscreen, his bent little fingers sticking out to catch the wind.

Beyond the last telephone pole we crossed wasted acres of black-ened fields, once a teak forest, and replanted here and there with sickly rubber plants. Blood-red scars were gouged into the hillsides where the topsoil had been carried away. We passed a bloated cow, its eyes sticky and weeping, being coaxed downhill to Hsipaw for treatment. In places our vehicles needed to wheel up onto the bank, the roadbed having been eroded by the rains too.

At a bamboo roadblock a round-faced teenager in Palaung State Liberation Army uniform and flip-flops joined us. He sat on the spare tyre and held his long-handled knife in pudgy hands. Phahte said nothing to us all morning, and the Chief of Police never met our eyes. I concluded that both of them were horribly hungover.

Our driver too stared ahead, though with rapt concentration. His aquiline features seemed to be shaped by the act of looking, his eagle's beak sensing a way around the massive craters and potholes. He drove quickly between the broken stretches of road, braking hard to leave us teetering above each chasm, easing into first gear to skirt around it and then accelerating away in an attempt to reach top gear as quickly as possible. The speeding-stopping cycle was relentless, straining our arms and rubbing our hands raw from clinging onto metal handles and seat backs. Every moment in motion was punished by wrenching dips. Branches and fronds whipped against our faces. It became impossible to appreciate our surroundings. Our mangled discomfort and the intense heat distracted us from the passing scene, from the waterfalls and plateaux and mile after mile of verdant jungle.

At noon we lurched up to a sun-baked long house, too numbed to be excited by the bowls of festering noodles and garlic-fried insects on offer. Phahte sat in the shade and drank his first Foster's of the day. A butterfly spring had snapped on the Land Rover, filling the air with the stench of burning brakes. While the drivers attempted to repair it, their greasy tools spilling out of a plastic Yum Yum Noodles carrier bag, we retreated to the shade at the back of the open building. A cockerel scratched at the dust. There couldn't be much for it to eat along the dry verge. Then we heard the sharp crack of gunshot. The chicken jerked off the ground and crumpled onto its side, bleeding from a shattered leg.

'Morning cock crows three times,' said Phahte, lowering his automatic. 'First time to say get up, second time to say light fire, third time to say cook breakfast.' The drivers had stopped their repairs. The cook had stopped stirring his pot. The only sound was the manic beating of wings. 'But no more. Now I say eat lunch.' Phahte raised the gun again, took his time, letting the bird suffer, then killed it.

'Never mind,' he told us, and took off his shirt. He crunched a garlicky cicada between his teeth. The drivers turned back to the brake shoes.

We had no appetite, so sipped at our bottle of 'Ultraviolet Safety' water and watched our host down two more beers. The Chief of Police joined him, and as they talked Phahte became boisterous. He ordered the PSLA boy soldier to stand the empty beer cans on an embankment, then picked each one off with a single, precise shot. Katrin, disgusted, looked away, but I whistled to assure him of our continued camaraderie. There was a sense that Phahte's mood could change on the slightest whim. His displeasure would have been, at the least, an inconvenience.

'My friend, we ride together,' he decreed.

'Thank you,' I said, trying to sidestep the dubious honour. 'But my wife and I are fine in the second car.'

'Second car now first car.' He waved away the damaged Land Rover, and we watched the Chief of Police lumber away towards it. 'Don't worry. We Christians ride together.'

Phahte fell into the front seat, bringing with him his automatic and the stink of beer. Our driver collected the discarded shirt, folded it, smoothed it and pressed it upon his lap. The Willys started first try but the Land Rover's engine would not turn over. It needed to be hand-cranked to life. 'God follows me,' concluded Phahte, his arrogance explaining away random nature. The cook waved us off with a broad smile. No money changed hands. The dead chicken lay in the dust.

As we climbed through the sweltering afternoon heat the condition of the road deteriorated. Each time we felt we could not imagine a poorer trail, it became still worse again. The hardened surface gave way first to an eroded lane, and then a pitted track. It began to resemble a boulder-strewn riverbed more than a highway. Hairpin bends snaked around the hills' contours, their edges unguarded by barriers or stones. Bridges were rough planks laid over gullies. In the places where streams crossed the road our wheels kicked up great fists of mud. Elsewhere a burning yellow dust caked our arms and legs, coloured our clothes and hair. I found myself thinking of the medieval torture which sealed the condemned into a nail-pierced barrel and rolled them downhill. It would have been a horrible way to die, but at least one would have reached the end sooner.

The drink had put Phahte in good if volatile humour. On the riverbed road peasants, walking between unknown and unknowable destinations, applauded his passing. In a three-hut village he bounced a newborn baby on his knee, its young mother wary of his wild laughter. He stopped every overburdened lorry to interrogate its operator. While he inspected the load our drivers retuned our vehicles' engines. One lorry took Phahte's fancy and he ordered it – along with its dozen hushed passengers – to turn around and follow us to Namhsan.

At the head of his wobbling, seesaw convoy, Phahte rode on the edge of his seat, his gun pointing out the window, his hand and crooked finger bent around the windscreen. 'My friend,' he announced, drunk now that the case of Foster's was finished, 'in Namhsan I will buy you a basket.'

I thanked him and explained, 'We just want to see if they are still made, Phahte.'

'Never mind. I will have one to be made.' He began to sing, slurring his words into a meaningless mash of tones. 'Onward, Christian soldiers, marching as to war . . .' The shrill sawing of countless cicadas scorched our ears. In our heated imaginations it seemed as if the road would never end. We began to fantasise that there was no place called Namhsan. The town took on the aura of a unreal destination. '. . . with the cross of Jesus, going on before.'

Phahte soon bored both of hymns and his royal progress, and at a bend he instructed the driver to reduce speed. As the next stretch of road came into view, he raised his automatic and took a shot at a pigeon. He hit it, and the PSLA boy soldier, anxious to please, scampered ahead to retrieve it. The men joked in Shan as they inspected the rust-brown corpse, and the driver risked teasing Phahte that it was a rather small specimen. At the next turn the convoy slowed again, and Phahte spotted a crow. He settled the gun against the windscreen and fired. The bird dropped off its bamboo perch and into the bush. The gun boys and drivers hopped down from the vehicles, beating through the undergrowth in their flip-flops to find the prize. Phahte walked swiftly forward on his short legs, the gun slung across his shoulders. He hooked his arms around barrel and butt, leaving his fists dangling, looking like one crucified. His skin rubbed against the gun metal. Our driver found the crow, which was as big as a large hawk, and the kill again lifted Phahte's spirits.

For the next two hours we crawled forward, stopping and starting every few minutes, while at our feet there gathered the corpses of pigeons, doves and an emerald-green parrot. Our driver offered Phahte encouragement, pointing out new prey, abetting the game. Phahte grunted the rare times he failed to hit his target. 'I am sorry,' he said to us after one unsuccessful shot. I did not understand his apology. Was it because he had missed? Because of the callousness of the killings? Or because he recognised that we – like the birds – were trapped by him? The sweet, aromatic scent of betel was sickly in his beery mouth. 'God loves you,' he added.

Phahte was a thug. Like the Rangoon generals, he bullied to mould behaviour and to dominate. But it was not brutality alone that had given him power. Vulgarity had not provided his arms or his eleven vehicles. At one checkpoint, a palm-thatch hut atop a barren hill as bare as a monk's head, Phahte peeled off banknotes for the ragged *Tatmadaw* guards. The gun boy handed over the Kalashnikov and a dozen rounds of ammunition. The soldiers dipped and bowed with obsequious, fearful loyalty. The shuck-shuck of hoes and shovels tumbled down the slope behind them. One square metre of teak sold for $200 in Burma; less if it was cut illegally. Over the border in China or Thailand it fetched $600. A complete, mature tree could be worth over $30,000 on the open market. In place of the ancient forests eucalyptus was planted, for firewood and oil, but the fast-growing trees drained the soil, and in a handful of years the land became exhausted.

As wealthy as the teak trade could have made Phahte, it alone could not have bought the friendship of both the SLORC and ethnic rebel groups like the PSLA. There had to be another reason for his influence.

Two-thirds of the world's heroin comes from the Shan State. The poppy fields are the only insurance against starvation for many families. Armed convoys of up to seven hundred mules carry the opium crop across the Golden Triangle to Thailand, unmolested by the *Tatmadaw* or the insurgent armies. Over the last decade, $80 million of US aid has failed to capture or stop a single convoy. Why?

Since the end of the Second World War, ethnic liberation factions had waged war against Rangoon. As late as 1992 as many as thirty-five rebel groups were fighting the Burmese army, as well as one another. Their battle for independence needed to be financed, and to buy arms the Shan armies – like those of the Wa, Pa-O and Kokang – levied a 10 per cent tax on their farmers. In most cases the only crop farmed in the northern hills was opium, and so, from the start, the pursuit of autonomy was dependent on drug trafficking. It was only after the opening of trade with China that the *Tatmadaw*, equipped with new, imported weapons, gained the upper hand. Military truces, though not political settlements, were negotiated, and in most parts of the country hostilities ceased. But despite the truces, and the surrender of the Shan drugs baron Khun Sa, the trade in opium blossomed. This was because the Burmese army had no wish to eliminate it. The *Tatmadaw* chose instead to cooperate with its former adversaries and to share in the spectacular profits. It is difficult to appreciate that the flow of heroin onto the streets of New York, Los Angeles and London could be stopped on the orders of Rangoon's generals.

Not that anyone could prove it. We passed no teak-laden lorries, saw no fields of Yunnan poppies. We spotted no farmers scoring the bobbing heads, collecting white sap, refining it into opium and loading sacks onto mule trains. Nevertheless, fortunes were being made in this impoverished wilderness. Phahte was not without money. To me he appeared to be an opportunist, a warlord, an insurgent fighter without any insurgents left to fight.

*   *   *

It was late afternoon by the time we reached Phahte's fiefdom, the old Palaung capital of Namhsan. The road snaked along the spine of the hills, 5,532 feet above sea level, as if along the back of a sleeping serpent. Tea plantations fell away down their steep flanks. Twisting donkey paths wound towards the surrounding ring of hill villages. Our convoy rocked into the single-street town of dark teak buildings. On broad verandahs and in small yards the day's gathering of tea leaves spread on woven mats caught the last rays of the setting sun. Our arrival flushed a handful of children out of the unlit interiors of the unpainted houses. Well-wishers waved from behind the ornately carved doors and beneath the overhanging eaves. The attentions of the town's few inhabitants distracted Phahte; there were courtiers and self-important messages awaiting him, and he grew bored with our company. When the convoy paused by the town water-pump he indicated that we should get out. 'We go back tomorrow,' he announced. 'Car here 8 a.m.'

'But we have to find the basket, Phahte,' I said. Our backs were blue with bruises. Our limbs ached. We hadn't travelled all this way only to turn around and go back home.

'I buy you basket. No worry.' The driver snapped the Willys into gear. 'Sharp 8 a.m,' repeated Phahte, and was suddenly gone, leaving us with the knowledge that he represented our only way back to Hsipaw.

We stood alone on the cobbled hilltop street, caked in dry, tawny dust, racked from the torturous journey. Two or three curious faces peered at us from over balconies. A pair of white-bloused girls blinked at us from their bamboo sleeping platform. A hobbling man stared as he drew an empty wooden-wheeled cart past us. There were no signs or posters, no written words, anywhere to be seen along the sunburnt road. We took a step forward, no longer certain of our destination. We had reached the end of our journey without having yet arrived.

Before the war Namhsan had been a busy British tea station. The Bombay Burma Trade Corporation had operated the drying factory here. But in 1941 the town had been destroyed by the Japanese. It had been rebuilt, but we were among the first foreigners to reach the town in over thirty years.

On a stool outside his stall an elderly Indian tailor stopped paring his toenails. His shop sign was a few remnants of patterned cloth hanging from the teak lintel above his head. 'You are His Majesty's subjects, I believe,' he hazarded, the words rusty on his tongue. 'I was educated by an English gentleman at St John's School.'

Katrin pulled the tattered photograph of Scott's basket from the knapsack, our vital marker in a place without signs. The sight of it took me back to that morning in the British Museum storeroom, to the remembered smell of jasmine and caraway, to the sound of the cold London rain beating on grimy windows. We had carried the photograph halfway around the world, watched it pass through a hundred hands, let its image guide us north from Rangoon, to Pagan, Mandalay and into the Shan State. The heat and handling had cracked its emulsion and it looked almost as worn as Scott's basket itself, but as a pointer it still served us well.

'We are looking for this,' Katrin said. 'We were told that we might find it here in Namhsan.'

The tailor handled the photograph with care, then spoke to a boy, who ran off up the street. 'I know a Mrs who will be of assistance to you. Please would you be so kind as to idle here a moment until her arrival.'

We had nowhere else to go, hardly knew where we were, so we waited. A few minutes later a stout matron came panting down the lane towards us. I had hoped that the 'Mrs' would be Palaung, that she would be wearing the traditional scarlet hood and ankle-length velvet coat, that her hips would be wrapped in silver bands. But instead of the blues and purples of the hills, Nancy – as she introduced herself – brought with her the colour of the tropics. Her blouse was a riot of yellow and pink flowers, her *longyi* was printed hibiscus-red and her cardigan dyed deep rainforest green. As she caught her breath she apologised for not meeting us sooner. 'It was most inconsiderate of me. I am sorry.' Her candid concern touched us. 'Ali's son has told me that you are looking for a basket,' she puffed, not intending to make our search sound frivolous. The tailor nodded on our behalf, and gave her the photograph. 'I will be pleased to help, but before, I am sorry, I must ask you first, how have you come to Namhsan?'

'A man called Phahte drove us here.'

'Phahte?' She hesitated, my poor pronunciation confusing her. 'You mean the man with the gun?'

'That's the one,' said Katrin.

'He is here?' she asked, then turned to the tailor for confirmation. 'But he's not due back for another week.'

'You know him then?' asked Katrin.

'I do, yes. He is my son.'

With the photograph in her hand, Nancy – her real name was Nan Si Si – led us up between the dark houses. Her presence made us less threatening, and we began to attract cautious spectators. A rake-thin spinster walked with us, craning her neck to see the photograph. Children held our hands, glancing to one another for reassurance as we walked. Ali the tailor followed on behind, still carrying his scissors. But we paid little attention to our companions. We were too startled by Nancy's revelation. A parent and child could not appear more different.

'You are certain that this basket is Palaung?' she asked.

'Our friends in Lashio and Hsipaw said that it is.'

'Maybe it is an antique from the British time?' I explained about the British Museum. 'Then it is possible. A lot of our old customs have been forgotten.'

'You are Palaung?' asked Katrin, looking at her gaudy outfit.

Nancy nodded, hearing the surprise in Katrin's voice. 'I'm sorry, but no one wears the folk costumes any more, except maybe on market day. A *longyi* is more practical than those old coats and caps. Listen to me, I'm talking too much already. I always talk too much.'

'But your son – Phahte – told us that he was Karen.'

'My husband was Karen. He fought against the Japanese during the war.'

'And Phahte takes after him?'

'Except that my son fights against everyone.'

Behind a pair of folding teak doors, in a sort of wardrobe that opened back from the street, we found the basket shop. Our arrival, which filled the wardrobe with a large proportion of the town's residents, startled its dozing owner awake. Nancy passed him the photograph while we inspected the fine *pock chard* working baskets, palm-leaf whisks and unworked rolls of inner-palm bark. There was nothing in the shop which resembled Scott's basket. The owner yawned, and Nancy translated.

'He says that your basket is made from sooted bamboo. It is peeled into strips, soaked for two weeks then sooted in the chimney. He calls it *tin-ma*, which means very hard.'

'We were told that all Palaung women have these baskets,' sighed Katrin, wearied by the search.

Again Nancy translated. 'He says they might have been made like this when he was small. But today we don't see them. Maybe your friends have not been to Namhsan in a long time?'

'Maybe they just didn't want to say no to us,' I suggested, knowing that Burmese kindness meant not wishing to disappoint expectations.

'That is possible,' acknowledged Nancy. The owner considered the photograph again and, through Nancy, informed us that sooted bamboo was insect-proof.

'That is useful to know,' said Katrin.

'He tells me too that the old styles take so long to make. There just isn't enough time these days.' I couldn't imagine anywhere less pressured by the rush of time than his wardrobe shop.

'Are there any older basket-makers in Namhsan?'

Nancy and the owner discussed the possibilities, becoming excited in the process. 'There *is* one elderly man who we think still knows this work. He might even be able to make you a copy.'

'That would be great,' I said.

'His house is a half hour's walk away. Can we go tomorrow?'

'I wish we could, but Phahte wants to go back to Hsipaw in the morning.'

It seemed that no one could disagree with Phahte, not even his mother, so Nancy suggested that we should hurry. Like the Pied Piper, she led us and our followers up towards the town's Patamya Pagoda. The day had began to dissolve into the rosy embrace of evening. Cooking fires burnt inside dim rooms and candles flickered beside household shrines. Through the gaps between the houses, over the corrugated roofs, we watched the encircling lines of hills fall into deep shadow beneath a ruby sky.

'Are you Christian too?' I asked Nancy as we climbed.

'No, I am a Buddhist, though not very devout,' she smiled. 'I am too much of a free thinker, I'm afraid. Or at least, I try to be.' The lane curved beneath the edge of the pagoda. Novice monks played football in the dusk and a pig rootled in its sty. 'It is not much further,' Nancy puffed. We skirted the edge of a large, open square, when the snap of whiplash laughter halted us.

'My friend, you are welcome,' shouted Phahte, both happy and drunk again. There was a can of Foster's in his hand. 'You will eat with me.'

We hesitated as he wheeled towards us, pausing to accept the gift of a bottle of Thai Mekong whisky. I calculated that if we carried on walking, if we hurried, he might remain distracted long enough to forget us again. We were within minutes of meeting the old basket-maker and maybe completing the search. But unlike our other escorts, who vanished into darkened doorways and lanes, Nancy would not walk away. The moment passed. Phahte turned left then right, saw us again and stumbled forward. 'You will eat with me,' he repeated.

'Thank you, Phahte, but this woman' – I gestured to Nancy – 'is helping us to find a basket-maker.'

'Come,' he insisted, indicating that we should climb the outside staircase to his office, where the meal awaited. 'Basket later. Never mind.' He said nothing to his mother.

'We don't have time,' said Katrin, 'if you want us to leave with you tomorrow morning.'

Nancy began to speak softly, kindly, in Palaung to her son. At first he didn't seem to hear. But then he spat a sting of words at her, and although we didn't understand them, we were struck by their venom.

'I am Chief,' he told us, emphasising the point by flourishing his beer can. He wielded power with a cocksure, medieval brutality. 'You will have dinner with me.'

We followed his wiry form up the steps, opportunity slipping through our fingers. The long, sullen room was divided into sections by hip-height partitions. There were military maps and naked Pirelli pin-ups on the wall, crates of lager and a sweaty tousle of mats on the floor. The drivers and the gun boy stood silhouetted against the window. In the dark Nancy whispered to me, 'We're like that, Phahte and me. We always have to bite a little.'

'This is my *haw*,' Phahte announced. *Haw* is the Palaung word for a palace. 'It is your home. You are welcome here.' As he led us past his armoury, which included a well-worn grenade launcher and a dozen cherished AK-47s, Nancy told us that once insurgents had blown up the building, but Phahte had survived and earned the love of the people.

'Never mind,' he said, defiant, confident.

I again mentioned the basket, and Phahte, taking the photograph from his mother, instructed one of his drivers to find the town's Education Officer.

'But I want to see the basket-maker's workshop,' said Katrin.

'You my friends,' insisted Phahte. 'You stay in palace. Education Officer come. Don't worry.' But we never met the Officer, or saw the photograph again. 'Now you eat with me.'

The gun boy called down the stairs and a cook appeared, bearing a burnished aluminium cauldron. It steamed and spat as he set it on the table. Phahte ordered us to sit down, and we took our places. He pulled open his khaki shirt and raised the lid of the hotpot. A thick, soupy ring of meatballs and bobbing islands of fat stewed around a cooking coal core. Phahte wielded his chopsticks to stir in green chilli and *keng-khe* leaves, then dished out four generous servings. The skull of a small bird floated in my bowl. He spooned rice onto our side plates and poured us great glass goblets of beer, attending to our needs like a solicitous Home Counties hostess dispensing tea for a visiting vicar. His baby finger stuck out in a manner which would have pleased the most pedantic stickler for etiquette.

'Good?' he asked, irritated that we had not volunteered our praise. The dish was, in fact, delicious, though we had little appetite. I could only think of the basket-maker sitting down to his own meal a few minutes' walk away. 'Do you like Burma?' Phahte asked Katrin suddenly.

'I like the Burmese people,' she replied.

'We are a welcoming people,' he declared, overlooking for a moment the pistol holstered on his hip. 'And Burmese papayas,' he continued with intemperate sincerity, 'are they not better than Thai papayas?'

'They both taste pretty similar,' said Katrin.

'In Thailand they use chemicals, but not in Burma.'

'Maybe the farmers can't afford chemicals here.'

'No chemicals is good.'

'Yes, it is good.'

'So they are better,' Phahte concluded with childish simplicity, translating for the cook, driver and gun boy. 'She prefers Burmese papayas,' he crowed, then raised his glass towards us. 'My friends!' The others applauded.

For the next hour Phahte talked, and we listened. Conversation was not a social skill that he had developed. Our occasional questions failed to engage him, and it became apparent that he had not brought us to Namhsan out of kindness, but rather as means of elevating his own status. In Rangoon we had been told that the Burmese considered tourists to be 'like the stars in the night sky'. Phahte also hoped a little of that light would shine on him, so his subjects might see him as reflecting the promise of liberty. To serve this end, our obedient, obsequious presence alone was required. He would have preferred it if we did not talk at all. We were stuffed mascots of hope, and he ignored us for the most part.

'Phahte,' I managed to interrupt when he paused in his praise of

Burmese tomatoes, 'isn't it possible for us to delay our return to Hsipaw? Just for a few hours.'

'Maybe you go back by "cha-la-la-la"?' he roared, imagining us rattling south on a sixteen-horsepower motorised wheelbarrow. Even at full throttle it would take a week to cover the distance.

'Is there no other way back?'

'Or maybe by feet?' he suggested, finishing his glass. He pushed his heart-shaped face towards us. 'But then you get shot dead.'

'You have come to a country that is very isolated,' explained Nancy. 'There are bad men living here. It is better that you go together tomorrow.' It would also be an insult to Phahte if we travelled by any other manner.

'Are there still insurgents in the hills?' asked Katrin. Our repulsive host had disgusted her, but it had not occurred to us before that there might be men in the area more dangerous than him. 'I thought the government had signed ceasefire agreements in the north.'

Phahte slammed his pistol on the table. 'My friends, don't worry. I will die but I protect you. You are like family.'

Nancy looked at him from under her eyebrows, frowning at his unruly behaviour. 'His father never used to drink so much,' she whispered. 'I lost him too.'

As Phahte sang 'Jesus loves God's little children,' the gun boy refilled his glass. 'You are Christian?' he demanded again, pointing a twisted finger at me.

'Yes, Phahte,' I confirmed. I had had enough. 'But I am a frustrated and annoyed Christian.'

As a rule I disapprove of weapons at the dinner table. Now I was anxious for our safety and wanted out, yet in Namhsan there was no handy telephone, no secure hotel and no authority greater than the unstable, over-armed drunkard who leered at us from across the table. It seemed to me that our only hope of salvation would be in manipulating his sense of honour as he had manipulated my naïve trust.

'We are tired now, tired and disappointed,' I said, and he seemed to listen. I tried to be bold. 'We have been looking for a long time to find the basket which is probably a few hundred yards from here, but you won't let us go to see it. You promised to help. But now I do not think that you are being fair to us.'

Phahte hit the table so hard that the lid jumped off the soup and small pieces of bird slopped onto the cloth. 'Yes!' he barked, 'Yes!' In the shadows the gun boy snapped to attention. 'So I not pick you up sharp 8 a.m. tomorrow.' His eyes gleamed with drunken purpose. For a moment there seemed to be the possibility that he would give us the time to meet the basket-maker. We might finally find Scott's basket. 'No, my friend. I pick you up at 6 a.m. and we go to church to pray. I mountain man. You gentle-man. No matter. We Christians together.' The drunken chief of the Palaung militia waved his pistol in the air and fired. 'God follows me,' he shouted as shards of roof tile clattered down around us.

EIGHT

Bound to Love

THE CRY CAME long after midnight, soon after he had fallen both into her arms and to sleep, and almost scared the life out of her.

'Who's there?' Nan Si Si whispered, now frightened again. 'Who is it?' The moon did not shine and the room was black, black as burial, and Saw Htoo was suddenly awake. 'It's not time yet.'

Saw Htoo sprung up and crossed the room. His feet were silent on the boards and Nan Si Si felt rather than saw him move. Only at the door, where he froze to listen, did she hear him release the rifle's safety catch. The breath of night air stirred the leaves of the calendar on the far wall. He stepped down onto the path and circled the house. 'Be careful,' she thought. 'Please take care.' There wasn't another sound. She wished that it was not so late. She told herself it was her fault that he had not taken more rest.

'There's no one there,' he said when he returned.

'I heard a voice,' she insisted. It had been a man's voice. He had spoken softly, as if reciting an incantation in the monastery. She had heard him whisper a single word.

'It was probably a bird,' Saw Htoo said casually, and lay back down beside her. He pulled her close but she knew he was listening. She felt him listening. She shivered, even though the night was warm. 'It was nothing, Nan Si Si. Go back to sleep.'

He needed his sleep. She knew that he needed his sleep. In two hours it would be dawn and he would be gone. He and the other Karens would march south, moving behind the Japanese lines and down from the hills towards the railway. He had hidden the English soldier's pack under the floorboards. She told herself that Saw Htoo had to rest, not to pander to the selfish fancies of a woman. The Karen think that the Palaung are a parsimonious people. Nan Si Si had never in her life considered herself to be mean, but when she met him it became true. She turned selfish. She didn't want to share him. She couldn't let go of him.

'It's so late,' she said into the dark. 'Who would disturb you at this time?'

'Don't worry about it.'

'I couldn't make out what he was saying.'

'Go back to sleep.'

'Maybe it *was* a bird,' she conceded, hoping that her agreement would draw his thoughts back into the house. If he relaxed, if she could put him at ease, he might doze for an hour. She felt his senses still roaming outside, detached and prowling away from his body, making sure that they were safe. The fire had burned out but she was wide awake. Her heart pounded in her chest as loudly as a child beating a tin-can drum. Its rattle had to be keeping him awake. He needed to sleep. She wanted to taste him on her lips. She wanted him to wrap his senses around her like a living, pleasing cloak.

'It must have been a bird,' he said, but he had not believed her. She shouldn't have said it was a voice. 'A bird or a bat.'

'I wish they would leave us alone, the birds and bats, tonight of all nights,' she moaned, then added, 'Sleep, Saw Htoo. Try to get some more sleep.'

He sighed and felt for a cigarette. 'He's weary of war,' she thought, 'and maybe even of me.' The flare of the match made the shadows dance around the room. Saw Htoo must have decided that there was no one outside, even though she knew that the prowler had not been a bird. He inhaled and in the glow of the cigarette his skin took on the smooth, burnished colour of a newborn baby. It made him look younger than his nineteen years, almost like a little child, and she wanted to cradle him in her arms. 'Don't go,' she longed to tell him, but instead she asked, 'Don't you want to sleep more?'

'With you awake beside me?'

'Maybe you would prefer to have another girl beside you?' she said, lifting herself up onto an elbow. She loved his heart-shaped face, his wide forehead and tapered cheeks. It gave him a look of meditative serenity. 'Maybe you'd like Nan Ihla? You once said that Ihla was like a little bird. Or did you say a bat?' Saw Htoo laughed out loud, so she continued, 'She is fat like a paddy-mortar. And she snores, you know. Did you know that?'

'Maybe it was her sneaking around outside the house.'

'No, it was a man,' she said, and then regretted it. 'If only I would think before opening my mouth,' she told herself. He drew deeply on the cigarette, and she felt his senses reach out again beyond the walls. The jungle was still and made no sound. She pulled at his waist to draw him back to her. 'I'm sorry,' she whispered. 'I'm just a little scared. There's no one there.'

'No one at all,' Saw Htoo said with certainty.

He smoked his cigarette, every measured breath one less for them to spend together. She counted their passing in the silence between their words. 'You know Ihla?' she said after a moment. She felt bad about her lie. Ihla was her friend. It was true that she was plump, but she had made up the story about her snoring. 'And her father?'

'The mat-maker?'

'He used to have a terrible temper,' she said.

'He seemed nice enough to me.'

'It used to be so bad that his wife encouraged him to travel away from Namhsan for months on end. Until one day, when he was away and Ihla was little, Ihla came into our house weeping. "Come quickly," she said. "My mother is lying on the floor crying. You have to help her." My mother and I ran to their house and found that she was in labour. The mat-maker didn't even know she was pregnant.

' "Please don't tell my husband," Ihla's mother pleaded with us. "He will beat me. We cannot afford another child."

'She planned to give it away to some cousin in Panglong. My mother said nothing, and helped her with the delivery. Saw Htoo, I had never seen anything like it. But after the baby was born my mother told the woman, "Mind that you keep and love this child. If you don't I'll come and take him from you, for I've lost two girls of my own."

'I didn't know your mother had lost two children,' said Saw Htoo, gentler now. Nan Si Si hadn't told him. Many women lose babies. Often couples who have been robbed of their children dedicate the newest-born to the monastery in the hope of saving its life. The evil spirits might then not have the power to take that baby away. 'What did the mat-maker say when he came back?' he asked.

'He held the child in his arms, not looking at it, but with tears in his eyes. I went home and cried the rains.'

They both fell quiet again, only now Saw Htoo was with her. He no longer listened to the outside or even reached ahead to the morning's march. She placed her hand across his waist. She realised that in the excitement of her storytelling she had woven the quilt around herself alone. Saw Htoo lay uncovered and naked, so she wrapped his body in her own.

Since that first birth Nan Si Si had often tried to picture herself as a mother. She had tried to imagine a life growing within her. She needed to feel the pain of delivery and the deep bond of shared flesh. She didn't care if she had a baby boy or a girl, even though boys are born with more merit. But she did wish for the good fortune of a birth at the full moon, and not for a Saturday-born child who would bring her unhappiness or poverty. She imagined that she would wash her baby in clean, cold water before its first sunrise and, when it was a few days old, give it its first taste of rice. She would chew the steamed – not boiled – rice into a smooth pap and then, as her mother had done for her, feed it to her child like a kiss. By its sixth month he or she would eat as much as three teacupfuls of rice a day and so grow strong like a stone and live long like water.

Her child would be the embodiment of love. It would sleep between her and her husband on its own little mat. She would carry it to the harvest and, as it grew older, they would teach it to herd cattle and to clear weeds from around the tea plants. Her husband would make it a clay whistle. It would learn the old rhyming tales which her mother had taught her. Its skin would be smooth all over like a mouse.

Every mother wishes for healthy, happy children. But if her baby remained weak she would make offerings so that its spirit might acquire merit and, when it died, live longer in the body next inhabited. She held onto Saw Htoo and kissed him, knowing that in less than two hours her arms would be empty. She wanted a child, so deeply that she could taste it.

'But I am not going away to sell sleeping mats, Nan Si Si,' said Saw Htoo. 'I might not come back.'

'We could hide,' she hurried, rising onto her knees before him. His cigarette had been snuffed out and it was again pitch black in the room. 'I know places in the hills. We could go there. No one would find us.'

'I cannot hide. I am fighting for a Karen state. Isn't that a beautiful sound? The Karen State.' He rolled the words around his mouth to savour them. 'It is what we've been promised.' And again his thoughts fled away from her.

She lay back down into her own solitude. When she was young, before her fourteenth year, the young men of Namhsan had come calling. As was the custom, each man wrapped himself in a large grey blanket which enveloped both body and head, a disguise designed to hide his identity from all but her. By the fireside they whispered their names, which all those assembled knew in any case, and in turn she gave them betel-nut and cheroots. Once five men sat together with her and they gossiped all evening, in between their formal rhymes of courtship. Ihla never had more than three suitors serenade her. The next day on the hills the men, who picked tea on different terraces, sang love songs to her and the other girls. She told them all to take a long drink of water to stop the flow of words. A Palaung girl is free to marry whoever she pleases, provided that the man shares her wish, but no neighbour took Nan Si Si's heart, and so the courtship soon lost its interest for her. She was not afraid to look to the left and to the right, that is to flirt with men, but she became lazy in her responses to their questions. Once she even yawned, when the carpenter's son Sai Wai was telling her what he had eaten that day. He later stole a thread from her coat and took it to the wise man to cast a love charm. It was then that she began to lock the entrance-door so none of them could come into her house, until her mother found out and scolded her.

It was not that she disliked the compliments, rather that she could not determine their true value. The whispered promises made her emotions sway like bamboo in the monsoon, yet the shower of kind words did not begin to satisfy her thirst. Excitement inevitably led to disappointment, laughter was always followed by tears and any real meaning remained changeable and unclear. She chose to wait for fate to bring her the man who would hold her heart.

When the war began it was not only the old traditions that died. There was no longer time for courtship ceremonies, or even for the morning sharing of night-time's dreams. The English tea-planters and bureaucrats escaped up into the hills, losing thousands of their people on the high jungle trails that led to India. Nan Si Si's mother, who had before abused with blasphemy the British Empire, gave the poor women and men food as they passed by the house. It was not that she cared particularly for the English. She had always condemned the three 'M's of their colonial ways: their missionaries, merchants and military. Rather, there was simply no vengeance in her character. She would have done the same for the Japanese if their refugees had been retreating, had they not cut short her forbearance by bombing Namhsan. She had died in the fire which swept through the marketplace. It was Nan Si Si who found it difficult to forgive them now.

'There, Saw Htoo!' she hissed in terror, startled back to her senses. 'Listen.'

'Quiet,' he whispered, already on his feet, the gun in his hand. 'I heard it.'

'That wasn't a bird.'

Saw Htoo crossed the inner room in two strides, then reached the door in a single step. He shouted a challenge at the darkness, first in Karen and then in Palaung, but no answer came back. He sprinted around behind the house, from where the voice seemed to have come. His bare feet drummed on the hardened earth. He, like all the other Karen soldiers, rose at the prospect of a fight. He seemed anxious to defend both his faith and his nation with his life. She prayed that the unknown intruder wasn't stronger than him. Saw Htoo pushed deeper into the night and she heard the thrash and snap of branches. 'Saw Htoo?' she called, suddenly alone. 'Saw Htoo?'

She stood up from the mat and tried to find her clothes. It was foolish to have undressed, she scolded herself. The Palaung usually sleep fully-clothed, women removing only the scarlet hood, but the Karen throw off their garments and sleep naked, like animals, in the skin. She wished now that he had spared her that habit. It was so foolish, if pleasing. She found her cap but nothing else. Her clothes were not where she had left them. At the start of the night, after she had laid out their bedding, she had asked Saw Htoo to look away and had undressed quickly, folding her smock and dress and setting them beside the hearth. Now she could not find them. He might have hidden them as a joke. She should have stayed dressed and let him sleep, stayed dressed so he might stay alive.

'Saw Htoo?' she whispered. There were no sounds outside the house, not even the breath of the wind. She felt for his matches but they too had vanished. He must have knocked the box aside. She could see nothing. She held up her hand in front of her face, close enough to touch her nose, but it was too dark even to make out her fingers. She bit them for the reassurance that it really was her here in this room in this house in the jungle. She licked them and tasted him.

She remembered an old woman who had appeared at the head of the cradle on the evening after Ihla's mother had given birth. Nan Si Si had not recognised her, as she was too young, and assumed that she was the cousin from Panglong. At first only the swiftness of her arrival had seemed unusual. Panglong was more than a day's travel from Namhsan. But the woman had sat among them, sharing in the examination of the child. There was always the time to talk in those days. Before the war it was still thought that a deep hollow at the nape of the baby's neck indicated a selfish and miserly character. Large ears, on the other hand, were considered a sure sign that the child would be good and wise. The visitor had explained that the position of birthmarks, with which Palaung and Shan children are often born, indicated something of the previous existence of the reincarnated spirit. The signs were discussed and their meanings interpreted, and towards the end of the examination the old woman stood up and left. It was only then that the other women fell silent. Later Nan Si Si learned that the visitor had been Ihla's mother's own grandmother, who had been dead for almost thirty years. The old woman's ghost had appeared to the family before, sharing in the birth of both Ihla's mother and Ihla herself. Now she had come to welcome their newest-born. Ihla's mother had then rubbed a finger of soot off the bottom of the rice-pot and made a black mark between her baby's eyebrows.

'Saw Htoo?' Nan Si Si heard his steps follow the path, climb the verandah and cross the room. She reached out in the dark to seize him.

'I could find no one.'

'He called your name, Saw Htoo. Your name.' The stranger's voice had shocked her. It had spoken as if from half-sleep, intimate yet distant, murmuring Saw Htoo's name again and again.

He was shaking. She could feel him shaking. But he answered her alarm in a controlled tone, 'You must not worry. We are tired. We should try to rest a little.'

They lay together, skin to skin, and now she felt thankful for Karen ways. She did not want to hear again the calling of his name. She buried her head in his chest and listened to his heart, traced its pulse, felt his body damp from the jungle dew. The intimacy reassured her, pushing the voice out of her mind and away from them. Saw Htoo's concentration drifted too, dulled by his tiredness, and they may have slipped off into the refuge of sleep.

'I can't believe it's less than a week since we met,' he said. She did not know if a minute had passed, or a whole precious hour. She gripped him, startled awake. His calm, confident manner comforted her.

'It's all happened so quickly,' she said. 'Maybe too quickly,' she thought.

'I remember seeing you that first time.' He had slipped into the tea factory among the pickers who weighed and emptied the day's harvest into long mounds near the door. Nan Si Si had noticed him caught in the great white beam of light that slanted down from the upper window. 'You were standing at the oven, staring at me.'

'I was *not* staring.' She had been trying to brush the dust and steam from her eyes. 'I was just looking.'

'Looking like you were staring, then,' he said. She had been working her way along the hot metal plates, judging the tea's dryness, turning the moist, shredded leaves with short flicks of her hands. The bright lines of fresh green leaves were the only colour in the dusty shed. Ihla had been beside her, tending the clay oven's fires. 'But I was staring at you,' admitted Saw Htoo.

'As well as fat old Ihla.'

'She will keep some man happy and warm through the rains.'

'And I will not?' She turned away from him and he held her, wrapping her in the safety of his arms.

'You will,' he breathed into her ear. She closed her eyes. 'The boy who was there on the first day, packing the sacks – what was his name? Sai Wai?'

'The carpenter's son?'

'He seemed to be soft on you.'

'He is just plain soft, as soft as a pumpkin.'

'One day I believe he will make a fine husband and give you many healthy children, all born with your gentle eyes . . . and his flat feet.'

She turned back to beat him then, pounding her fists against his chest until he laughed his whiplash laugh again and pulled her so close that she thought the breath would be squeezed out of her.

That first evening, when Saw Htoo had come to her father's house to talk of driving the Japanese from the country, she had known that he was the man she would marry. The revelation had come to her with great clarity, as certain as bamboo is strong. The dangers and complications had not occurred to her. She had not considered that his bravery might get him killed, even though she admired him for risking his life, or that he wished to return to his southern village of wooden clapboard churches after the war. She knew simply that she wanted to bear his child, their child, so that his laugh and courage and heart-shaped face would live for ever.

'I can't breathe,' she gasped. 'Let me breathe, Saw Htoo.' He let her go and she strained for air.

'I'm sorry.'

'I like it when you hold me, but not that tight.'

'I wasn't thinking.' It was not true. He had been thinking, only not of her.

'It's not fair,' she complained as she caught her breath. 'They shouldn't disturb us tonight.'

'It must have been some boys from the village.'

'It was a man's voice. Maybe the other Karens?'

'Damn kids,' he swore, but without anger, and she realised for the first time that he too was frightened.

He lit another cigarette. His matches had been under the mat. He looked at his watch. Its minute-hand seemed to be racing ahead, counting off the last hour. She took his hand into her own and shook his wrist as if to slow down the clockwork march of time. 'It is running too fast,' she thought.

'I never told you about my friend Ko Kyin Pe,' said Saw Htoo, exhaling. The smoke curled up towards the roof tiles. 'We grew up in the same village, and did everything together. We played together, hunted together, and when the war started we joined the Burma Rifles together. Last month he was shot' – Saw Htoo placed her hand on his stomach – 'here.'

'I'm sorry.'

'It took him two days to die. We had no morphine. He pissed blood until there was no blood left in him. The Sergeant too, who was from Loikaw, died the same morning. He stepped on a landmine. I found him leaning against a tree, staring at the ground looking for his legs.' He took another draw on his cigarette. His words were gentle now, spoken no louder than a whisper. 'When it happens to me I'd like to die quickly. Here,' he said, and placed her hand on his heart.

'It won't happen to you. I want you to come back to me. Remember that.' He didn't answer her. 'Please remember.'

'I'll remember.' The words were spoken in the same flat tone of voice as if he had said 'The tea is ready.'

'It must have been the village boys,' she insisted, angry now. 'I'll tie them to their houses in the morning. They shouldn't make trouble for new couples.'

'Damn them. God damn them.'

'It must have been them fooling around.'

'It's too late now to try to sleep.' He looked again at his watch. 'Much too late.' He went to put out his cigarette, even though it was not half-smoked, and the room slipped again into darkness.

Nan Si Si and Saw Htoo had eloped, as was the tradition, though without the customary long engagement. Their courtship had lasted four days. A girl's parents can object only to a match with a man from another clan or village. Her father did not approve of Saw Htoo despite his strengths, telling her not to set a stone on a slope. He feared that ill would befall the daughter who married a defiant, foreign man. 'A tree growing in the middle of the bamboo is useless,' he had told her. The Palaung are a quiet and peaceable people, despising all those who take human life. He would never have approved of her marriage to a Christian guerrilla fighter, no matter how defensible his principles, no matter how her mother had died. But she believed that Saw Htoo was a good man. She knew that he would care for her and protect her. He was a man willing to shout at the silence of the night.

'I have not built you a house,' Saw Htoo had apologised. It was the custom, when parents objected to a marriage, for the man to build a home for his lover. But there hadn't been enough time. So her uncle had loaned them this hut in the jungle instead. An elder had chosen an auspicious hour for the elopement, with due regard for the days of the week on which they had each been born. Ihla had helped her to carry her clothes and her bedding – a mat, a quilt and a small pillow. Her cooking pot had come too. Her uncle had acted as their escort. Saw Htoo had left tobacco for her father but he had refused to accept the gift. They had come to this house only a few hours before, and then had not slept at all. They had talked together, eaten a little curry and rice, and then he had told her that he needed to rest. She had known it but she had kept on talking, and had taken him again and again into her arms.

One day there would be a wedding, and all the village would sit before their lacquered bowls. One day a baby would sleep in her lap. One day Ihla too would have a child, maybe fathered by Sai Wai, the heartbroken carpenter's son, and the two young women would sit together watching their children play.

'You will come back, Saw Htoo,' Nan Si Si said, 'and we will have a family.'

'Maybe,' he replied. 'But maybe we should wait.'

'It's too late. You have me now.'

'But don't you think it's selfish?'

'What?'

'Wanting a family.'

'You *will* come back,' she pleaded. She didn't want to talk about death again. It was a time for beginnings, not for conclusions. She wanted her man alive. 'I will find the bone of the socket of a tiger's eye to make you a ring that will protect you. I will buy a sambur's sprouting antler to give you courage. You will come back to me.'

'And I *will* die, either later this morning or in fifty years' time. It doesn't matter when. In making a new life we are only trying to perpetuate our own, defying death. To me that's selfish.'

She had never considered love to be selfish, although there was a greed in her need for a baby. 'Maybe it is at first,' she admitted, 'but in it are the seeds of selflessness, of creating and nurturing and teaching and then – when the child becomes an adult – of having the generosity to let go.' She began to wish for the dawn. She wanted the black, broken night to be driven away by the rising sun. 'And it does matter when you die,' she added. 'If it didn't, if there wasn't any future, I wouldn't be here with you. I wouldn't be yours.'

'I just don't want you to be left alone,' he said.

'If you'll light the fire again I'll make us some tea.'

As the water boiled Saw Htoo dismantled his rifle. He slid the bolt free and counted his cartridges. They flashed with a terrible, evil beauty in the firelight. He cleaned each part and reassembled the weapon.

'The Palaung believe that we are descended from the sun and a dragon,' she told him. Their wait for the dawn had lulled them into silence. She tried to fill it with an old legend. 'A dragon princess – a *naga* – who lived deep down in the earth decided that she wanted to see the light of day. So she changed form and became a beautiful girl, and when the sun prince saw her, he came down to her and loved her for seven days. But then he tired of her and returned to his home in the sky.'

'I won't tire of you.'

'In time the princess, because she was really a *naga*, laid three eggs and, in her rage at the prince, threw them away. The first fell onto the Gangaw Taung. It broke and turned all the mountains that it touched into jade. The second egg landed at Mogok, which is why the hills there are filled with rubies and sapphires. But the third egg was caught in a tree and did not break. The sun warmed it until it hatched into the first Palaung.' When Saw Htoo chuckled she told him, 'We believe it to be the real history of our origin. It is no less fanciful than your loaves and fishes or walking on water.'

'You believe that the first Palaung was born in an egg?'

'We wear clothes in stripes to recall the *naga*'s scales. Our hoods remind us of the dragon's head. Our dresses are of the early morning sparkling. The daytime green and midnight black honour our parents. I believe this; at least I would if I could find my clothes. Where did you hide them?'

'You don't need dragon's scales when you are with me.'

'Saw Htoo, I need my clothes. It's nearly morning.'

He laughed and took her then, at last, by the fire as the tea brewed, and afterwards slept deeply, briefly, like an ox. At dawn a crow cawed away to the north-east of the house. It was a bad omen. While Saw Htoo slept Nan Si Si made a mark on him with a piece of charcoal, as the old woman had taught her, knowing that if he was killed and a baby was born to her with a birthmark in the same position, his spirit had entered into the body of the child.

They ate the last of the rice for breakfast. Taste is the most social of the senses, and the most intimate. Mouths are used to talk and to kiss, as well as to eat. Flavours cannot be savoured from a distance. Taste brings pleasure, from mother's milk to a last curry, from lovers' first embrace to their children eating around the family table. Nan Si Si found her clothes under the house, hidden with the pack of explosives. She dressed while Saw Htoo prepared his kit. 'Come home,' she told him as the sun rose above the trees, 'and do not fear.'

'I am not afraid, Nan Si Si.'

A man's voice whispered outside the house. It summoned him, and this time did not frighten them. They were prepared for its call. Saw Htoo went out into the morning and met his platoon. He divided the supply of cartridges and charges. She rolled up the bedding.

'I heard you calling my name in the night,' he joked in Karen to the youngest soldier. 'I would have thought you'd have more manners.'

'It wasn't me, sir,' replied the soldier, surprised by the accusation. 'I didn't leave the village all night.'

'I can't think what kept you awake,' teased the Lieutenant, noticing Saw Htoo's tired eyes, and the other men laughed with him.

Saw Htoo came back inside and kissed her goodbye. It was time. 'It wasn't the village boys,' he decided. 'It was the Lieutenant. I should have known. He's such a joker.'

'You will come back, Saw Htoo,' she whispered. She hadn't told him about the charcoal mark.

Nan Si Si – and the angry dragon child within her – watched him walk away up the path towards the far horizon.

NINE

Stitch and Pair

WE AWOKE to the sound of lapping waves, to the smell of sweet water, to the caress of cool morning breeze. My tongue tingled in anticipation of more papaya and honeydew melon. Katrin slipped out from under the sheet to open the bedroom curtains. Her bare feet padded on the terracotta-tiled floor. I blinked away the sudden brightness. Two dark-haired lovers drifted in the bay, the man held in the woman's arms like a child at her breast. The water's calm, mirrored surface reflected the whiteness of the sky. Beyond the lake, high above the floating islands woven from the stems of hyacinths, we watched a single, black bird circle the embrace of misty hills.

The evening before we had arrived at the Gypsy Guest House in the dark, seeing nothing, hearing nothing, not knowing the place where we had chosen to stop and recuperate. The electricity supply had fused and I had tripped on the stairs and dropped our luggage. Katrin had walked into a cupboard while looking for the bathroom. We had eaten our midnight feast of fresh local fruit in silence and by torchlight, until the batteries had run out. We had undressed and found the bed by touch alone, falling into a dead sleep of utter exhaustion.

Less than a week earlier we had been in Namhsan. Our single, fearful night there had passed punctuated by the scamperings of rats and Phahte's fitful snores. Once in the small hours he had shouted out loud and Katrin had gripped my hand. She hadn't let go, even when we ourselves had dozed off on the dark edge of dawn, startling each other awake an hour later to find him gone. He had not marched us off to church, so we stole away instead for breakfast with Nancy, that is Nan Si Si. The evening before over supper she had stood up to her son, and even though she had been shouted down, he had listened to her reason in the end. He had put away his pistol and let us alone. We had slunk off to our sleeping mats, hounded only by his tirade against the feebleness of 'gentle-men'. It could have been far worse. Nancy had acted as our intermediary, intervening on our behalf, and had tempered the worst of his excesses. We had been grateful to her, and for the hour's peace spent over milky morning tea apart from her son. 'We need to bite at each other,' she had repeated to us, hinting at both her distaste for his belligerence and the depth of her devotion to him. 'It is our way.'

Yet, much as she had wished to help us, she had not been able to find the basket-maker. He had been sent into the fields to help pick tea and would not be returning for a week. We had no option but to leave Namhsan without meeting him. While we waited in Phahte's Willys, Nancy had wished us a safe journey home. 'The world is round,' she had said, then added with a dash of hopelessly hopeful Burmese optimism, 'Maybe we meet again one day.'

On the drive back not a word had passed between us. The journey took almost ten hours. Phahte had acted with the grace of a spoilt child, stopping and starting every few hundred yards, shooting over twenty-five birds along the way. In Hsipaw, when his driver had dropped us off, he had not even turned around to say goodbye. We never saw if he had a birthmark on the place where Nancy had once marked his father, Saw Htoo.

'I was fearful for your safety,' the gardener had said after the jeep had driven away. We had been surprised to find him awaiting our return. 'My conscience could not let me leave before setting eyes on you again.'

'That man is dangerous,' I had flared, turning my anger at myself on him. I had been enraged by my casual acceptance of his assurances of safety. 'If you ever again help tourists, do not let them travel with Phahte.'

The gardener had nodded in sincere appreciation. 'Thank you for your advice. But it is not to Phahte that I was referring. It is his enemies who must be feared.'

'I don't understand.'

'It is considered bad business to shoot a guest,' he had explained, 'even your enemy's guest. Phahte was not so much protecting you, as you were protecting him.'

It seemed that our host travelled by armed convoy because he was frightened. The gardener had learned that years before Phahte had been an ambitious *Tatmadaw* sergeant who had seen the chance to advance himself in Namhsan. The army lacked the resources to police the Shan Hills, so, by fighting off the insurgents and brokering a kind of peace, Phahte had been able to carve out a fiefdom for himself in his mother's land. The government had been pleased to grant authority to one who, if not reliable, was at least consistent in his greed. Phahte would rule until the *Tatmadaw* had the men and arms to control the area itself. Or until his enemies – who were jealous of his profits – killed him.

The memory of our ordeal had stayed with us on the rocking, retching train ride back to Mandalay, and along the switchback bus trip through Kalaw and Aungban, renowned among Shan truckdrivers for its infamous brothels. We hadn't had the strength to think of anything else. We had risked so much to reach Namhsan, yet had failed in our objective. Our journey had become an end in itself, but the recollection of my stupidity haunted me. In a display of faith which would have pleased Phahte, I thanked God for our escape from him, and from his enemies.

I ate two mangoes and four sweet, thumb-sized bananas for breakfast. From the guest house balcony we gazed out across picturesque Inle Lake, Burma's only real holiday destination. Elderly Americans took happy snaps of water buffaloes bathing at the boat landing. A French tour group compared the merits of the Yadana Man Aung Paya with the pagodas of Laos. Nyaungshwe, the waterside tourist town of hotels and souvenir shops, offered fresh food but few smiles. The restaurants had more diners than flies. The bars stocked

Carlsberg rather than Steinbräu – 'brewed by the Sino-German Wuhan Yangtze River Brewery Company Limited'. Shops sold Western goods smuggled over the border from Thailand. An Oral-B toothbrush cost fifty kyat. $50 bought vintage Moët et Chandon champagne. The twice-daily flight from Rangoon was packed with foreigners. Onboard one heard no Burmese spoken. At the Inle Hotel three families of giraffe-necked Padaung women had been put on display like animals in a zoo. They were housed in a compound and tourists paid $3 to photograph them, saving themselves both the time and the trouble of travelling into the hills. Smiles had been unconditional elsewhere in Burma, but in Nyaungshwe faces were harder. No one attempted to pay our bus fare.

We had lost much weight during our travels, and needed to rest. We didn't have the energy for new challenges. We decided to rent a power canoe and to spend the day sightseeing on the lake. Our guest house found us a boat and boatman. I didn't try to negotiate the price. The YMC 'New 195' diesel was hand-cranked into life and, spitting great clouds of exhaust and a spray of water from its long, proboscis-like prop, sliced us out onto the smooth, calm waters.

The local Intha people built floating fields using water hyacinth, staked to the bed of the lake with bamboo poles. The farmers paddled down the channels that ran between them, reaching into the narrow fertile strips, gathering the harvest of green beans and fiery chillies to their canoes. Dragonflies mated above the rows of tomatoes. Incoming freighters rode low on their waterlines, laden with cabbages, aubergines and gourds. Fishermen fished for *nga-pein* carp from their light teak flatboats, balancing on blunt-beaked bows with one leg, rowing with the other, casting their nets with both free hands. Others dropped conical snares into the water and speared trapped eels with a trident. The tourist canoes cut between the fishers and the fields, prows tilted up, nosing at the sun.

Our destination was Nga Phe Kyaung, the 'Jumping Cat' monastery, built on stilts in the centre of the shallow lake. Inside, the monks bullied and shoved angry, tail-snapping cats through hoops for the entertainment of tourists. Stocky Korean students left their air-cushioned Darth Vader footwear at the door and bumbled around the ornate wooden interior. Japanese holidaymakers in cycling shorts politely applauded, then chatted among themselves. A sun-blond Californian and a broad-beamed Bavarian shared pointers on the best Patpong sex clubs. Here too, as in Pagan, were Burmese tourists, the nephews of soldiers and the daughters of businessmen, who like the foreigners were determined to have a good time.

Katrin and I wandered away from the performance to sit by the water. At its edge a French tourist had begun to feed the fish. She broke off pieces of *petit-coeurs*, carried by hand from Paris or Marseilles, and dropped them one by one onto the placid surface. The carp darted forward in ones and twos, circling around and around, snapping up the morsels of biscuit. The taste excited them, and more fish followed, drawn like a current into a whirlpool. The woman crumbled whole biscuits into the lake and the feeding grew frenzied. Dozens of carp swept together in ever tighter circles, swimming closer and closer until the eye of the spiral burst the surface. The water foamed with gleaming scales and gaping mouths. I saw the flash of wild eyes, imagined the gasping for breath. I squeezed off a couple of photographs to capture the moment. We looked up from the froth of fins and gazed out over the lake.

'May I sit with you?' asked a slender monk, and we moved aside to make room on the ledge. As he eased himself down beside me I noted his hollow, sunken cheeks and jet-black eyes. 'I saw your camera,' he said, gesturing at my heavy, twenty-year-old Canon.

'You must see lots of cameras here.'

'Many new ones, yes. But not this model.'

He said nothing more, so I asked, 'Would you like to hold it?' I had read that monks were forbidden to ask for anything. Scott had written about their dependence on offerings alone. The custom was intended to impart dignity and to repress desire.

'If I may.'

I handed him the camera and he turned it in his hands with familiarity, felt its weight then lifted the viewfinder to his eye. He seemed pensive, reflective.

'The jumping cats are' – I struggled to find the right word – 'entertaining.'

'We try to please our guests. Visitors enjoy the distraction of a show.' There was no financial motive behind the performance, no requests for donations were made, even though plates of crispies and fresh fruit were always on offer. 'It helps to relax minds. It also provides us with the opportunity to practise our English.' As he handled the camera I sensed, beneath his air of meditative serenity, a hint of unholy longing. 'I used to have this model,' he added.

'You hold the camera like a professional,' I said.

'I was once a photographer, long ago.' I then noticed the two old, deep scars: the first slashed across his throat, the second at the point where the skull met the spine. Both had been stitched together with broad, rough sutures. 'I became a monk in 1988.'

His words reminded me of the man pushing a green bicycle, the demonstrators marching under multi-coloured banners, the crude news sheets spread out on the pavement in front of Rangoon's city hall like a mosaic of truth. I remembered the photographers who passed rolls of film to foreign journalists. As tourists jostled behind us I recalled too that it was disrespectful to step on a monk's shadow, especially the shadow of the head, and wondered if it was also considered discourteous to ask direct questions.

'You want to know why?' he asked for me. 'Because as a layman my life lost meaning. I needed to search for the truth.' I tried not to stare at the scars. I could only guess at the horrors which so many Burmese had endured. He relieved me from further speculation by asking, 'Do you think that our visitors are searching for something similar? Or are they maybe running away?'

I glanced back at the other travellers, then thought of those we had met in Pagan and Rangoon. 'There are people who do just want to escape,' I said, knowing that for the affluent modern tourist, travel is not a necessity. Few of us really need to strike out into the unknown, except out of desire to inject the exotic into our regulated existences. 'But I think many travellers are looking for a truth too, trying to know themselves by understanding parts of the world that are unfamiliar to them.' I shrugged, 'It isn't a particularly original thought.'

'Is that why you are here?'

'I suppose I'm trying to untangle the threads that tie together the disorder.'

The monk focused the camera on me and released the shutter. 'Once I came very near to dying. In that experience I realised that it was only for my body that I had been working. I had wanted good food, better clothing, the best house; and all that covetousness led to greed, which frustrated me and made me angry with others. I could not differentiate, or judge.'

'And now?'

'Now I strive to work off these evil things. Today I have only four needs: one meal each day, a robe, medicine and shelter – all of which are here in the monastery.'

I admired his clarity and abnegation. Its simplicity appealed to me. But it made me question my feelings. What does the fortunate visitor feel, travelling among the betrayed? Embarrassed by the chance of birth? Or guilty? Even fearful? How does the maltreated local react to the invasion of tourists? With anger? With bitterness? Or maybe with relief at being able to speak out against the stifling darkness? 'To us you tourists are like stars in the night sky,' the Rangoon *biryani* bar owner had told me. 'We hope a little of that light will shine on us.' Burma's history had seemed so distant from our own. Yet the bitter tragedy of the nation, the vain hope of its people, the greed of their rulers affected me so deeply that my emotions rose and fell like the wind before the monsoon. The Burmese dreamed of a better tomorrow, for without their hope and labour there would be no future. I felt the injustice, and wanted to help. But not with platitudes. Or sympathy. Or by donating money. Such gestures seemed only to draw attention to our material comfort and their distress. It seemed to me that maybe the only way to redress the balance was by listening and seeing, by trying to understand the betrayals, by accepting responsibility for preserving their memory, and stitching the past to the present to find a new way forward.

A longboat sped a group of Israeli tourists away across the broad waters. 'In our travels around your country we have learned a little about the tragedy of 1988,' I said to the monk, more quietly now despite the roar of the diesel.

'The Burmese say that if a man has no education he becomes a soldier. If he has no brains he joins the police. And if he has no luck he goes into a monastery,' smiled the monk, handing me back the camera. 'As you will have seen, there are many monks in Burma.'

Our canoe sliced away from the monastery and into a canal. Channels wound through the fields, between the hyacinth and betel vines, to far pagodas. Stilt houses hovered above the water, the family boat moored beneath as cars park under raised houses elsewhere. Our canoe came ashore at Mang Thawk. Its lakeshore produce market attracted few foreigners. The monk had suggested that, after our travels, it might be of more interest to us than the souvenir-hawking touts at the Ywama tourist emporiums.

We scattered an armada of ducks off the muddy landing and ambled up between the half-hearted, half-empty stalls. A fisherwoman sold carp by the brace, lashed through the gills with a twist of bamboo. There were a few baskets of peanuts and tamarind sprouts, a single platter lined with banana leaves full of Inle watercress and mustard leaf. A sleeping ironmonger sold nails by weight. A pair of Palaung women hawked odd containers of tea leaves. There seemed to be little to arouse our curiosity. We began to idle back to the boat, thinking with pleasure of an afternoon nap between clean white sheets, when the market's meagre 'gift' stall caught our attention. On a dirty blue cloth the stallkeeper had laid out a few tired items. There were the usual reproduction opium weights, a tatty carved Buddha, a tarnished set of monks' gongs – and two dusty baskets. We blinked at them in disbelief. They were both identical to the one in the British Museum.

'This ... these are Palaung?' I asked, too shocked to say much else.

'Pa-O,' yawned the stallkeeper, gesturing away to the east. The Pa-O were ethnic cousins of the Karen, another of Burma's twenty-one distinct racial groups. 'From the hills about a three-mile walk from here.'

'Three miles?' We inspected the baskets: the design, shape and weaving were a perfect match. 'Are you sure they're not Palaung?'

'Palaung baskets are different,' replied the stallkeeper, shaking his head. 'Palaung baskets have no lid.' He took one of the baskets to show us. 'This is Pa-O.'

'And the maker? Would you be able to take us to meet the maker?'

'Not possible,' he laughed. 'The baskets are maybe one hundred years old. All the makers are dead.' We asked him the price. 'Maybe $20?'

'Can we afford it?' asked Katrin. In Burma it took a labourer three months to earn $20. At home $20 wouldn't fill our Escort's petrol tank. I shrugged away the question. Of course we could afford it. In comparison with the stallkeeper we were wealthy, and the discrepancy as usual made me feel uncomfortable.

'You can bargain,' he volunteered, misinterpreting our hesitation. He was anxious for a sale. 'You could offer me, say, $10.' His negotiating technique lacked resolve.

Katrin spoke first. '$20,' she said.

The stallkeeper looked surprised. 'Forgive me, lady, but I only asked for ten.'

'Yes,' I said, 'but we'd like to pay twenty.'

'$10 is a fair price,' insisted the stallkeeper. 'I cannot sell it for more.'

I pulled two crisp ten-dollar bills from my wallet. We had decided on which of the two baskets we wanted. 'Twenty,' I said. 'For this one.'

'It isn't in good condition, sir,' he whispered, showing us the worn corners. 'And there is a tear in the weave here. $10 will be sufficient for me.'

'We have been looking for this for a long time,' explained Katrin. She put the basket on her shoulder, let it swing by its carrying strap and rest against her hip. It told us that James George Scott had probably travelled to Inle. 'But we will only buy it if we can give you twenty.'

The stallkeeper stared at us, then at the basket and the money. He blinked twice. He bit his lower lip. 'Lady, sir,' he said slowly, 'if you wish you can give me twenty.'

'Good.'

'I will keep ten for myself, for the basket, and give ten to the monastery.'

'Won't you keep it for your family?' I asked.

'Or to buy your wife a present?'

'The gift will be better spent earning merit in the next life,' he decided, 'so our faces will be open and all people will welcome us.'

We paid the stallkeeper. To bring good luck he then slapped the bills over each item in his shabby display.

'Are you happy?' I asked.

'Very happy. I make good business today.'

The rain came long after midnight, falling in torrents, the great fat drops of water drumming on the hotel window and coaxing rich, humic smells up out of the earth. I half-expected to awake to find that our basket had been caught by a gust of wind and blown away into the lake. But in the morning it sat on the table, looking dusty and not particularly special. Its discovery still seemed too remarkable to be true. After enduring dysentery, Phahte's pistol and a cornucopia of medicinal drugs, the object of our search had been found – at a tourist destination an hour's flight from Rangoon. If we'd booked a one-week package holiday from London to Inle we would probably have happened upon the Mang Thawk market. The basket would have been found with ease.

But there were other discoveries that would never have been made on a package tour. Our journey had enabled me to understand the dichotomy between the Burmese people's kindness and their unelected masters' cruelty. In the past Burma's kings had exercised a brutal authority, but only within their court. At the same time a tolerant, affable Buddhist lifestyle had prevailed in the country's heartland. But the tools and weapons of the modern state enabled the SLORC to extend its control beyond the central court. It would be an over-simplification to suggest that the generals were upholding a regal legacy. Their motivation to seize power was personal, 'un-Buddhist' ambition. In stark contrast to their claims, the State Law and Order Restoration Council – and their arrogant army – were the main obstacle to the country's progression towards a just, pluralist society.

The search for the basket had shown me that it was the influence and identity of Buddhism which defended the Burmese against both domestic injustice and the acids of imported materialism. The people had also remained good-natured and quiescent through the decades of political repression because of their natural optimism, which had been heightened by the opening of their tarnished land to tourists, and because of their desperate need for outsiders to understand the horror of their situation.

Another revelation had come at Mang Thawk market when Katrin put the basket on her shoulder. The gesture had carried me back to the first morning in the storeroom in Dalston, to the smell of jasmine and caraway. At the time I had noticed that the museum card index had listed Scott's find as a 'shopping basket'. I was familiar with shopping in the West. Katrin and I have trailed through the markets of London and Tuscany dragging overladen carrier bags, clutching great heads of cauliflower, granary loaves and half a dozen Granny Smith apples. Scott's basket had always seemed to me too small for the task. But our travels through Burma had shown us that most Asians survive on much less than us. Their baskets carried home from market only a little rice, a handful of soot-black soyabean cakes or the few ingredients for a peanut curry. In many cases it was all that could be afforded. In Asia physical space – in a line-bus, in a house, even in a basket – is a luxury.

Our search had never been for the basket alone, although it was a beautiful keepsake. Instead it had been an attempt to understand the ordering mind and the controlling hand. Baskets reveal our long-ing for organisation and completeness, our attempt to take charge of the world, to contain and to be contained. They, like love, make order in the chaos.

On our last day in Burma we walked past the guards and into the leafy walled garden on Rangoon's University Avenue. At that time the gate was still open. Troops had not yet re-erected the barriers. The Military Intelligence officers only glanced at our passports. We sat with others under a bright canopy, listening to a doctor speak about maintaining a healthy heart. The authorities had permitted his talk because of its 'educational' value, but rather than its medical tips it was his advice on staying true to one's own heart that the audience heeded. The speaker's ambiguous turns of phrase made the Burmese laugh like the bulbuls that hide in the green groves of peepul trees. In spite of the cordon of soldiers, the garden was the one place we had seen in all the country where people behaved as if they were not confined. In the front row, smiling with her countrymen, sat Aung San Suu Kyi.

At the time 'the Lady' was not under house arrest. The military did not forbid her from leaving her family home. But when she did go out they arranged for her car to be stoned by thugs. When she tried to travel to Mandalay her carriage was disconnected from the rest of the train. So she remained behind the garden wall, deprived, like most other Burmese, of her freedom. She was a prisoner of conscience, but her courage reached far beyond her containment. It drew the country and the world to her – and to her party – through weekly speeches and meetings.

The tragedies and wrongs encountered during our journey had convinced me that there was no hope for democratic reform. The Burmese were too subdued, the generals too well armed. But when the talk finished and Aung San Suu Kyi walked through the crowd to welcome us to her home, I believed that their evil would be defeated.

She wore an elegant purple *longyi*. Her fine black hair was woven around yellow blossoms. She asked us about our travels. I responded by praising the generosity of individuals. She told us that, as visitors, we would not have seen their fear.

'We have sensed it,' I replied, 'and have tried to understand.'

'We've seen a great deal of personal courage,' said Katrin.

In a light voice, at once controlled and thoughtful, she said, 'That is what we must do: maximise courage, minimise fear.' Behind her an NLD – National League for Democracy – supporter wore a T-shirt which read 'Fear is a habit; I am not afraid'.

I didn't ask Aung San Suu Kyi any probing questions. I didn't query her about her clarity or her faith. I didn't pry into her six years of imprisonment, into the aching isolation from her husband and sons. The questions had all been asked before. Instead I wanted to give something to her. So I told her what we had seen: that the people needed her, that they felt her love protected them, even if she might not be able to free them, that she was the embodiment of their hope. I tried to tell her that she upheld the only force, apart from fear and greed, strong enough to bind the diverse Burmese into one nation. She knew all this, of course, though she was too courteous to say so, but it was all that I had to offer.

'Concepts such as truth, justice, compassion,' she once wrote, 'are often the only bulwarks which stand against ruthless power.' Her kind, determined eyes were set in a slim, delicate face. 'We will get there in the end,' she told us, the good mother convinced that the family would prevail, 'but it will take time.'

On our journey we had fought against bad roads and bureaucracy, against evil and illness. The physical effort of travel had so exhausted us, and the hygiene had been so poor, that our nails and hair had stopped growing. We had battled to communicate in a system designed to hinder interaction, to isolate individuals and to cripple free thought. But throughout the trip, with the possible exception of the single night in Namhsan, we had had a choice. When it suited us, we had the freedom to leave, to step onto an aircraft, to fly out of the country. We could escape from the sadness and the pain, unlike Ni Ni, Ma Swe, May and Nancy. We could forget the greed, fear and waste. I could write up my notes in public, eat clean food without fear of infection, say Aung San Suu Kyi's name out loud. And it made us so sad.

Yet the Burmese showed no envy or bitterness towards us, despite our liberty of movement. The despair which we most often encountered was our own. We were welcomed, as I had been welcomed ten years before, as family.

One hundred years ago James George Scott related a story of how, in the distant age of legend, Buddha came upon a starving tigress. Her two little cubs were whining for nourishment, dying for the lack of food.

'If I feed her, who shall lose but I?' Buddha asked himself. And so large was his heart, so great was his compassion, that he threw off his robe and offered himself to the animal. He allowed the tigress to eat him. His sacrifice saved her and her cubs, preserving that which is most precious, that which the Buddhists call 'this breath of fleeting life'.

ACKNOWLEDGEMENTS

Much of old Burma had been lost long before the generals began to defile the golden land, and to illuminate the stories of earlier times I relied on the observations of Sir James George Scott and Leslie Milne. My research was brought up to date by the writings of Aung San Suu Kyi, Anna J. Allott, Bertil Lintner, Martin Smith and the reports of the PEN American Center and Asia Watch (The Women's Rights Project). The trip itself would have been more arduous without the advice, translations and Valium provided by Vicky Bowman. It would have been poorer without the correspondence, warmth and karaoke of the Rivers family. On the journey through the book my editor Michael Fishwick proved to be the wisest guide. I am grateful for his enthusiastic support, as I am to Rachel Calder and JoAnne Robertson for their invaluable encouragement and contribution. The generosity of the Arts Council of England is appreciated. But above all it is the courage and compassion of the women and men who cannot be named which must be acknowledged. May the day come when we can meet again in Burma.

Rory MacLean

The Oatmeal Ark

From the Western Isles to a Promised Sea

*'We met, my great-grandson and I, more than a century after my death
. . .'* The Reverend Hector Gillean is a ghost. At the start of the last
century he built a ship and sailed west from the Hebrides to
search for a promised land in the heart of the Canadian wilderness. Two hundred years later his great-grandson retraces the
hopeful voyage from Scotland to Nova Scotia, across Canada by
water and through three generations of extraordinary family
history.

A wave-rocked, wind-tossed travel adventure of ghosts and
boats unfolds. The minister-mariner, a paddle-wheel publisher
and a boat-building broadcaster propel their living descendant
across the world's second-largest country. *The Oatmeal Ark*
voyages into the deepest places of the heart, exploring love and
hope and loss, and unravels the history of a divided nation
whose parts have grown greater than its whole. Its story is at
once a record of a remarkable pilgrimage, a fantastical narrative
and a glimpse at the universal quest for a better world.

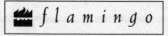